Revolutionary New York

Revolutionary New York
250 Years of Social Change

Edited by
BRUCE W. DEARSTYNE

excelsior editions

Published by State University of New York Press, Albany

© 2026 State University of New York

All rights reserved

Printed in the United States of America

No part of this book may be used or reproduced in any manner whatsoever without written permission. No part of this book may be stored in a retrieval system or transmitted in any form or by any means including electronic, electrostatic, magnetic tape, mechanical, photocopying, recording, or otherwise without the prior permission in writing of the publisher.

Links to third-party websites are provided as a convenience and for informational purposes only. They do not constitute an endorsement or an approval of any of the products, services, or opinions of the organization, companies, or individuals. SUNY Press bears no responsibility for the accuracy, legality, or content of a URL, the external website, or for that of subsequent websites.

EU GPSR Authorised Representative:
Logos Europe, 9 rue Nicolas Poussin, 17000, La Rochelle, France
contact@logoseurope.eu

Excelsior Editions is an imprint of State University of New York Press

For information, contact State University of New York Press, Albany, NY
www.sunypress.edu

Library of Congress Cataloging-in-Publication Data

Name: Dearstyne, Bruce W. editor.
Title: Revolutionary New York : 250 years of social change / edited by
    Bruce W. Dearstyne.
Description: Albany : State University of New York Press, [2026]. | Includes
    bibliographical references and index.
Identifiers: ISBN 9798855804911 (hardcover : alk. paper) | ISBN 9798855804935
    (epub) | ISBN 9798855806922 (PDF) | ISBN 9798855804928 (pbk. : alk. paper)
Further information is available at the Library of Congress.

Contents

Editor's Introduction   vii

1 Daniel Koch, The Oneida Rebellions, 1763 to 1784   1

2 Bruce W. Dearstyne, New York State's Birth, 1777   17

3 Thomas C. Rosenthal, MD, Cyrenius Chapin: Buffalo's
   Doctor and Hero in the War of 1812   31

4 Brad L. Utter with Thomas X. Grasso, Clinton's Ditch:
   The Birth of the Erie Canal, 1825   49

5 Nancy Newman, The Anti-Rent Rebellions, 1839 to 1846   69

6 Albert M. Rosenblatt, The Lemmon Case and Slavery in
   New York State, 1852 to 1860   85

7 Kelly Hayes McAlonie, Welcome to the Club: Louise Blanchard
   Bethune, Breaking Barriers for Women in Architecture, 1885   103

8 Daniel Kornstein, The Triangle Fire and the Velvet Revolution
   in Workplace Safety, 1911   121

9 Anthony F. Gero, Black New Yorkers in World War I:
   The Extraordinary Achievements of the 369th US Infantry,
   the Famous "Hellfighters," 1916 to 1918   139

10	Susan Ingalls Lewis, How New York Women Won the Vote, 1917	157
11	Ellen NicKenzie Lawson, Prohibition in New York City, 1920	175
12	Dennis Gaffney, Radical Roots: The Rise of the United Federation of Teachers and the First Teachers' Strike in New York City, 1960	195
13	C. R. Roseberry, The Empire State Plaza and the Remaking of Downtown Albany, 1963	213
14	Ashley Hopkins-Benton, The Stonewall Uprising and the Fight for Gay Rights, 1969	229
15	Bruce W. Dearstyne, The 9/11 Attacks and New York's Resilience, 2001	243
16	Kevin C. Fitzpatrick, Inside the COVID-19 Era in New York: New York City Parks as Witnesses, 2020 to 2022	257

Selected Bibliography	271
About the Contributors	277
Index	281

Editor's Introduction

Bruce W. Dearstyne

Revolutionary New York: 250 Years of Social Change is a timely book, published as New York and the nation celebrate the 250th anniversary of the American Revolution.

The book was proposed and assembled by SUNY Press Senior Acquisitions Editor Richard Carlin.

The anniversary of the Revolution is a time to look back to the launch of both the state and the nation and to study the origins, conduct, and results of the Revolution. But it is also an opportune time to reflect on historical changes since then. *Revolutionary New York* explores "unfinished revolutions" in the Empire State—the two-and-a-half-century struggle to realize the Revolution's ideals and bring increased freedom and opportunities to previously marginalized populations.

New York is, in a sense, a state where the revolution never ends. This book reflects the theme of the *New York State 250th Commemoration Field Guide*, issued in 2024 by the New York State Museum and the Association of Public Historians of New York State. "By thinking about this commemoration beyond the American Revolution itself, we are able to consider the ever-evolving history of our state and nation over time." The guide notes that "over the past 250 years, New York has been the battle ground for a variety of struggles over concepts of freedom and equality. . . . Reconciling the ideals of the Revolution with the continuing struggle towards a more just society allows 250th planners to broaden the focus of the commemoration to include other movements towards social justice."[1]

---

1. New York State Museum and Association of Public Historians of New York State, *New York State 250th Anniversary Field Guide* (Albany: New York State Museum, 2024), 6, 16.

Revolutionary New York

The book presents the pageant of revolutionary New York in the form of sixteen historical stories about conflict, change, and turning points. Some of the chapters have been adapted and updated from previous SUNY Press books, as the headnotes indicate. The others are new, written just for this volume.

I provide a brief introduction, in *italics*, for each chapter, connecting it to the central theme.

In a few cases, the copyeditor or I have made very minor editorial changes to ensure clarity or bring the texts into alignment with current usage; for instance, the book uses the terms *American Indians* or *Native Americans* rather than *Indians* and *enslaved people* rather than *slaves* to reflect current usage, which has changed in recent years.

The selected bibliography at the end of this volume includes books cited by the authors. It does not include page numbers, articles and other materials, or all the sources cited in the SUNY Press books excerpted here. Those sources can be found by consulting those books directly.

Chapter Summary

Chapter 1, Daniel Koch, "The Oneida Rebellions, 1763 to 1784," relates the story of the Oneida American Indian tribe, from the colonial wars through the Revolution to their fate at the hands of the new state and nation.

Chapter 2, Bruce W. Dearstyne, "New York State's Birth, 1777," presents the story of the state's origin year, a harrowing transition from rebelling British province to something new and unprecedented: a *state* deriving its powers from the people.

Chapter 3, Thomas C. Rosenthal, "Cyrenius Chapin: Buffalo's Doctor and Hero in the War of 1812," relates the exciting story of a patriotic doctor and militia leader who rallied American forces in defense of Buffalo and the New York western frontier against attacks by the British in the War of 1812.

Chapter 4, Brad L. Utter with Thomas X. Grasso, "Clinton's Ditch: The Birth of the Erie Canal, 1825," is the story of the canal, the greatest state public project of the nineteenth century, that spurred development of New York and the nation.

Chapter 5, Nancy Newman, "The Anti-Rent Rebellions, 1839 to 1846," covers tenant farmers' determined resistance to an archaic and oppressive land system in the mid–Hudson Valley.

Chapter 6, Albert M. Rosenblatt, "The Lemmon Case and Slavery in New York State, 1852 to 1860," describes the rise and demise of slavery in New York and a key court decision, on the eve of the Civil War, that maintained that enslaved people from states where slavery was legal would be free if they were brought into New York.

Chapter 7, Kelly Hayes McAlonie, "Welcome to the Club: Louise Blanchard Bethune, Breaking Barriers for Women in Architecture, 1885," relates the struggle to achieve professional recognition for women in the profession of architecture.

Chapter 8, Daniel Kornstein, "The Triangle Fire and the Velvet Revolution in Workplace Safety, 1911," describes a tragic factory fire in New York City and the factory safety and health requirements enacted in its aftermath.

Chapter 9, Anthony F. Gero, "Black New Yorkers in World War I: The Extraordinary Achievements of the 369th US Infantry, the Famous 'Hellfighters,' 1916 to 1918," tells about heroic Black soldiers in World War I who were treated shabbily when they returned home because racism continued after the war.

Chapter 10, Susan Ingalls Lewis, "How New York Women Won the Vote, 1917," relates the history of the fight for woman suffrage in New York and activists' victory in 1917.

Chapter 11, Ellen NicKenzie Lawson, "Prohibition in New York City, 1920," is the story of resistance to Prohibition in the nation's largest city, a major contributing factor to its repeal in 1932.

Chapter 12, Dennis Gaffney, "Radical Roots: The Rise of the United Federation of Teachers and the First Teachers' Strike in New York City, 1960," describes the origin of the United Federation of Teachers in New York City and its first strike, in 1960, a milestone in the history of public employee unions.

Chapter 13, C. R. Roseberry, "The Empire State Plaza and the Remaking of Downtown Albany, 1963," is the history of the development of the state office complex and its transformation of Albany.

Chapter 14, Ashley Hopkins-Benton, "The Stonewall Uprising and the Fight for Gay Rights, 1969," is the story of how a police raid on a gay bar in New York City accelerated the campaign for gay rights in New York and the nation.

Chapter 15, Bruce W. Dearstyne, "The 9/11 Attacks and New York's Resilience, 2001," describes the devastating terrorist attack on New York City on September 11, 2001, and the city's extraordinary resilience and recovery.

Chapter 16, Kevin C. Fitzpatrick, "Inside the COVID-19 Era in New York: New York City Parks as Witnesses, 2020 to 2022," explores the impact of the COVID-19 pandemic on the New York City Department of Parks and Recreation, including how the agency took on new responsibilities during the crisis.

The Continuing Revolution

Each of the chapters stands alone, presenting its own dramatic story. But they have traits in common that illustrate the "continuing revolution" theme:

- They are inspirational, against-the-odds stories wherein a determined individual or group struggled against the status quo to improve social conditions, move toward equality, or effect social justice.

- It usually took several years and extraordinary patience and perseverance by the New Yorkers in these stories to achieve the change they wanted. Even in the face of indifference, opposition, or hostility, their determination kept them going.

- Most of the stories are about ordinary New Yorkers who rose to the occasion in their time and achieved extraordinary results. Famous people from history are for the most part absent from the stories.

- The chapters present "New York stories" but have implications or ramifications beyond the state's boundary, for the nation. In some, ideas that took root in New York spread across the country; in others, Americans beyond our state were inspired by what New Yorkers did.

- They have reverberations today, as some of the same issues linger, though in different forms, making the stories not only interesting but doubly valuable for the parallels and insights they offer us.

New York seems to always be undertaking, in the midst of, or finishing some sort of revolution or another. Restless New Yorkers rarely feel complacent, just accepting the status quo; rather, they are inclined to alter the state of affairs to (hopefully) make things better. New York has often seemed on fast-forward, ambitious, eager to advance its prospects, impatient with delay, and inclined to go it alone if the rest of the nation does not share its vision.

Historian Allan Nevins's 1955 assessment of New York City is also applicable to the state as a whole: "it is too protean, too subject to incessant phantasmagoric change. . . . Its architectural and social record is a palimpsest. Over its skyscrapers hangs some demon forever waving his wand and exclaiming 'Presto, Change!' At his command, the change comes—comes through growth, the successive waves of immigration from abroad and migration from within, the passion for rebuilding."[2] New Yorkers walk and talk faster than other people, visitors from outside comment. The phrase "in a New York minute" describes the restlessness and haste in the city. Exuberant New Yorkers want to be heard. "They talk very loud, very fast, and altogether," Massachusetts's patriot leader John Adams recorded in his diary after a bracing visit to New York City in 1774. "If they ask you a question, before you can utter three words of your answer, they will break out upon you again—and talk away."[3]

New York has a lot of history to be proud of and talk about. It is arguably the nation's most historically significant state. Its original Indigenous inhabitants, usually called Indians by those who came after them, began residing here thousands of years ago. Its oldest cities, New York (called New Amsterdam by the Dutch, the original colonizers of the area) and Albany (called Fort Orange by the Dutch), go back more than four centuries.

New York is renowned for its cultural, financial, and political influence. For many years, it was the most populous state, and it has always been a leader, influencing the rest of the nation. New York has over a thousand historical monuments and over five hundred historical societies and museums (far more than any other state). It is the only state with officially appointed local historians and one of the few with a state historian.

Yet New Yorkers sometimes seem too busy *making* history to slow down and *study* history. Students in New York schools learn little about their state's past. New York has an official New York State History Month (October) designated by law, but it passes every year with little public fanfare. State policymakers seldom draw on the state's long history for precedents,

---

2. Allan Nevins, "The Golden Thread in the History of New York," *New-York Historical Society Quarterly* 39, no. 1 (January 1955): 7.

3. Quoted in David McCullough, *John Adams* (New York: Simon and Schuster, 2001), 25.

parallels, and insights when formulating new policies. Allan Nevins wondered at New York's stunning history alongside its "want of reverence for the past."[4]

Historians have sometimes shortchanged New York, too. The state historian Alexander C. Flick, in his book *The American Revolution in New York* a century ago, lamented that "New York's role in the Revolution has been ignored, misrepresented and misunderstood."[5] Other states get the majority of the credit, said Flick. Americans tend to think that the *real* revolution took place in Massachusetts (the locale of the Boston Tea Party and Paul Revere's ride), Pennsylvania (the site of the Declaration of Independence), and Virginia (Thomas Jefferson's home state, where Patrick Henry shouted "Give me liberty or give me death!," and where the Revolutionary War ended at Yorktown in 1781).

Of course, New York's role in the revolution was critical. Nearly one-third of the major engagements of the war were fought here. The British spent a great deal of time and resources taking and holding New York City and trying without success to conquer the rest of the state, failing at the great Battle of Saratoga in 1777. The American victory there turned out to be the turning point of the Revolution—four years later.

That's one subtheme of the New York story: Events here have revolutionary-dimension reverberations later. The spark of historical change has often been lit in New York.

New Yorkers, though, have seemed to just shrug their shoulders, indifferent to their state being upstaged in the grand historical pageant. The problem Flick described has been chronic; New York has not tended to catch the popular historical imagination, and historians have often preferred to focus on other states (where the story is more compact and easier to tell) or the national scene (where history played out on a grander stage and could be painted with broader strokes).

Framing Revolutionary-Scale Change

"Here is a really interesting story," wrote the historian Dixon Ryan Fox in a 1933 essay, "for where is there a history more dramatic, more richly

---

4. Nevins, "Golden Thread," 7.

5. Alexander C. Flick, ed., *The American Revolution in New York: Its Political, Social and Economic Significance* (Albany: State Education Department, 1926), 1.

varied, more instructive? In every stage it illustrates the history of the whole United States."[6]

David M. Ellis, in his book *New York: State and City*, agreed: "throughout the past two centuries, New York has been where the action is. Wherever we look, we encounter . . . people who have formed a society of infinite variety, complexity, and change. As America's society grows increasingly pluralistic, it may be able to forecast its future from New York's experiences."[7] New York's historical story defies easy telling and the imposition of grand theories that "explain" it. Sometimes it might seem New York has at least three historical narratives—New York City, "upstate" (north of the city), and Long Island. New York contains the nation's largest city and also Adirondack Park, at six million acres the largest in the contiguous United States. The Town of Hempstead is the most populated town in the nation, but the Town of Piercefield has around three hundred inhabitants.

Historians have been challenged to come up with a statewide conceptual framework that encompasses New York's history and embodies both continuity and change. The New York State Museum tried with a booklet published during the bicentennial of the Revolution entitled *Forces: Three Themes in the Lives of New Yorkers*, designed to identify key traits in the historical character of New York.[8]

One theme was materialism: "New Yorkers have fashioned, used, invented, acquired, lusted after, traded for, and aspired to a literally infinite number of material things. . . . All bespeak a prodigious productivity and achievement reflecting a people's quest for a material definition of success."[9]

The second was diversity. New York has been built by millions of immigrants. This has made it an ethnic, religious, and cultural mosaic. Its cities reflect a cosmopolitan flavor and an inherent tolerance. There is a good deal of variation from one region to another, and every city has its distinct traits.

The third theme was change. This theme, even more than the others, conveyed the revolutionary character of New York. The war disrupted New York's economy and society. But "within two generations, New York would

---

6. Dixon Ryan Fox, foreword to *Wigwam and Bowerie*, vol. 1 of Alexander C. Flick, ed., *History of the State of New York* (New York: Columbia University Press, 1933), vi–vii.

7. David M. Ellis, *New York: State and City* (Ithaca: Cornell University Press, 1979), 24.

8. David R. Gould, *Forces: Three Themes in the Lives of New Yorkers* (Albany: State Museum, 1977).

9. Gould, *Forces*, 7.

earn a place in population, commerce, transportation and agriculture second to none." It was populated by farms, factories, and nascent cities by then. "Change of this magnitude is typical of New York's past. . . . The fact of change has brought with it the expectation and encouragement of change as opposed to its mere acceptance. In New York, from an early date, change has not been simply a result of societal development, but rather a massive motivating force."[10]

The booklet continues, "In the history of change in America, New York was often the innovator. The creation and perfection of the transportation networks was the key to New York's commercial and industrial triumph."[11] For instance, New Yorkers invented or perfected an impressive list of transportation firsts, *Forces* explains. These included turnpikes (1802), the first successful steamboat (*Clermont*, 1807), passenger-carrying railway (Mohawk & Hudson, 1831), major trunkline railroads, and the Roebling suspension bridge (Niagara Falls, 1854). New York's innovations catalyzed change. "These improvements spread quickly beyond New York's borders, and everywhere raised property values, stimulated agriculture, commerce, and industry by slashing freight rates and made the settlement of the continent possible."[12] The rapidity of growth was accelerated by the triple forces of immigration, industrialization, and urbanization.

In 1785, early in the history of New York state, George Washington called it "the seat of Empire," a phrase later rendered into its popular nickname, "the Empire State." The name has stuck to this day. It has come to denote New York's spirit of leadership.

The New York Central Railroad named its flagship luxury passenger train that, from 1892 to 1967, ran from New York City to Buffalo and then to Cleveland the Empire State Express. The train's cars were named after New York governors. The train became so famous that the postal service issued a stamp to commemorate it. Its most famous engine, "999" (built in the Central's yards near Albany), set a speed record of over one hundred miles per hour on a run from Batavia to Buffalo in 1893. In 1931, the Empire State Building, then the world's tallest building, opened for the first time. The state called its magnificent new Albany office building complex completed in 1978 the Empire State Plaza.

---

10. Gould, 39, 41.
11. Gould, 41.
12. Gould, 41–42.

Leading in Industry and Finance

New York has led the way in wide-ranging transformations.

The New York Central Railroad, created in 1853, the nation's second-largest railroad, was a pioneer in modern management techniques, connecting New York with seven other states and two Canadian provinces. By the turn of the twentieth century, the Central's lines stretched from Chicago through the nation's agricultural and industrial heartland in the Midwest, to Buffalo, on to Albany and Boston, south to New York City, and north into two Canadian provinces.

It was aviation pioneer Glenn Curtiss of Hammondsport, New York (not his contemporaries the Wright Brothers, who have overshadowed him in history), who developed modern flight controls (some still in use today) and who made the first preannounced, publicly witnessed, press-covered, professionally certified airplane flight, in 1908. Curtiss also made the first Albany–to–New York City flight in 1910. He invented pontoons and seaplanes and is known as the "Father of Naval Aviation" for his role in training Navy pilots and building the first planes for the United States Navy.

Endicott, New York, was the home of the Computing-Tabulating-Recording Company, founded in 1910. It later evolved into the International Business Machines company (IBM) in 1924. IBM became one of the most successful and influential companies in history, leading and shaping the fields of information processing and information management, serving as a model of customer service, and pioneering in enlightened employee practices. It sparked the dramatic expansion of information technology, leading to the internet, the World Wide Web, and the computers and cell phones of today.

Schenectady was often called "the city that lights and hauls the world." General Electric, the nation's leading producer of electrical goods and products, was founded there in 1892. It was a pioneer in light bulbs, electric engines, commercial power stations, vacuum tubes, jet engines, and recently renewable energy and health care.

The American Locomotive Company (ALCO) was founded in Schenectady in 1901, an outgrowth of the Schenectady Locomotive Works, established in 1848. Before its demise seven decades later, ALCO manufactured hundreds of locomotives. It led the advance in technology from coal-fired steam engines to diesel, then to electric.

Rochester was also a leading industrial city. Bausch & Lomb, founded there in 1853, soon became the nation's leading producer of optical goods.

Rochester was where the Kodak camera was invented and where Eastman Kodak was organized in 1892. The company was a leader in innovation and the most important maker of cameras and film in the predigital era. Inexpensive, easy-to-use Kodak cameras made photography—and, later, movies—commonplace in the United States.

Buffalo was for many years the largest grain port in the nation. Grain was offloaded from ships and railroads from the west into huge elevators for shipment and distribution elsewhere. In the late nineteenth and early twentieth centuries, the Buffalo region was a major producer of steel.

New York City was the nation's leading manufacturing city until around the mid-twentieth century. It led in several areas, most notably garment manufacturing. New York is also the hub of the nation's finance industry, as several of the largest banks and the New York Stock Exchange (founded in 1792) are located there. It is sometimes called the financial capital of the United States and the world. As such, it has provided the capital resources for much of the world's commercial development and activity for more than a century.

The Brooklyn Navy Yard was a beehive of activity in the twentieth century. It employed around seventy thousand workers at its peak during World War II. It was at the yard that the first ironclad battleship, the *Monitor*, was outfitted and commissioned in 1862. The USS *Arizona*, sunk during the Japanese attack on Pearl Harbor on December 7, 1941, was built in Brooklyn in 1915. So was the USS *Missouri* (1941), where the enemy surrendered in 1945.

New Yorker J. P. Morgan, the most powerful banker and financier of the late nineteenth and early twentieth centuries, reorganized railroads and industrial companies to make them more stable and profitable. He also financed leading-edge companies such as General Electric and managed the consolidation of several large steel companies to form U.S. Steel in 1901. His actions helped ward off depressions and stabilize the economy in 1893 and 1907. In fact, Morgan grew so strong and so adept at controlling financial markets that people became apprehensive of his power. He is perhaps the best example of the outsized ambition and influence in the state's history, and it was beyond the state's capacity to rein him in. That took federal action, particularly the creation of the Federal Reserve in 1913 and the Federal Trade Commission and the Clayton Antitrust Act in 1914.

New York has led on another front as well. It has long been regarded as the media capital of the world, a fountain of ideas that affect people everywhere. It has been the most important publishing and broadcasting center in the nation. This means, among other things, that New York writers have something of a hometown advantage and that New York editors and producers can often determine which ideas get broadcast and which do not. It has been the home of the nation's most influential newspapers, including *The New York Times*, *The Wall Street Journal*, and the *New York Post* (the oldest continually published daily in America, founded in 1801). The *New York World* was one of the most widely read, influential papers in its time (1883 to 1931). The editorials in the *New York Tribune* (1841 to 1924) helped shape public opinion; its editor Horace Greeley ran for president in 1872 on the Liberal Republican and Democratic party tickets (he lost to Ulysses Grant).

The nation's major book-publishing houses call New York home. These include Penguin Random House, Simon & Schuster, HarperCollins, and W. W. Norton. *Time*, *Newsweek*, *New York Magazine*, and *The New Yorker* are all immensely influential. In the past, journals such as *The New Republic* and *McClure's Magazine* have publicized important reform ideas.

The television industry took root in New York. ABC, CBS, NBC, and the Fox News Channel are all headquartered there.

Leading in Social and Political Reform

New York has been on the leading edge of major social and economic developments that have affected the entire nation. That has also made it a leader in reforms to deal with these transformative forces.

For instance, during the Progressive Era, circa 1900 to 1920, New York was the first state to come to grips with the ramifications of urbanization, industrialization, immigration, and the glaring differences between the very rich and the very poor.

Our state became a leader in labor reform, business regulation, and social welfare programs. For example, the State of New York established a comprehensive labor department (1901), a health department (1901), personal privacy protection (1903), a comprehensive education department (1904), and the nation's strongest public utilities regulation (1907). It enacted a model tenement house law (1901). New York was the first to outlaw night work by women in factories (1899, reenacted 1903), proscribe child labor (1903), pass workers' compensation (1910), and legislate a comprehensive workplace safety and fire code (1912 to 1915). It regulated the carrying of concealed weapons (1911). The state began construction of a new cross-state canal in 1903 and started a state highway program in 1909.

In the years that followed, many other states—and eventually the federal government—followed New York's lead and used it as a model for their own reforms.

This was particularly notable for the New Deal in the 1930s, which enacted a battery of reforms to combat the Great Depression and promote social welfare. That was no surprise. President Franklin D. Roosevelt (1933 to 1945) was a former New York state senator and governor. He developed the state's Temporary Emergency Relief Administration in 1931 to combat the Depression, and a number of New Deal agencies, including the Federal Emergency Relief Administration, were modeled on it.

Frances Perkins was an investigator for the state Factory Investigating Commission, which studied factory safety issues after the tragic Triangle Fire in 1911 that killed many workers. She helped shape a battery of safety regulations between 1912 and 1915. She went on to serve as industrial commissioner under Governor Roosevelt and then as the first female secretary of labor, from 1933 to 1945. In that role, among other things, she was a major architect of the Social Security Act of 1935.

Robert F. Wagner, state senator from 1909 to 1918, led the enactment of several progressive reform laws. Later, as US senator from New York, he was the principal author of the National Labor Relations Act, commonly called the Wagner Act, in 1935. It guaranteed the right of employees to organize and bargain collectively and to take collective actions, including strikes.

Leading in Diversity and the Quest for Equality

America is a nation of immigrants and descendants of immigrants. New York has been a gateway to the United States; more people have entered through New York City than any other port—over a million in 1907 alone. Many moved on, to upstate cities or into the interior of the country via the Erie Canal and, later, rail lines and highways linking New York to the rest of the nation.

But many stayed on in New York City, and their descendants did, too, bringing a rich array of religions, customs, and skills. The borough of Queens was, and still is, one of the most diverse areas in the nation. It is made up of white, Asian American, Black, and Latino individuals. Nearly half of Queens residents are foreign-born. Over a hundred languages are spoken there. Immigrants to New York changed their outlook to accommodate their new surroundings, but they also leavened their communities with their own cultures. That is one of the things that have made New York great.

Writer E. B. White, in his 1949 book *Here Is New York*, referred to the city's newcomers—he called them "settlers"—as people "who [were] born somewhere else and came to New York in quest of something." This group gives the city its vibrancy and, according to White, accounts for New York's high-strung disposition, its poetical deportment, its dedication to the arts, and its incomparable achievements. Commuters give the city its tidal restlessness; natives give it solidity and continuity; but the settlers give it passion. And whether it is a farmer arriving from Italy to set up a small grocery store in a slum, or a young girl arriving from a small town in Mississippi to escape the indignity of being observed by her neighbors, or a boy arriving from the Corn Belt with a manuscript in his suitcase and a pain in his heart, it makes no difference: each embraces New York with the intense excitement of first love, each absorbs New York with the fresh eyes of an adventurer, each generates heat and light to dwarf the Consolidated Edison Company.[13]

New York's record on race is tarnished by its retaining slavery until 1799, when a law mandated its gradual termination by 1827. But the city and state were, in comparison to most other places in the nation, models of inclusion and tolerance. New Yorkers were, and are, packed so closely together in New York City and in other cities, and so busy with work and getting on with their own lives, that they had little time for hate. They were more inclined toward acceptance and inclusion.

Black New Yorkers built a thriving community in Harlem, heralded by the Harlem Renaissance in the 1920s and 1930s, a burgeoning of creativity by Black writers, artists, musicians, and others. New York was a leader in the civil rights movement and was the first state to prohibit discrimination in employment based on race, creed, color, and national origin, in 1945. Two years later, in 1947, Jackie Robinson became the first Black man to play on a Major League Baseball team, the Brooklyn Dodgers.

New York was the place where the campaign for women's equality began (in Seneca Falls in 1848). It was not the first to grant women the right to vote—that did not happen until 1917—but the victory in New York was the decisive factor in victory at the national level three years later. It was the place where the modern gay rights movement took flight; after a

---

13. E. B. White, *Here Is New York* (New York: Harper and Brothers, 1949), 26.

brutal police raid at a gay bar called Stonewall Inn in New York City, the patrons fought back, and several days of unrest followed.

The National Association for the Advancement of Colored People (NAACP) was established in New York City in 1909 to combat racism. In 1920, the American Civil Liberties Union (ACLU) was founded in New York City to protect the promise of the Bill of Rights and to expand its reach to people historically denied its protections. The state has protected civil liberties in many laws over the years and recently did so in an amendment to the state constitution approved by the voters in 2024.

New York Women Lead

Many change makers were women, though men often got the credit when they came up with similar ideas or were in positions of power and therefore able to implement the ideas women had initiated.

Several of the chapters in the book illustrate women's leadership, particularly in the struggle for suffrage and equal rights. But New York women could be cited for their outsized influence in other areas as well.

Over a century before Rosa Parks's famous stand against transportation segregation in Montgomery, Alabama, it was a New Yorker who first established the principle of integration of public transportation. There was de facto segregation in public transportation in New York in the first half of the nineteenth century. It was understood that Black riders would be limited to certain sections of horse-drawn streetcars, or to separate cars. On a hot morning in July 1854, Elizabeth Jennings, a Black schoolteacher in New York City, refused a conductor's order to move out of a segregated car. When she stood her ground, she was forcefully removed by the conductor, a police officer, and some passengers. She sued in court, and the court awarded her damages and ruled that Black customers had the same rights as others. That decision led to the desegregation of public transportation in the city. In 1873, the state legislature passed a law that explicitly outlawed discrimination on public transportation in New York City.

Edith Wharton was a master at capturing upper-class society at the end of the nineteenth century in her novels *The House of Mirth* (1905) and *The Age of Innocence* (1920). Her books were unflinching in their portrayal of societal norms in her era. Her books are the basis for much of the public's perception of that era, including for the recent TV series *The Gilded Age*.

Florence Kelley was a broad-scale social reformer who fought for woman suffrage and laws to abolish child labor and protect women workers in the Progressive Era (ca. 1900 to 1920). She headed the National Consumers League, which lobbied factory owners to improve working conditions. She was also one of the founders of the NAACP.

Crystal Eastman was another multifront reformer. She was a suffragist, but once women got that right, she pushed for full equality in education, the professions, and social life generally. She was a pacifist during and after World War I. Her book *Work Accidents and the Law* (1910) laid the basis for New York's employers' liability law, the first in the nation. With seemingly boundless energy, she studied and wrote about socialist revolutions around the world and was one of the founders of American socialism.

Many people contributed to the environmental movement. But it was Lois Gibbs, a resident of the Love Canal section of Niagara Falls, who helped propel environmental issues into the arena of public awareness. Love Canal had been a dump site for toxic chemicals before it was covered and houses, including Gibbs's, were built there. Chemicals oozed to the surface and caused health problems. Gibbs organized her neighbors, brought in the press, kept lobbying until the state investigated, and, in the early 1980s, achieved the goals of getting the state to buy up contaminated houses and the company that had buried the chemicals to pay for the cleanup of the site. Her high-visibility campaign was a major factor in the creation of the federal Superfund in 1980 to locate and clean up toxic dump sites. Gibbs, a model of citizen activism, went on to found and direct a national nonprofit organization to train and support local activists in their environmental work.

Into the Future

As the 250th anniversary approaches, some people believe New York might be losing its historic luster and momentum. Older manufacturing industries have closed down. The state's population is declining.

But New York, always resilient, is a leader in education, finance, insurance, health care, and professional and business services. It is a pioneer in next-generation industries such as semiconductors and nanotechnology. The state is one of the nation's leaders in environmental policy, moving away from fossil fuels and adopting clean energy.

New immigrants are entering in sizable numbers. New York's public education system continues to be one of the best in the nation. Its political leadership is determined to keep New York moving.

The musical *Hamilton*, about New York revolutionary leader (and later the first secretary of the treasury) Alexander Hamilton and written by New Yorker Lin-Manuel Miranda, debuted in New York City in 2015. It was a runaway success. In the fourth scene of the play, set in 1776, "The Schuyler Sisters" introduces Hamilton's future wife, Eliza, and her two sisters, the three daughters of revolutionary leader Philip Schuyler. They hail from Albany, but their songs are an ode to Hamilton and Miranda's hometown, New York City. To be sure, there are disparities of wealth in New York ("There's nothing rich folks like more than going downtown and slummin' it with the poor," sings New York patriot leader and future vice president Aaron Burr). But the city exudes energy, creativity, determination, and progress. The Schuyler sisters chant, "Work! Work!," a constant theme in New York's history.

"Look around, look around at how lucky we are to be alive right now!," sings Eliza. The ensemble magnifies the New York theme: "The revolution's happening in New York . . . the greatest city in the world!" At Alexander and Eliza's wedding four years later, in 1780, the guests sing, "In New York you can be a new man!"

In a 2020 press conference, Mayor Bill de Blasio explained that the city was beating the COVID-19 pandemic and bringing in new businesses. That should not surprise anyone, the mayor said, citing New York's historical confidence and resilience: "people should never bet against New York City and our strength and our people and our talent. . . . Look, the bottom line about New York City has been true for generations. It's more true than ever. Extraordinary talent here. Extraordinary creativity. If you want to get anything done, come to New York City because this is where it happens."[14]

Since the time of the Revolution, New York has been "where it happens." The city and the state have been ahead of their time, jettisoning outmoded customs and institutions, trying new things, and charting the way to the future. That is what the chapters in this book are about. We can expect New York's "revolution" to continue.

---

14. Bill de Blasio, "Transcript: Mayor de Blasio Holds Media Availability," August 4, 2020, City of New York, https://www.nyc.gov/office-of-the-mayor/news/568-20/transcript-mayor-de-blasio-holds-media-availability.

1

The Oneida Rebellions, 1763 to 1784

Daniel Koch

Adapted from Daniel Koch, "Land of the Oneidas: Central New York State and the Creation of America, from Prehistory to the Present" (SUNY Press, 2023).

The American Revolution led to the displacement of the Oneidas and other Native American tribes from their traditional homelands in New York. This is an important but often-neglected revolutionary impact of the Revolution in New York.

New York's strategic location made it an arena of battle in the Revolution. The Oneidas, a Native American tribe in central New York affiliated with the Haudenosaunee Confederacy (formerly called Iroquois), like other American Indian tribes, were caught between contending forces and buffeted by the winds of war. At the end of the colonial wars between France and England in 1763, in which England was victorious, the American Indians negotiated with English authorities. As New York and the other English colonies drifted toward independence in the 1760s and early 1770s, they were faced with a choice of allying with the English or with the American patriots or trying to stay neutral.

Both sides of the Revolutionary War tried to attract their support. Some of the confederacy supported the British, but most of the Oneidas sided with the patriots.

After the Revolution, their fate was in the hands of New York and United States authorities. The Oneidas, like other tribes in the confederacy, under pressure from white settlers, were gradually forced off their ancestral lands through a series of treaties.

Editor's note: In this chapter, the terms "Native American" and "American Indian" are used to conform to current usage.

☙

The Oneidas inhabited, hunted, and traveled over a homeland that stretched up through the center of what is now New York state. In the heart of the country is Oneida Lake. To its south is a hilly plateau, with long, rounded-top highlands, in which the Oneidas had built their principal villages for centuries. Through the center of their territory ran a flat corridor—the only significant break in the Appalachian Mountains that divide the Atlantic coast from the interior of North America. In the eighteenth century, Euro-Americans fought for control of the "Oneida Carry," a short stretch of dry land between the Mohawk River and Wood Creek and thus the strategic point in an otherwise all-water route connecting the Atlantic, via the Hudson and Mohawk Rivers, to the Great Lakes.

Britain had used its tenuous military control of that corridor to thwart France's ambitions during the French and Indian War. At the war's end in 1763, France handed over its North American territories to the British. With no further threat from the French and their Native American allies in the region, the Oneidas feared there would be nothing to restrain settlers and squatters from moving onto their lands. They had witnessed the way that speculators bought up most of the Mohawk lands to their east and then opened the lands up to settlers over the preceding decades.

When Sir William Johnson—Britain's superintendent of Indian affairs—passed through in 1761, he met the Oneida chief Conoghquieson with upwards of thirty other Oneidas and Tuscaroras at German Flats. The Tuscaroras, originally from lands farther south in what are now the Carolinas, had been invited to Oneida lands earlier in the century and had become the sixth nation in the Haudenosaunee Confederacy. Conoghquieson said to Johnson, while presenting rows of ceremonial wampum, "This land, which was given us by the Divine Being, we love as our lives and therefore hope you will secure the possession of it to us, which has been ours from the beginning, by preventing any more of your people from settling higher in the Country."

Britain was buoyed by its victory against the French in North America but also burdened by it. Its war debts were enormous, and nearly as soon as the war with France ended a new one against Native American adversaries began as the British tried to take control of the Ohio territory. In

1763 the Ottawa chief Pontiac launched an attack on now-British Detroit, the opening act in a widespread offensive against nearly all of Britain's trans-Appalachian forts. Protecting these frontier outposts from American Indian raids over nearly the entire eastern half of North America, from Hudson Bay to the Gulf of Mexico, would be a mammoth, expensive task. Protecting hundreds or thousands of new colonial settlements over the same area would be impossible.

Although the Mohawk Joseph Brant and some Oneidas fought on the side of the British, others—particularly the Senecas, geographically closest and therefore most vulnerable to attack if seen by anti-British tribes to be aligned with the enemy—were wavering. Many of their warriors joined the rebellion. The British were aware that the western five (at least) of the Six Nations could join the ranks of their enemies if something were not done to alleviate their most urgent concern.

In 1763, King George III signed a royal proclamation declaring that all lands west of the Appalachians would be off limits for settlement. The proclamation also stipulated that land east of the boundary line could no longer be bought directly from American Indians; only the British government via its royal governors or the superintendent for Indian affairs could buy land from American Indians. Land purchasers and speculators would thenceforward need to buy from the government. Theoretically, this would protect American Indians from the sort of exploitative land sales they had been forced to accept in years past. This helped turn the original Five Nations more clearly to Britain's side in the later stages of Pontiac's War. In the end, however, it would contribute to turning many white colonists against the king.

The 1763 line was ill-defined and needed clarifying to make it legitimate in the eyes of settlers. For one thing, there were already some settlements and patents west of the Appalachians in Pennsylvania and Virginia. A revised line, henceforward known as the Line of Property, was drawn up by Johnson and proposed to a grand conference of representatives from American Indian nations throughout eastern North America at Fort Stanwix, on the Oneida Carry, in 1768. The line was moved westward in most places in exchange for a range of presents and promises that royal enforcement of the boundary would be rigorous. It ran right through Oneida territory.

Although no white settlers in the Mohawk Valley lived west of what is now Herkimer, New York, in 1763, some of the Oneida lands had already been sold—not to hardy pioneers but to wealthy speculators who had no intention of living on them. The most significant example was the Albany official Pieter Schuyler, who procured the "Oriskany Patent," a large tract of land that included the Oneida Carry in 1705. He sensed its future value, even though at that time it was an isolated parcel deep in Native American territory and at the mercy of French raiders.

The most difficult part of the 1768 proceedings at Fort Stanwix was the placement of the Line of Property in Oneida country. For Johnson it was imperative that the line be placed to the west of the Oneida Carry, so that the now-crucial route to the continent's interior could be secured for the future. The sticking point was that the Oneidas were arguing the legitimacy of the 1705 patent. At Stanwix, the Oneidas "said they had the greatest reason to doubt [that] an Indian Deed" had been legitimately made in 1705. Johnson argued that the patentees were men of good character, but the Oneidas dug in. If the Line of Property were set at the western end of the Oriskany Patent, large areas of the Oneidas' ancestral hunting ground that had not yet been patented would be east of the line and vulnerable to squatters.

Most annoyingly of all for Johnson (foreshadowing troubles to come), two "New England Missionaries who attended the Congress . . . used every means in their power with the Oneidaes . . . to prevent their parting with [the Oriskany Patent], poisoning their Minds with a thousand Storys." The missionaries had been sent by Eleazar Wheelock, a Connecticut Congregationalist preacher who hoped to build a grand Indian school there and aggressively advised the Oneidas not to give up any ground. The Presbyterians, Congregationalists, and other nonconformists of New England—dissenters from the official Church of England—would come increasingly into conflict with the Crown and with Johnson as its major representative west of Albany.

In the end, Johnson prevailed in getting the Oneidas to forfeit the Oriskany Patent, drawing the boundary just to the west of it. From there it ran southeastward to the west branch of the Unadilla River, near present-day Bridgewater. The Oneidas were paid an extra £1,000 for making this concession, and nine Oneida families living on the tract who earned money by helping transport goods were allowed to remain. After 1768 the gaps between existing patents and the Line of Property were filled almost immediately.

Johnson's work to secure the Line of Property was a success in the short term. It made King George III's Proclamation of 1763 a reality. But for many American colonists the proclamation itself felt like a high-handed decree forbidding their movement west onto land they felt they had helped

Britain to win. Land purchases from American Indians would still be the preserve of high-ranking royal officials and aristocrats. For the Oneidas, the Line of Property cut across their hunting grounds. A repetitive cycle of land sales that constantly divided the nation between pro- and anti-sale factions had begun.

The centuries-old Oneida tradition of living in a single main village, in longhouses, had changed completely by the time of the Fort Stanwix Treaty. Their last traditional village site at Primes Hill housed between eleven and twelve thousand people in 1714. It was surrounded by traditional twelve-foot-high palisades. By the 1730s, the Oneidas, like most of the Haudenosaunee, had divided themselves into several smaller hamlets and homesteads. Officials still referred to the most densely populated of their settlements as "castles," but by the middle of the eighteenth century the traditional Oneida village was no more.

While most Oneidas stayed within about twenty miles of the Primes Hill site, some scattered farther afield. By mid-century, the main Oneida settlement itself had split in two. The larger village was Kanonwalohale, at a ford of Oneida Creek where the village of Oneida Castle is today. It was founded in the 1740s by warriors who had grown more powerful within the nation. Its name, meaning "enemy's head on a pole," cast a fear-inspiring picture. But the Oneidas at Kanonwalohale did not build palisades and had moved down from the defensive positions afforded by the high hills where the Oneidas had lived for centuries, onto the main east–west land route from Albany to Oswego. They were generally accepting of Euro-Americans. The village resembled a colonial settlement more than a traditional Haudenosaunee one in most ways. There was no longhouse. Some sixty houses with one or two families each sat spread apart from each other, with orchards and enclosures for livestock in between. About seven hundred Oneidas lived in Kanonwalohale, roughly half the population.

A smaller but significantly sized settlement known as "Old Oneida" was in the hills several miles south of Kanonwalohale, in the vicinity of the old Primes Hill village site. Probably a scattered group of about forty homesteads rather than a concentrated village, it was the stronghold of the traditionalist faction of the tribe: Oneidas who wanted as little as possible to do with colonists and who largely rejected Christianity, particularly when it gained a greater hold in Kanonwalohale during the 1760s.

Just as the nature of Oneida settlements was changing indelibly, Protestant Christianity was becoming firmly entrenched. The Anglican missionaries at Fort Hunter had been successful in the Mohawk settlements and had made some inroads among the Oneidas, but it was Presbyterianism that would make the biggest impact. Presbyterianism had its origins in the puritanical rejection of the Church of England's preservation of some Roman Catholic practices. The Presbyterians created their own organization that sent missionaries to the American Indians, called the Society for the Propagation of Christian Knowledge.

Presbyterian missionaries found their first success among the Oneidas at Oquaga. Elihu Spencer was the first to arrive, in 1748. He started writing an Oneida vocabulary but left within a few months. Another Presbyterian, Gideon Hawley, went to Oquaga in 1753, where he learned the Oneida language and became a well-established figure. Visitors noted that his services were being attended by over one hundred Native Americans. Psalms were sung and sermons delivered in both English and Oneida. Services were solemn and dignified, but Hawley was less strict than other Presbyterian missionaries were. Dancing and feasting were not prohibited, though alcohol and war were preached against strongly. He left in 1756.

Although the Oquaga mission was flourishing, the Christians in the Oneida heartland did not have a minister of their own. Some went to Fort Hunter or to Oquaga and participated in Christian services there, but these were long and difficult journeys. Christianity was embedded enough in the main Oneida villages that it survived, at least among a significant faction within the tribe, between the visits of the Anglican missionaries in the 1750s and the arrival of a new and different kind of missionary, Samuel Kirkland, in 1766.

Kirkland's faith had been forged in the Great Awakening, a period of evangelization in the American colonies, which inspired him to spread the Gospel even if it meant martyrdom. When Kirkland came to Kanonwalohale, he built a small cabin, tilling his own garden and surviving on very little food in his first year there. This, he said, earned him "contempt" from villagers who saw his way of life as unprofitable and effeminate. Agriculture was still seen as women's work. However, in 1767 he began to win some ground in the community. He mastered the Oneida language and began teaching the Oneidas to read and write it. He showed courage in standing up to alcohol abuse, even wrestling to the ground an Oneida man who tried to strangle him after he destroyed a cache of rum.

Food became scarcer in the 1760s, partly due to settlers' encroachments on traditional Oneida hunting grounds, and partly due to failed harvests. Kirkland stayed close to the people and saw their suffering, offering kindness and what charity he could. He gained new status with the

Oneidas as someone who knew and understood their problems. By 1771, he reported that three or four hundred American Indians were attending his worship services at Kanonwalohale. Although there were fluctuations in faithfulness and very few conversions among the traditionalists at Old Oneida, Kirkland had become a powerful and respected presence among the People of the Standing Stone. He baptized respected warriors, including one in 1767 who would be a lifelong follower, Shenandoah. Kirkland gave him the Christian name John.

In the years between 1766 and 1774, the Oneidas' relationship with Kirkland deepened, just as their relationship with William Johnson became more and more strained. Johnson, although beloved by the Mohawks, had already tangled with the Oneidas at Stanwix. To the latter, it was obvious that while he promised to protect their lands, he was simultaneously keenly interested in buying large pieces for himself and for wealthy friends. Kirkland, by contrast, showed no interest in procuring land and indeed promised the Oneidas that he never would attempt to buy or take a single acre. The Oneidas began to resent what looked like Johnson's preferential treatment of the Mohawks.

When Johnson tried to block the building of a place of worship that would be financed by Presbyterians in Boston rather than via him (the representative of the king and the Anglican Church), the Kanonwalohale village council, backed by Kirkland, insisted they would go forward with building it anyway. The new meeting house was constructed in 1774. It was a two-story structure with glass windows, thirty-six by twenty-eight feet, with a steeple towering sixty feet high—the most impressive building in Iroquoia. Johnson was incapable of stopping it. To save face, he donated a church bell. Johnson and his Mohawk protégé, Joseph Brant (brother of Johnson's mistress and Kirkland's former classmate), were also meddling in Oquaga in 1773, trying to turn as many Native Americans as possible away from Presbyterianism and toward the Church of England.

Kirkland and Johnson themselves became representative of the two increasingly polarized camps in the political life of colonial America: those unwaveringly loyal to the Crown and those for whom Britain's control over the colonies seemed increasingly intolerable. Kirkland was a New England Presbyterian whose immediate employers were in Boston, the epicenter of anti-British agitation in the American colonies. Just as these tensions were beginning to crest, Sir William Johnson died in 1774. His nephew Guy Johnson, equally committed to the British Crown, succeeded him as superintendent of Indian affairs. Guy Johnson tried to downplay the tensions to the Haudenosaunee; Kirkland, however, was drawing the Oneidas' interest to the colonial cause, but he was not the only one. The Oneidas were dependent on their colonial neighbors, particularly at German Flats, for vital trade. The Palatine Germans resented British taxation, and when fighting broke out, they would take the side of the rebels.

In April 1775, British soldiers marched to Lexington and Concord in Massachusetts, where colonial militias were building stockpiles of arms. It began America's War of Independence. Soon after the Battles of Lexington and Concord, Guy Johnson attempted to argue the virtues of George III with some Mohawk Valley patriots and ended up in a brawl. Palatine Germans drew up a petition to the king and declared solidarity with the people of Boston, where further battles between British forces and colonial militias were taking place. The Johnsons sensed their time was up and evacuated to Canada.

The Oneidas and most of the Haudenosaunee attempted to stay neutral in the conflict for as long as possible. Some individuals chose their own way. Many warriors were keen to gain reputations that would come with fighting. Some went to Montreal, eager to join in campaigns on the British side against the rebellious Americans. Others, like the half-Oneida Thomas Spencer, advocated strongly in favor of fighting against the British. Many Oneidas sympathized with Kirkland, who saw the Americans' conflict as just, but they knew they had little to gain by taking sides in this war between "two brothers," as they saw it. They promoted neutrality vigorously among the Haudenosaunee. For the Haudenosaunee nations to the west, there was little to endear them to the American side. Their trade was less dependent on the Mohawk Valley and Albany (which became a rebel-controlled city in 1775). They could trade with the British via the Great Lakes, Niagara, and the Saint Lawrence, and they had not been influenced by a "patriot" figure like Kirkland. The Mohawks, too, were drawn far more to the British than to the American side. Their most prominent figure, Joseph Brant, was intensely loyal to the Johnsons and carried many warriors with him.

When Johnson fled to Canada via the Oneida Carry, he attempted to give gifts to the Oneidas, sensing that they would be the biggest obstacle in tipping the balance in Iroquoia toward the British. The Oneida chief Shenandoah refused to accept them, and the Oneidas did not meet with Johnson at a conference he held with Indians at Oswego. However, in response to petitions for support from rebels of Massachusetts, the Oneidas sent forth clear declarations of neutrality. An Oneida delegation also went to Kahnawak in Quebec in 1775 to urge their relatives there to remain neutral.

Other Haudenosaunee began accusing the Oneidas of being too sympathetic to the colonists in 1776. Kirkland had clearly attached himself to the rebellion, becoming a Native American agent for the Continental Congress. Shenandoah accompanied Kirkland on a visit to the patriot forces in Boston the year before, where he met George Washington. The Cayugas were outraged that to demonstrate their neutrality, some Oneidas had handed over to the patriot leader Philip Schuyler a war belt that Johnson had presented to Haudenosaunee warriors in Montreal. In 1776, successful colonial attacks in Canada meant the western Haudenosaunee were deprived of their usual trade with the British and took out their anger on the Oneidas. It was clear by the end of a Grand Council meeting in Onondaga in March 1776 that Haudenosaunee neutrality was hanging by a thread and that the Oneidas were clearly the odd one out. That summer, Philip Schuyler (on behalf of the Continental Congress) and John Butler (on behalf of the British) held rival conferences at German Flats and Fort Niagara, respectively, each giving gifts and trying to gain the trust and partnership (or, in Schuyler's case, neutrality, at least) of the Haudenosaunee nations.

The American patriots, at the same time, reoccupied Fort Stanwix as a means of protecting the Mohawk Valley settlements from potential British incursions via Oswego. By tolerating American patriot soliders' presence on their soil, the Oneidas knew that both British and American Indian observers would see it as yet another sign of the Oneida's pro-American leanings. However, they also felt a need for protection. The Oneidas and American colonial officers at Stanwix, which was rechristened Fort Schuyler during the war, built up a positive relationship. The Oneidas were able to trade and buy supplies at Fort Schuyler, and the fortress offered at least some hope of refuge if Kanonwalohale were to come under attack. By 1777, even while the Oneidas were still technically united in neutrality, their leaders were divided between pro-American and pro-British support.

The British plan for 1777 was to destroy the Revolution with a three-pronged attack, converging at Albany. General Burgoyne would head south from Montreal with eight thousand men. General Howe would proceed north from British-controlled New York City. Barry St. Leger would lead a force on ships from Canada down the Saint Lawrence and across Lake Ontario to Oswego. There they would meet up with Joseph Brant and his American Indian force, which would bring together a combined total of sixteen hundred fighting men. From there they would traverse Oneida country, take Fort Schuyler (Stanwix), and proceed down the Mohawk. At the height of summer, Burgoyne's offensive appeared to be going successfully.

They took Fort Ticonderoga on Lake Champlain in July. They were then poised to move on to Fort Schuyler. In the beginning of August, they laid siege to the fort. By the end of the Battle of Oriskany, as it came to be known, hundreds of dead bodies littered the road. Most of them were white members of the American militia. But there were significant numbers of Haudenosaunee dead, including several dozen Seneca warriors who fought on the side of the British.

The remnants of the British forces retreated to their camps around Fort Schuyler, where the siege continued. While the battle was raging at Oriskany, an American sortie had gone out of Fort Schuyler and looted the campsites of the British and Haudenosaunee who were involved in the fighting, meaning that when the weary fighters returned, their food, blankets, and possessions were gone. Messengers reported that a powerful new force of battle-hardened patriot soldiers under Benedict Arnold was coming up the Mohawk from Albany, striking fear into the increasingly demoralized British and their American Indian allies. They abandoned the siege and retreated toward Oneida Lake, but not before making a raid on Oriska, stealing what they could and burning it to the ground.

By the end of August, British forces were gone from the Oneida heartland, but there was no saying whether they'd be back. At Oriskany, Haudenosaunee of the Six Nations on opposite sides of the Revolutionary War had fought and killed each other. The Oneidas received a bloody hatchet from Onondaga, signifying that they were now at war with the rest of the Haudenosaunee Confederacy. But the offensive that would have cut the colonies in half and almost certainly ended the war if it had succeeded was stopped. St. Leger's retreat killed the British pincer movement's momentum. It meant that Burgoyne's force was now on its own, deprived of vital support from the west that might have resulted in a triumphant occupation of Albany by the autumn. Instead, he was defeated at Saratoga in October 1777. It was the key battle in the preservation of the revolution. The soldiers, militiamen, and Oneidas who fought at Stanwix and Oriskany had laid the foundation for America's victory.

In September 1777, Oneidas and Tuscaroras met in another council with Philip Schuyler. He offered a war belt to confirm that that they would fight side by side against the British; it was accepted. The fighting with the other Haudenosaunee, however, weighed heavily. The Oneidas declared their objective in future fighting would be to capture British prisoners, which they would exchange for Haudenosaunee warriors that had been captured by the Americans. About 150 Oneida warriors then went to Saratoga, where the decisive phase of the battle between Schuyler's and Burgoyne's armies was underway. The Battle of Saratoga was a disaster for the British. On October 17, 1777, Burgoyne surrendered, ending all hope of success in the New York campaign.

The Oneidas were understandably worried about attacks from other Indians and asked for fortifications at Kanonwalohale. The Marquis de Lafayette, a French aristocrat who had enlisted to fight with the Americans against Britain at the rank of major general (despite his age, twenty in 1777), was in Albany. After a meeting with the Oneida chief Grasshopper at Johnstown in March 1778, he sent three Frenchmen to Kanonwalohale to engineer a fort. The Americans' hope was that if they were able to provide the Oneidas enough security, they would in turn send warriors to Valley Forge to help Washington, who requested the help of the Oneidas, knowing that their skills would be of particular use against small British raiding parties that were harrying the countryside in Pennsylvania.

In April, forty-seven warriors, nearly all Oneidas, met at Fort Schuyler and began their trek with Louis de Tousard to Valley Forge. When they arrived, Washington met them personally. They fought alongside Lafayette, and at least six of them died at the Battle of Barren Hill in May 1778. The fort building at Kanonwalohale stalled, however. The three Frenchmen stayed for a month in April 1778, but the project was abandoned due to lack of manpower.

During the summer of 1778, patriot settlements at Cobleskill and German Flats were raided by a pro-British band of Haudenosaunee and Loyalists led by Joseph Brant. The predominantly Loyalist town of Unadilla was raided by Oneida warriors in September. American soldiers raided and burned down the mixed American Indian village of Oquaga, which Brant had been using as a base, sending refugees either to the British camp at Niagara or to the Oneidas at Kanonwalohale, depending on the side to which their sympathies leaned. A final raid by Brant and Butler's American Indian–Loyalist force on the village of Cherry Valley in November turned into a massacre, and women and children were among the victims. Given the escalating violence in and near Oneida territory, Congress reinitiated the plan to help fortify Kanonwalohale. Fifty troops led by Captain John Copp from Fort Schuyler were sent to help the Oneidas build a picketed wooden fortification big enough for the residents to use for shelter in the event of attack. It was completed between January and February 1779.

To prevent further massacres on the frontier, Washington determined to destroy the Haudenosaunee. A large force under General John Sullivan began to assemble in Pennsylvania. A plan coalesced whereby General James Clinton would march his forces through New York to meet Sullivan's troops in Tioga, bringing the total number of soldiers to some four and a half thousand. They would then take the war into the Cayuga and Seneca homelands. An initial strike against the Onondagas was led by Goose Van Schaick from Fort Schuyler in April 1779. The Oneidas were not consulted, and indeed the arrangements were deliberately kept from them. After the destruction of the Onondagas' village, refugees fled to Niagara or to Kanonwalohale, as had happened after the burning of Oquaga. Throughout the month of September 1779, the Sullivan–Clinton expedition destroyed every Cayuga and Seneca village, home, field, and food store it came across. Brant's small group of volunteers was unable to challenge an army of over four thousand. Four Oneida warriors accompanied the expedition, but the majority stayed away, citing that they would be needed to defend their own homes in case of an attack on Kanonwalohale.

By October, nearly all the Seneca, Cayuga, and Onondaga people were living as refugees at Fort Niagara, dependent on the British crown for the food and clothing needed to survive the winter. With so many warriors thirsting for revenge, the Oneidas knew Kanonwalohale would be under attack as soon as the spring weather came in 1780. Two of the most respected Oneidas—Shenandoah and Good Peter—along with two neutral Mohawks went to Niagara to try once more to persuade the Haudenosaunee there to stop fighting on the side of the British. They were not only ignored but imprisoned and lowered into a dungeon beneath the fort, where they languished for five months in four-by-four-foot cells. One of the Mohawks died.

As summer came and the delegation did not return, the Oneidas knew that Kanonwalohale would be targeted. The fortress there was small and had no cannons, so there was a final choice to be made. Those who wished were permitted to go to join the British and the Haudenosaunee at Fort Niagara. Some did, for a range of reasons. Shenandoah's family went to be closer to him. Some Onondagas and Tuscaroras and thirty-two Oneidas, including the sachem White Skin, joined the British, perhaps for self-protection, perhaps out of fear of or loyalty to the greater body of Haudenosaunee. The rest of the Oneidas in Kanonwalohale and Old Oneida fled and set up temporarily outside Fort Schuyler.

In July 1780 Brant set out with three hundred men, including Shenandoah and Good Peter, who had been released from the dungeon on the condition that they try to persuade the Oneidas to turn their backs on the rebels and join the Haudenosaunee at Niagara. When they found Kanonwalohale empty, they burned it to the ground. They then went to Fort Schuyler, where they convinced 132 Oneidas—including twenty warriors—to join them, while the rest rushed into the fort for protection. The six hundred or so Oneida refugees then went to Schenectady, where they were promised housing in former barracks. They passed a miserable winter there amid shortages of food, fuel, and clothing. In town, despite what they had done to help the American cause, they were subjected to anti-Indian sentiments that had been stirred up over the murderous raids of the previous year. In that winter there was no substantial American Indian habitation anywhere in the Oneida lands or—for the first time in centuries—anywhere between Schenectady and Niagara.

Several skirmishes occurred in the Mohawk Valley in 1780 as Brant and Sir John Johnson continued to harry the area around their former homes. In 1781 another British–American Indian raid on Cherry Valley crossed the vacated Oneida lands. But the focus of the war that year was in Virginia, where Washington's forces, including three Oneidas who had been meeting patriot leaders in Philadelphia earlier in the summer, forced the surrender of Cornwallis's troops at Yorktown. This decisive showdown made it clear that Britain was not going to win the war. The Oneidas spent another winter in Schenectady. They celebrated the arrival of George Washington when he visited the area in June 1782. In London, Parliament had already signaled that they would seek peace, though it would take months of deliberations before the final Treaty of Paris was signed, officially ending the war. The Americans attempted one final strike to dislodge the British from Fort Oswego in February 1783, traveling from Fort Herkimer through the frozen Oneida country. Two soldiers died in the freezing temperatures, and the assault was abandoned after the Americans became lost in the woods near the fort.

Washington visited Fort Schuyler and inspected the carry over to Wood Creek. It was shallow and narrow, but Washington already knew this muddy river was essential to America's future. It had no grand vista, as anyone who has seen Wood Creek will know, but Washington contemplated "the vast inland navigation of these United States" and saw the distant bounds "to a New Empire." Washington's great preoccupation in his postwar life and presidency would be the binding together of America as it began to expand across the Appalachians and away from the eastern cities. The great channel formed by the long-disappeared outlet of Lake Iroquois was about to take center stage.

The Treaty of Paris that ended America's grueling War of Independence was signed on the September 3, 1783. A boundary line separating British Canada from the United States was drawn through Lake Ontario. Britain also recognized American control of lands west of the Appalachian Mountains, extending all the way to the Mississippi River. Exhausted by eight years of war, both sides had accumulated heavy debts and lost thousands of men in the struggle. The Haudenosaunee were not mentioned in the treaty, and, indeed, there had been no official end to their war. They still lived as refugees, either in Schenectady or at Niagara, and it was unclear when or if they would ever return to their homes.

Two conferences were held at Fort Stanwix (as it was called again after the war) in 1784 with representatives from each of the Six Nations to make peace. The first was a meeting with commissioners from the State of New York. New York's Governor George Clinton initially hoped to secure some land cessions from the Haudenosaunee to strengthen New York's claim over the area. They were competing against Massachusetts, who had a rival claim to Iroquoia based on its 1630 Royal Charter. Clinton distrusted the federal government, which he felt would probably bend toward pleasing more populous New England. New York's Indian Commission had been set up in 1783 to make a deal with the Oneidas and Tuscaroras in which they would give up their land and move west. But they also did not want to let the cat out of the bag too early. They agreed to take precautions with the Oneidas so as not to alarm them "with apprehensions that there is the most remote Intention to deprive them of the enjoyment of the District belonging to them."

The Oneidas and Tuscaroras were warned that the state was hopeful of getting their lands and resettling them further west. Kirkland himself was reported to have told them of the state's design, much to the annoyance of Clinton. The state commissioners agreed "for Reasons which are obvious . . . not to mention any thing to [the Oneidas and Tuscaroras] at present with Respect to the Purchase or Exchange of their Lands" at the conference. Instead, Clinton tried to persuade them that they wanted to know the boundaries of their lands so that the state could protect them. Clinton was unable to achieve very much but did begin to establish a relationship with the Haudenosaunee, which he would later turn to his advantage. He also left behind vast supplies of rum to help frustrate the proceedings at the next conference.

The second congress, in October, was with the commissioners of the United States. A delegation of elites from the Continental Congress came to

Fort Stanwix, who were met by 613 American Indians who camped outside the fort. The majority were Oneidas or their dependents; only twenty-seven were representatives from the Seneca, Cayuga, and Onondaga Nations. The Haudenosaunee were forced to recognize United States primacy in American Indian affairs, to return all prisoners held at Niagara, and to renounce any claim over the Ohio Country to the west. Forts Niagara and Oswego were signed over to federal control. The US stated that under these conditions, the Haudenosaunee could return to their homelands to rebuild their villages. Many Senecas, Cayugas, and Onondagas did so, but the Mohawks opted to remain in Canada. Whereas the other Haudenosaunee were treated as defeated enemies, the Oneidas and Tuscaroras were treated as friends and allies. They were promised money to rebuild their church. Article 2 of the treaty granted that "the Oneida and Tuscarora nations shall be secured in the possession of the lands on which they are settled."

However, while the Oneidas had none of their land taken from them and procured some promises to help rebuild, they had not gained anything by supporting the American side in the war. Their population had declined from twelve hundred in 1775 to one thousand in 1783, and thirty-six of their warriors were killed in combat. Some Oneidas never returned to their homeland, instead joining Brant and other Haudenosaunee who decided to settle permanently in Canada. Some had died of disease during the exile in Schenectady. Those who did return to Oneida in 1784 tried to rebuild their lives there, but factionalism within the tribe, poverty, and alcoholism prevented any form of unity from reemerging. Instead of one village, there were five. The houses put up were makeshift structures. Kirkland lamented that the Oneidas had "depreciated" and now seemed "filthy, dirty, Nasty creatures a few families excepted." They nominally had command over some six million acres but also knew that with their tiny population they would be unable to stop settlers squatting on their lands without the assistance of the state. Clinton was sure to use this to his advantage and would lose no time while the Oneidas were in a position of weakness, division, and hunger.

The period 1763 to 1784 is framed by two conferences with the Haudenosaunee at Fort Stanwix. The first was a British attempt to preserve Haudenosaunee land, or at least to spare themselves the problem of policing too rapid an expansion of colonists into American Indian territory. The 1784 conference, or conferences, rather—one with the State of New York and one with the United States—were altogether different. The state clearly had designs on Oneida lands, and although it did not achieve its aim of procuring them at Stanwix, it would in the years to come. The United

States dealt with the Haudenosaunee as defeated enemies, apart from the Oneidas and Tuscaroras. It exercised restraint in a bid to induce some of the Haudenosaunee at Niagara back into the US and rob the British of the loyalty of their warriors, but there was certainly no renewal of the protections the British had offered in 1763. Within a generation, almost all of what had once been Iroquoia would be in the hands of white Americans in the State of New York. It was, at least for some of the Revolution's leaders and soldiers, what they felt they had fought for.

2

New York State's Birth, 1777

Bruce W. Dearstyne

Adapted from Bruce W. Dearstyne, "The Spirit of New York: Defining Events in the Empire State's History" (SUNY Press, 2nd ed., 2022).

In January 1777, betting on New York state to survive and triumph would have been risky. The odds against its success seemed long. It had formally joined the revolution the previous year, the last state to adopt the Declaration of Independence. But its largest city, New York City, was occupied by the British, who would soon launch three invasions to subdue the upstart New York revolutionaries. British army and naval forces seemed invincible.

The year 1777 proved to be truly revolutionary, New York's "Miracle Year." Its dramatic high point was April 20. That was the day that the Convention of Representatives of the State of New York, an ad hoc revolutionary group elected the previous summer, completed work on New York's first constitution. That act, in effect, officially and formally brought the new state into existence. Before year's end, New York had established its first state government, sustained a war effort, and defeated the British invasions.

New York's birth year turned out to be tumultuous and triumphant.

⁂

New York: From Province to State

New York had been a British province since 1664, when the British had seized New Netherland from the Dutch. But on April 20, 1777, the *province* was relegated to the past, and something new, New York *state*, asserted itself into existence as a self-proclaimed independent geopolitical entity.

The New York constitutional convention had done its work on the fly, scurrying north from White Plains to Fishkill to Kingston ahead of advancing British military forces. Delegates voted for approval of a final draft that still had strike-outs and marginal corrections.

Given the perils the new state faced, furthermore, it just wasn't practical to give "the people" a chance to vote on the new document that established "their" government. The convention simply proclaimed the constitution would take effect two days later, on April 22.

There was no time to spare to even make a clean copy. The document had to be rushed to the printer, corrections and all, so that copies could be distributed for public readings. (The original document, with the strike-outs and marginal notes, is preserved in the New York State Archives.)[1]

Seldom had a government been established in such forlorn circumstances with such seemingly dim prospects. The previous summer, British army and naval forces had easily conquered Long Island, New York City, and lower Westchester County. As the new constitution was being proclaimed, the British were planning three invasions—south from the British colony of Canada, north from occupied New York City, and eastward from Oswego and the Mohawk River—to rendezvous at Albany and split and subdue the fledgling state.

Even in the areas the newly proclaimed government controlled, particularly the Hudson Valley, there were large numbers of Loyalists (also called Tories), opposed to independence. Other people were indifferent or opportunistic, ready to ally with the newly minted state or swing their allegiance back to British colonial authorities, depending on the exigencies of the war.

From Loyalty to Rebellion

New York had gradually drifted from proud allegiance to the British Empire to a status of armed rebellion in the late 1760s and early 1770s. British taxes, trade restrictions, and regulations tightened London's control over colonial trade and commerce and violated what the colonists insisted were their rights as British subjects. New Yorkers elected three "provincial congresses" in 1775 and 1776 to deliberate on the growing crisis and what New York

---

1. A transcript of the 1777 New York Constitution can be found at https://avalon.law.yale.edu/18th_century/ny01.asp.

should do. The third one met only briefly, in the early summer of 1776, its sole accomplishment to arrange for the quick election of a fourth provincial congress to take up the issue of independence. By the time the fourth provincial council met at White Plains on July 9, the issue of independence had to be addressed. The Continental Congress had drawn up a declaration of independence on July 2, but New York's delegates, lacking instructions, sent home for direction.

The new provincial council quickly changed its name to the Convention of Representatives of the State of New York—an audacious leap of faith, since "the State of New York" technically did not exist yet. It instructed New York's delegates to vote for the Declaration of Independence, making New Yorkers among the last to sign. It appointed a committee of fourteen members to draft a constitution for the "state."

CREATING A NEW CONSTITUTION

The drafting committee got off to a slow start. The convention, which had migrated from White Plains to Kingston to keep away from the British, was serving as the de facto government of New York, and its members were busy with other things, including raising money for the war effort, dealing with Loyalists, investigating conspiracies, overseeing the state militia, and supporting continental army forces under General George Washington's command. Drafting did not begin in earnest until early 1777. The convention labored in cramped quarters on the second floor of the Ulster County courthouse.

Three extraordinarily capable delegates did most of the work—John Jay (1745 to 1829), Gouverneur Morris (1734 to 1806), and Robert R. Livingston (1746 to 1813). They were all among the educated elite, graduates of King's College, the predecessor of Columbia University. They embodied and reflected traits that would later be associated with the spirit of New York: elevating the public interest above their own welfare, blending energetic determination with an inclination toward compromising for the public good, and tempering idealism with pragmatism and a get-it-done mindset.

John Jay did most of the actual writing. Jay had been elected a delegate to the First Continental Congress in 1774. He was, in the words of the historian Richard B. Morris, a "prudent revolutionary" who at first counseled reconciliation and compromise.[2] Hoping for a change in British

---

2. Richard B. Morris, *John Jay, the Nation and the Court* (Boston, MA: Boston University Press, 1967), 6.

policy, Jay had written an "Address to the People of Great Britain," which the Continental Congress adopted in 1774. In the document, Jay asserted that Americans demanded restoration of their rights as Englishmen: "No power on earth has the right to take our property from us without our consent. . . . We will never submit to be hewers of wood or drawers of water for any ministry or nation in the world."[3]

The British were unmoved. Their intransigence and punitive policies transformed Jay into a revolutionary, and by April 1776 he confided to a friend that Americans really had no choice—"the sword must decide the controversy."

Elected to the fourth New York provincial congress, Jay quickly assumed a leadership role, proposing ideas, brokering compromises, and drafting language trying to move things along.

The constitution writers did not have much to draw on. Other colonies becoming states were drafting their own constitutions. The Articles of Confederation would not be adopted by the Continental Congress until November 1777. The US Constitution was a decade in the future. New Yorkers had to be pioneers in constitution writing. The delegates drew on their own experience in colonial government, some British and French political philosophers who had written about natural rights and the obligations of government, and a few American writers. The most prominent was Massachusetts rebel leader (and future president) John Adams, whose 1776 booklet *Thoughts on Government* summarized the purpose and structure of republican government.

The convention was at first divided. Some delegates wanted to move fast, but others advised delaying until the military situation shifted (hopefully) in the patriots' favor. Some wanted to use the Revolution to overthrow and replace the existing social and economic order, such as breaking up large estates and distributing their lands as individual farms. Others, though, wanted to preserve the status quo but under a new structure of self-government. The majority of delegates gravitated toward a middle course: move ahead expeditiously but in a way that did not upset the economic or social order in the new state they were creating.

Jay cultivated that viewpoint. He helped forge an unwritten consensus in the convention around several principles:

A written document. New York leaders had seen firsthand the limitations of the unwritten "British constitution"—a hybrid that included the

---

3. John Jay, "Address to the People of Great Britain," September 5, 1774, in Henry P. Johnston, ed., *The Correspondence and Public Papers of John Jay: 1763–1781*, vol. 1 (New York: G. P. Putnam's Sons, 1890), 17–34.

Magna Carta, laws, judicial decisions, and precedents. That "constitution" had proven too vague to protect colonists' rights. The New York constitutional statesmen wanted something concrete.

Clearly understandable. The constitution would be read by the literate, read to the illiterate, and broadly discussed by the citizens of the new state. It would help wavering New Yorkers decide which side to support in the great struggle. It needed to be written in language that people could readily understand.

Derived from the people. The document would specify that all governmental authority derived from consent of the governed. Everyone understood, though, that over half of "the people" would not actually have political rights: women were not included in the convention and would not be able to vote. Slavery, which had taken root during Dutch colonial days over a century earlier, would continue.

Suffrage by men with a stake in society. Men of full age who held property or paid taxes and therefore had a stake in society should have the vote.

Strong executive control, but with limitations. The new state would need a strong governor to win the war, create state government, collect taxes, secure the state's borders, execute the laws, and hold the new state together. At the same time, experience with a tyrannical king and overreaching colonial governors required that the governor's power be subject to checks.

Two-house legislature. There was a rough consensus on the desirability of a bicameral legislature. One house, with larger membership, elected by a sizable part of the electorate, would represent all citizens. The second, smaller and elected by men with more substantial property holdings, would be more representative of the upper levels of society.

An independent judiciary. The framers envisioned a tripartite government, the legal system of which would be related to the other two but also insulated from the political considerations that might affect the governor and the legislature.

Protection of citizens' rights. The constitution's architects were determined to protect civil rights, and in fact the drafting committee was given a specific charge to include a bill of rights.

The Grand New Constitution

Jay and the committee labored through five drafts and finally reported to the full convention on March 12, 1777. The debates over the next few weeks sometimes focused on principles, other times on the minutiae of word choices. The document approved on April 20 represented a blend of principles and pragmatic compromises. It had these features:

It provided a rationale for the document's—and the new state's—existence. The document began by citing a call from the Continental Congress to the states to establish state constitutions. It quoted the Declaration of Independence, which, of course, included a long list of accusations against King George III, as a reminder of why the revolution was necessary. This introduction put the new constitution into context—responding to a call for action from the congress, and also defending Americans' (including New Yorkers') rights.

A strong executive branch but with novel constraints. "The supreme executive power and authority of this State shall be vested in a governor" who shall "take care that the laws are faithfully executed." The governor would also command the state militia, advance recommendations for action to the legislature, and report annually to the legislature on "the condition of the State." But the document also included a "Council of Revision" consisting of the governor, chancellor, and judges of the state supreme court to approve or veto bills. It created a "Council of Appointment" consisting of the governor and four senators to approve all gubernatorial appointments (the governor could vote only to break a tie).

A balanced bicameral legislature. The convention created an assembly and a senate, the former broadly representative of the people and the latter meant to be more be attuned to interests of business and property. Action by both houses would be needed to make appropriations and pass bills.

An independent judiciary. The constitution said little about the courts, essentially continuing the colonial system but under the authority of the new state. The local courts of colonial days were adopted with little change, but a new "supreme court" was added at the top. The constitution continued a separate court of chancery, which had powers to adjudicate commercial disputes, appoint and supervise trustees of people needing judicial protection such as orphans and widows, foreclose mortgages, and settle disputes where there was no clear legal guidance or common-law precedent. Over both courts was placed a special appeals court, or "court of errors," consisting of the senate, the supreme court justices, and the chancellor but with the provision that neither the chancellor nor the supreme court justices could vote on appeals from their respective branches.

The document declared that "the free exercise and enjoyment of religious profession and worship, without discrimination or preference, shall forever hereafter be allowed within this State to all mankind."

The constitution guaranteed the right to trial by jury, but other rights are not mentioned, despite the fact that the committee had been instructed to include a bill of rights. The most plausible explanation for the absence of such a statement is that the framers decided that it might inhibit the new government's flexibility in dealing with Loyalists.

The scourge of slavery. A number of the framers, including Jay, were slaveholders, yet they acknowledged slavery was wrong and later freed their slaves. It was a contradictory blend of supporting human freedom and at the same time holding some people in bondage. Jay tried to get abolition of slavery included in the document, without success.

John Jay wrote in July 1777 that "unless the government be committed to proper hands, it will be weak and unstable at home, and contemptible abroad." Jay and his band of conservative-minded revolutionaries had created a constitution that did that, a groundbreaking document for the times. There were not major revisions until 1821, and even then the main changes were structural, such as abolishing the Council of Revision and the Council of Appointment in favor of the governor's power of legislative veto and appointment, similar to today.

Several of the framers went on to leadership roles. John Jay served as the state's, and later the new nation's, chief justice and as governor of New York, from 1795 to 1801. Gouverneur Morris helped write the US Constitution, one reason why that document parallels New York's in some ways.

The New Government Gets Down to Work

New York had now declared itself a state; what would happen next? The convention arranged for election of a governor and legislators in June, to take office in September, but it remained the de facto government in the interim. It designated a council of safety from among its membership to handle security and military matters. It set up the judicial branch of the new government on its own authority, building on the basic outline in the new constitution.

The summer elections went smoothly. General George Clinton from Orange County was elected governor (his only rival was Albany's General Philip Schuyler). The legislature convened in Kingston in early September.

Military responsibilities prevented the new governor from reporting to Kingston for his inauguration until September 10. In his inaugural speech, Clinton promised to govern with "vigour and dignity." He noted the constitution's "line between the executive, legislative and judicial powers" and explained, "It shall always be my strenuous endeavor on the one hand to retain and exercise for the advantage of the people the powers with which they have invested me; on the other, carefully to avoid the invasion of those rights which the constitution has placed in other persons."[4]

Governor Clinton then quickly returned to command troops in the field. He remained both a general in the patriot army and governor of New York during the rest of the war. The legislature got down to work, levying a tax on personal property and real estate to support the state's war effort.

Chief Justice John Jay assumed his official duties on September 9, 1777, when he delivered a speech to the first grand jury of the supreme court, held at Kingston. He used the occasion to instruct the new jurors on their responsibilities but devoted most of the document to expounding the principles embodied in the new state constitution. Jay intended the speech as a broad public educational document, and the new state government widely distributed it.

"All the calamities incident to this war will be amply compensated by the many blessings flowing from this glorious revolution," said the new chief justice. The constitution came from the people through their elected representatives. "From the people it must receive its spirit and by them be quickened. Let virtue, honour, the love of liberty and of science be and remain the soul of this constitution." The constitution protected "great and equal rights of human nature," including liberty of conscience and equal protection of the laws.[5]

Jay turned his attention to setting up the court system and presiding at court trials.

Turning Back Three Invasions

New York's prospects, dim in January 1777, were much brighter at the end of what would prove to be a tumultuous year.

Both sides of the war recognized New York's paramount strategic significance as a province and, after April 20, as a state. The British grand

---

4. Governor George Clinton, "Opening Speech," September 10, 1777, in Charles Z. Lincoln, ed., *Messages from the Governors: 1777–1822* (Albany: J. B. Lyon, 1909), 7–11.

5. John Jay, "To the Grand Jury of Ulster County," September 9, 1777, in Johnston, *Correspondence*, 158–65.

strategy was to invade from the west, north, and south and converge on Albany, thereby dividing and conquering New York. That would separate the northern colonies from the southern ones. The British reasoned that would make it easy to subdue the rebellion. Patriot forces, on the other hand, and particularly the new state government, recognized the need to hold New York at all costs.

The British strategy soon began to fall apart. In July, a force made up of British troops, Loyalists, and Britain's American Indian allies, under General Barry St. Leger, began moving eastward along the Mohawk River from the British site at Oswego. Patriot General Nicholas Herkimer confronted the enemy at Oriskany on August 7. A bloody battle followed. Herkimer's leg was shattered in what would eventually prove to be a mortal wound, but the general sat at the base of a tree and continued to direct the battle, a particularly dramatic example of New Yorkers' grit and determination. The ferocity of the American colonists' resistance discouraged the American Indians, many of whom abandoned St. Ledger. A few days later, when General Benedict Arnold arrived with patriot reinforcements, British forces retreated. Arnold chased the weakened invaders out of the Mohawk Valley. The invasion from the west was over.

Meanwhile, a massive British invasion force led by General John Burgoyne began moving south from Montreal, Canada, in June. Burgoyne's objective was the Hudson River and then Albany. Patriot General Philip Schuyler delayed the British through obstruction of trails and limited attacks that wore down the enemy.

But Schuyler was disliked and mistrusted by the New England troops that made up part of his command, a reflection of the occasional tension between New York and New England. After a subordinate surrendered strategically important Fort Ticonderoga on Lake Champlain, Schuyler was replaced by General Horatio Gates. Gates continued and intensified Schuyler's strategies and increased the size of his army. Burgoyne's advance was bogged down. Growing desperate, Burgoyne sent a force eastward to replenish his dwindling supplies, but they were defeated by a large patriot force at Walloomsac, New York, now called the Battle of Bennington because of its proximity to that Vermont city.

On October 17, 1777, Burgoyne, his way forward and retreat backward both blocked by the Americans, surrendered to Gates near Saratoga. It was the greatest patriot victory in the war so far and turned out to be its turning point. The Saratoga triumph convinced France to enter the war on America's side, which proved decisive.

General Burgoyne made it to Albany, but under an armed patriot guard. He was held under house arrest at Philip Schuyler's mansion in Albany—Schuyler graciously agreed to host him and a few aides even though Burgoyne had burned Schuyler's country house near Saratoga. After a short stay, the general was paroled and allowed to return to Britain, meaning he was released on the condition that he would not fight against the Americans again. His captured soldiers, though, remained prisoners of the Americans.

A third British invasion force began moving up the Hudson from New York City in early October 1777 with a view to linking up with Burgoyne in Albany. Washington asked Governor Clinton, who was also still serving as a continental army general, to take charge of defending two key forts near West Point that guarded a chain the rebels had strung across the Hudson to impede the British fleet. Clinton took command of one, and his brother General James Clinton assumed command of the other one. The British assault on October 6 overwhelmed both forts, but stout resistance organized by the Clintons inflicted unexpected casualties on the enemy.

As the British were breaching the front of his fort, Governor Clinton retreated out the back and descended a steep cliff to the Hudson in the darkness. As the British searched for him, Clinton hailed a boat that had just arrived from the opposite shore to rescue patriot survivors. Seeing that the boat was full to capacity, the governor prepared to swim across the river. The officer in charge, recognizing the governor, insisted on giving up his own spot. Clinton refused. With the British closing in, the new governor made an executive decision: he jumped into the already full boat and, very slowly, the overloaded vessel was rowed across the Hudson to safety. The new governor had demonstrated personal courage, a skill in rallying outnumbered forces, and an ability to inflict substantial losses on an overconfident enemy.

The British, undeterred, proceeded up the river to the rebel capital of Kingston. The legislature had plenty of advance warning, delegated its responsibilities temporarily to a committee of safety, and evacuated downriver to Poughkeepsie, where its members resumed working in early 1778.

British General John Vaughan landed troops near Kingston on October 15 and burned the town the next day. "Esopus [Kingston] being a nursery for almost every villain in the Country," Vaughan later wrote, "I judged it to be necessary to proceed to the town. On our approach, [defenders] were drawn up with cannon, which we took and drove them out of the place." Firing continued from the houses, and so "I reduced the place to ashes . . . not leaving a House."[6]

It turned out to be a hollow victory. Burgoyne had been defeated at Saratoga a day earlier, and the grand plan to link with him at Albany was in shambles. The British sailed back down the river to New York City. Vaughan hoped that destroying the capital would destroy the New York revolutionary movement. Instead, it inspired resentment, converted many wavering New Yorkers to the patriot cause, and buttressed the war effort. The three failed British invasions were to be their last major incursion into the territory under the authority of the new state government.

New York's independence was assured after the British defeat at Yorktown in 1781 and the Treaty of Paris in 1783, which recognized the United States as a sovereign nation. The new state got its biggest city back on November 25, 1783, when the last British troops departed from Manhattan. General George Washington, accompanied by Governor George Clinton, triumphantly led the victorious continental army into the city. Clinton proved to be a popular, effective governor, serving until 1795, returning for another term in 1801 to 1804, and then serving as vice president under both Thomas Jefferson and James Madison.

Gouverneur Morris moved to Pennsylvania, but Jay and Livingston stayed in New York. They grew apprehensive of Clinton's popular policies, including taxation of land, harsh treatment of Loyalists and sale of their confiscated lands, and issuance of paper money, which promoted inflation. They were alarmed by Clinton's ability to appeal directly to the public. Jay served as governor from 1795 to 1801. In part to counter the growing popular appeal of Clinton—and other popular governors like him in some of the other states who seemed like threats to the established social and economic order—the prudent New York revolutionaries who wrote the state constitution became strong supporters of the movement to create a strong *national* government.

The trio who were most influential in drafting the state constitution in 1777 soon identified as Federalists—men who supported the proposed US constitution, a strong federal government, and conservative fiscal policies. Morris, by then a delegate to the Constitutional Convention from Pennsylvania, drafted much of the document. Livingston was a prominent federal

---

6. George Dangerfield, *Chancellor Robert R. Livingston of New York* (New York: Harcourt Brace, 1960), 103–5.

proponent in New York. Jay was a leading advocate in the state. Along with Alexander Hamilton and James Madison, he wrote *The Federalist Papers*, a comprehensive treatise on merits of the proposed constitution.

The Test of Time

New York's first constitution endured without major revisions until 1821. It proved to be a versatile, flexible document, strong on principles and the outline of the structure of government, leaving the legislature and governor plenty of leeway to flesh things out. The constitution sustained the state through the initial establishment of state programs, westward expansion, the War of 1812, and the initiation of the Erie Canal in 1817, among other developments.

Even in 1821, the changes were modest. The Council of Appointment was abolished and state offices were thereafter filled by the legislature, the governor, or the governor with the consent of the senate. The Council of Revision, which had sometimes proved obstructionist and other times seemed overly politicized over the years, was abolished. The governor was given the power to veto bills, subject to reversal by the legislature.

Specific civil rights such as freedom of speech and habeas corpus, left out of the 1777 constitution but covered by 1787 legislation and firmly embedded in the common law and state court decisions, were specifically protected in the 1821 revision. Voting rights for men were gradually expanded through reduction and finally elimination of property-holding qualifications. Woman suffrage, though, did not come until 1917.

New York did not move to end slavery until 1799, when John Jay, who was by then governor, signed a law that gradually abolished it by 1827.

The 1777 constitution declared that the convention, acting "in the name and by the authority of the good people of this State, doth ordain, determine and declare that no authority shall on any pretence whatever be exercised over the people or members of this State, but such as shall be derived from and granted by them." In 1777, a document purporting to represent the consensus and will of the people was a startling, radical departure from the past.

It was a stunning achievement. John Jay noted in his speech to the Ulster County grand jury in September 1777, referenced above, that "the Americans are the first people whom Heaven has favoured with an opportunity of deliberating upon, and choosing the forms of government under which they should live."⁷ By just about any measure, the first New York State Constitution was a fulfillment of that opportunity.

Looking back, two and a half centuries later, with the benefit of hindsight, it may seem that the State of New York was destined to succeed from the beginning. But it certainly did not seem that way to the people at the time, who were actually making history. They were carrying out a revolution and were determined to make it succeed. The framers of the state constitution knew they were inventing something new and untried. They were well aware of the might of the British army and navy and their own personal risk—getting captured would have meant prison or, possibly, execution. Oriskany and Saratoga, in retrospect, look like inevitable victories due to Americans' courage, good strategy, and just plain persistence. But, at the time, they were against-the-odds victories. Saratoga turned out to be the first step on the road to victory due mainly to French intervention, but that was hard to foresee in October 1777, when more than three years of war lay ahead.

New York's revolutionary story is different from any other state's. The year when the Empire State was established, 1777, was epochal and something of a preview of the spirit, energy, vision, determination, and persistence that would make New York a leader among the states. It demonstrated New Yorkers' willingness to fight for principles they believed in. It set the stage for New York's rise to greatness.

---

7. Jay, "Grand Jury," 161.

3

Cyrenius Chapin

Buffalo's Doctor and Hero in the War of 1812

THOMAS C. ROSENTHAL, MD

Adapted from Thomas C. Rosenthal, "Cyrenius Chapin: Buffalo's First Physician and War of 1812 Hero" (SUNY Press, 2025).

Much of the history of revolutionary New York has been made by citizens of the state who stepped forward to lead in times of crisis. Buffalo's Cyrenius Chapin is a good example. He was one of the first physicians in Western New York. When the War of 1812—sometimes called the Second War of Independence—broke out, he organized a local militia to support American military efforts on the Niagara Frontier. His militia company developed a reputation for fearlessly attacking British forces even when vastly outnumbered. Chapin organized and led the effort—unsuccessful as it turned out—to prevent Buffalo from being burned by much larger British forces. Sometimes, he had to act alone, risking death, or accompanied by only a few soldiers. Chapin was captured and incarcerated by the British. After the war, he expanded his medical practice, trained young physicians, and organized the Erie County Medical Society and the Erie County Agricultural Society.

Chapin exemplified many traits that illustrate New York's steadfastness and resilience. He was a pioneer in his field at a time when most doctors were self-taught or learned through apprenticeships. He asserted leadership in a dangerous time when it would have been easier and safer just to sit on the sidelines. He rallied other New Yorkers to the patriotic cause. Regular army officers sometimes *accused him of being impetuous and leading his men into battle when the regular officers were hesitating and holding back their own forces. He was undeterred and kept pushing audaciously. That was one of the themes in his life.*

☙❧

It was December 10, 1813, and two men raged at each other in the entryway of Joseph McCarthy's store on Queen Street in the village of Newark, known today as Niagara-on-the-Lake, Ontario. Soldiers held back a crowd drawn by the intensity of the bedlam. One man, Brigadier General George McClure (1771 to 1851), was the ranking officer in charge of American troops occupying nearby Fort George. The other was forty-four-year-old Cyrenius Chapin (1769 to 1838), Buffalo's first physician. Both were part-time officers in the New York militia assigned by the United States' regular army to occupy Canada's Fort George (Berton 1981).

The fighting between American and British forces in what became known as the War of 1812 had been intense for much of 1813. Just a few weeks before their public argument, McClure had replaced Army Major General Wilkinson as commander of the troops at Fort George. Despite a previously sullied reputation, Wilkinson had been reassigned to lead a United States campaign down the Saint Lawrence River to capture Quebec and Montreal from British and Canadian forces. He took most of the regular army with him, leaving Fort George to the New York militia led by McClure, whose skill set leaned toward carpentry, land speculation, politics, and self-promotion. The frigid winds of winter were approaching, and most of McClure's soldiers, being militia members, were nearing the end of their term of service and eager to return home. General McClure, in a letter cosigned by congressman Peter Porter (1773 to 1844) and Dr. Chapin, requested that Fort George be reinforced with regular troops, but his request was denied. McClure then requested authorization from Secretary of War John Armstrong Jr. to destroy Fort George and vacate the Canadian shore. McClure also recommended the neighboring town of Newark be burned to prevent its residents from offering refuge to British troops (Ketchum 1854; White 1898).

On that cold December tenth day, McClure had ordered a contingent of Canadian defectors under his command to commence burning Newark. They knocked on doors, gave residents one hour's notice, torched all eighty village homes, and sent the population, mostly women, children, and older adults, into a Niagara Frontier winter.

Dr. Chapin had lived in Buffalo and the Niagara Frontier for a decade. The youngest of five children, he was born in Bernardstown, Massachusetts, on February 7, 1769. He married his hometown sweetheart, Sylvia Burnham, shortly after completing his medical studies in 1793.[1] Upon his arrival in Buffalo in 1803, there was such a scarcity of housing in Buffalo that he and his family rented a house in Canada while he built a flourishing practice on both sides of the Niagara River. By 1805 he had the resources to build Buffalo's sixteenth frame building that combined his drugstore, doctor's office, and home. Chapin was a big thinker whose original scheme had been to bring forty families with him to settle Buffalo. When those plans were rebuffed by the Holland Land Company, he purchased the first lot sold in the newly surveyed village of New Amsterdam, later renamed Buffalo.

Chapin learned medicine as an apprentice, though beyond bloodletting, intestinal purging, herbs, and opium, early-nineteenth-century medicine offered few effective remedies. Chapin's reputation was sustained by a commanding, paternalistic temperament that he backed up with a stubborn willingness to tackle any affliction his patients suffered. He was not described as ostentatious, but, at six feet, his height alone drew attention. Near-constant exposure to the outdoors gave him a rugged bronze complexion that set off arching eyebrows, piercing blue eyes, and a prominent Romanesque nose. His signature attire was a long cloak of blue cloth (Atkins 1898). Chapin's movements were quick and certain, guided by a dignified authority. Over the course of his career, numerous partners attempted to match his pace, but the majority only lasted a few months, exhausted by Chapin's long, busy days and his minimal need for sleep. Gorham Pratt, his longest tenured partner, agonized over Chapin's proclivity for denouncing most anyone he did not admire with direct statements that got him in trouble.[2]

On the night of December 10, when he and General McClure argued in the village of Newark, Chapin was incensed by the needless destruction being inflicted on its residents, some of whom had been his patients. As a civilian, Chapin was used to being listened to, so he thought little about challenging a superior officer. Chapin believed it was enough to destroy the barrack buildings at Fort George and the fifteen hundred tents stored there. He held nothing back as he used expletives to describe McClure as callous

---

1. C. Douglas Kohler, "Colonel Cyrenius Chapin: The Brave Soldier, the Good Citizen, the Honest Man," *Western New York Heritage* 12, no. 4 (2010): 28–36.

2. G. F. Pratt, "Biographical Sketch of the Late Dr. Cyrenius Chapin, of Buffalo," *Buffalo Medical and Surgical Journal* 8 (1869).

and spiteful. Burning Newark, he said, would accomplish nothing short of satisfying a wish to visit undeserved misery on noncombatants. McClure accused Chapin of being an unpatriotic partisan who typified uncivilized backwoods sodbusters (Berton 1981). Holding rank's upper hand, McClure charged Chapin with mutiny, ordered him arrested for treason, and had him escorted to jail at gunpoint. McClure's report on the incident reads, "There is not a greater rascal [who] exists than Chapin, and he is supported by a pack of Tories and enemies to our government" (Ketchum 1865). Chapin was an ardent Federalist and British hater, and nothing could have insulted him more than being called a Tory. Within hours, several of Chapin's backers confronted the guards at the jail and freed him without any resistance.

Quarrels between Dr. Chapin and McClure were not uncommon. A few days earlier, to prove that the British were lurking in the woods around Fort George, Chapin had defied orders and marched his band of soldiers into the countryside. As he suspected, his outfit was soon attacked by a British militia. Hemmed down, Chapin sent a messenger to Fort George asking for help. McClure refused to send anyone to support Chapin, telling his officers that he hoped Chapin would be captured, or worse (Berton 1981).

The day after McClure destroyed Newark, Chapin attempted to resign his militia appointment. His resignation read, "The ill-fated town of Newark was burned, under his [McClure's] orders, the night of the 10th of December, 1813. Here was exhibited a scene of distress which language would be inadequate to describe. Women and children were turned out of doors in a cold and stormy night; the cries of infants, the decrepitude of age, and the debility of sickness, had no impression upon this monster in human shape; they were consigned to that house whose canopy was the heavens, and whose walls were as boundless as the wide world" (Ketchum 1865).

The *Buffalo Gazette* sided with Chapin and excoriated McClure for the burning of Newark, sparking a widespread condemnation of McClure's command. Other newspapers, including the *Pittsburgh Gazette*, called McClure's order a "wanton and abominable act" (Berton 1981).

After retreating from Fort George and burning Newark, McClure abandoned Buffalo, withdrawing his entire army, totaling two thousand men, thirty miles inland to Batavia. When Buffalonians protested, McClure declared that if the citizens of Buffalo would arrest "that damned rascal Chapin [he would] keep his troops in Buffalo and defend the city." Buffalo's defense was left to a few volunteers who refused McClure's orders and pledged to follow Dr. Chapin (Taylor 2010). Once McClure reached Batavia, he surrendered his command to Major General Amos Hall (1761 to 1827).

Well before the burning of Newark, Chapin had proven himself capable of stirring rancor among his superiors, but he had also earned the animosity of the British. Seven months earlier, in May 1813, American Major General Henry Dearborn (1751 to 1829) and 4,500 troops he assembled at Fort Niagara had seized Fort George and the village of Newark (Taylor 2010; White 1898). According to the *Buffalo Gazette*, "Dr. C. Chapin, was in the vanguard." Chapin's militia was described as "showing up where they were least expected, always ready, and effective in their unique style of hit and run warfare." The British and Canadian forces retreated to Burlington Heights, sixty miles west of Fort George, leaving the Americans in control of the Canadian Niagara River shoreline (Taylor 2010).

Once the Americans were firmly entrenched at Fort George, Major General Wilkinson was assigned to hold Fort George for the Americans. By June 1813, Wilkinson was encouraging Dr. Cyrenius Chapin's "Forty Thieves" to conduct raids that became notorious throughout Canada's Niagara Peninsula (White 1898). The forty-four-year-old Chapin alleged that he only confiscated property that was public or held by British supporters. Nonetheless, Chapin accumulated enemies, and many Canadians who had leaned apolitical began viewing Chapin as a brigand (James 1818; Thompson 1897; Cruikshank 1912).

By June 1813, one ambitious British lieutenant, James FitzGibbon (1780 to 1863), became obsessed with stopping Chapin's raiding parties. Lieutenant FitzGibbon began his career fighting Napolean before being transferred to Upper Canada, where he was assigned to training Native American mercenaries. In return, they taught FitzGibbon the methods of unconventional warfare (McKenzie 1971).

FitzGibbon moved his regiment to a farm owned by John DeCou near Beaver Dams (now Thorold, Ontario), sixteen miles from Fort George, where he began his own brand of guerilla raids (McKenzie 1971). FitzGibbon's regulars, reinforced by several hundred Algonquin warriors, soon earned their own nickname, the "Bloody Boys" (Berton 1981; Barbuto 2014).

So it was that Chapin devised a plan to clear the Niagara Peninsula of FitzGibbon and free Canadian nationals, whom the British had jailed under suspicion of supporting the American invaders. Though he convinced the fort commander that his plan would work, there was doubt about Chapin's ability to lead a large military operation. Instead, Lieutenant Colonel

Charles G. Boerstler was charged with leading the attack on Beaver Dams, and Chapin's unit was placed under Boerstler's command. Though only thirty-five years old, Boerstler was old school. He believed that war should be fought in open fields by advancing troops and considered Chapin's methods of hiding behind trees to be uncivilized. He viewed Chapin as civilian rabble. However, Boerstler had to concede that Chapin knew the terrain well and placed Chapin's militia in front of the 570 troops, artillerymen, and two cannons assigned to the operation (Berton 1981). The operation began on June 13, 1813.

Two days before, Boerstler assembled his forces for the Beaver Dams assault near the village of Queenston, Canada. There, Chapin and several officers had dinner at a tavern owned by Laura and James Secord. The Secords knew Dr. Chapin well, and Chapin viewed the Secords as friendly to the American cause. Laura Secord was born in Massachusetts and moved to Queenston with her family in 1793 when her father received a Canadian land grant. Her husband, James Secord, was a second-generation Canadian of French Huguenot descent. Politics had not been a major interest of the Secords—that is, until the Battle of Queenston the previous October, 1812. Having been in the Canadian militia when the Americans attacked, James was wounded, and American soldiers looted their food stores (Berton 1981). After the Battle of Queenston, Laura Secord nursed her husband back to health, managed the farm, and discovered an abiding appreciation for the protections promised by the British Army.

The evening of Chapin's dinner, the thirty-seven-year-old Laura Secord proved a generous hostess. She was attentive to every need of Chapin's guests, pouring wine and refilling dishes. All the while, she carefully absorbed the details of their conversation. By all accounts, it was a pleasant evening loosened by considerable drink and heated by tactical debates about the imminent attack on FitzGibbon.

At four thirty on the morning of June 23, 1813, the petite but sturdy Laura Secord donned a bonnet and began a twenty-mile hike to Beaver Dams, driving a cow part of the way so no one would suspect the true nature of her mission. It was dusk when Laura reached the DeCou farm, but Mrs. Secord had stamina enough to provide FitzGibbon with all she had heard the night before. Then, having set the stage for battle, she walked back to her Queenston farm (McKenzie 1971).

Laura Secord lived a long life, but she never discussed her role in the battle and never confirmed that it was her friend, Dr. Chapin, who had divulged the American plans. Nonetheless, her efforts likely altered the outcome of what became known as the Battle of Beaver Dams (McKenzie 1971). While it is possible that Chapin's scouts got their numbers wrong, Canadian historians credit Laura Secord's warning for the sudden addition of five hundred Algonquins to FitzGibbon's forces at Beaver Dams (Thompson 1897).

As they approached Beaver Dams on a blistering hot June 24th, Chapin's scouts observed several of FitzGibbon's warriors sprinting across an open field to take up positions for an ambush. Chapin rushed to inform Boerstler, who dismissed Chapin as a coward and sent his unit to the rear, a relegation that would assure the glory of expected victory would be all Boerstler's.

Two miles short of DeCou's farm, precisely as Chapin had warned, Algonquin warriors sprang from trees in a sudden assault. Boerstler ordered his regulars to charge into the trees with bayonets drawn, but the warriors came from all directions, dodging from tree to tree, reloading their muskets under cover, and resuming their assault. For three hours, fierce combat continued. Thirty Americans lay dead with only five Algonquins killed when FitzGibbon sent a white flag demanding Boerstler's surrender. FitzGibbon's message claimed that, should any more of their warriors be murdered, the Algonquins could not be restrained and Boerstler's troops would be massacred. He added a bluff, claiming that another seven hundred fresh British regulars would soon join the battle.

Boerstler capitulated. He allowed FitzGibbon and his Algonquin warriors to take his 462 American troops prisoner, including Chapin. The Americans were immediately relieved of boots, swords, and uniforms, while the scalps of the American dead were removed (McKenzie 1971).

FitzGibbon agreed that the American officers would be paroled, until he realized that his nemesis, Dr. Cyrenius Chapin, was among the captives. By late afternoon, Chapin and his men were loaded on two large rowboats for transport along Lake Ontario to the British prisoner of war camp in Kingston, Ontario. What followed is best described in one of the few surviving documents written by Dr. Chapin himself. Chapin's version of the battle is corroborated by several participants in the Battle of Beaver Dams and was published in an 1836 pamphlet titled *Chapin's Review of Armstrong's Notices of the War of 1812* (Chapin 1836).

Chapin states he was placed in one rowboat and Captain Sackrider, his second in command, was placed in another boat for the Lake Ontario passage to Kingston. Sixteen British soldiers were assigned to guard twenty-eight captives in the two boats. A greater portion of men were in Sackrider's boat, and the rowing of both boats was delegated to the American captives (Chapin 1836).

Once out on the open waters of Lake Ontario, Chapin distracted the British guards by telling lewd stories. Curious about the laughter in the other boat, guards in Sackrider's boat allowed their boat to be maneuvered alongside the first. Suddenly, Chapin shouted an order to seize upon the British guards. The British guard closest to Chapin knocked the doctor to the bottom of the boat, threatening to kill him at the point of his bayonet. But chaos had its effect, and the British guards were quickly overpowered. Chapin's prisoner revolt started at four thirty in the afternoon, and by two thirty in the morning Chapin, his two captured boats, twenty-eight soldiers, and sixteen British prisoners arrived back at Fort George (Thomson 1818; Chapin 1836).

※

Now, in December 1813, McClure's abandonment of Fort George struck Chapin as an insult to those Americans who sacrificed their lives in capturing the fort and the torching of Newark as hurtful to innocent civilians. However, burning Newark did have a stinging effect on British and Canadian soldiers. Both armies were short on winter supplies, but now the British were desperate to feed themselves and Newark's refugees. Eight days later, on December 18, 1813, British and Canadian troops crossed the Niagara River and seized Fort Niagara. McClure's abandonment of Buffalo left only a few militiamen at the fort, located some thirty miles north of Buffalo. Most of them fled as the British approached, and British bayonets quickly eliminated the few who remained. The British loaded twenty-seven cannons, three thousand stands of arms, and massive quantities of ammunition and provisions in their boats and returned to their barracks in Canada. The stolen supplies comprised nearly all the American military stores along the Niagara River and postponed starvation for the British troops and their dependents (Taylor 2010).

Before their departure, the British and their Native American mercenaries burned every house in the nearby village of Lewiston, New York. When a few Native American Tuscarora men from a New York reservation rescued one family from assault, the Tuscarora village was also burned. The next day, as American troops returned to Fort Niagara, they found mutilated bodies, many decapitated and with their hearts torn out. Some were scalped (White 1898).

The meager response to the British raid on Fort Niagara confirmed what British spies had reported. McClure's withdrawal left the area undefended. Within days, Canadian informants told American authorities that newly reinforced British troops were staging an invasion of Western New York. By Christmas, General Hall, still refitting the two thousand troops McClure had abandoned in Batavia, made contact with Dr. Chapin to coordinate several hit-and-run raids on British positions in Canada, hoping to delay or at least confuse the British. General Hall's options were significantly restricted by the loss of supplies from Fort Niagara and the approaching winter.

Near midnight on December 29, 1813, nineteen days after the burning of Newark, British soldiers and their Indian mercenaries made another landing near Fort Niagara under the command of British General Phineas Riall (1775 to 1850). The American military crew who had returned to Fort Niagara were a hurried assemblage of independently led militia units responsible to General Hall, who was still in Batavia. Once again, Fort Niagara was hastily abandoned to the British. When word of the attack reached Chapin, he assembled a ragtag calvary and dashed toward Fort Niagara, where he confronted the Americans who had deserted the fort. One soldier described Chapin's arrival that night, writing, "The irascible doctor furiously damned the two colonels and their men for not having driven away the British, and delivered General Hall's order that they should immediately make an attack." But the British had already begun their destructive march south along the Niagara River to Black Rock and Buffalo. They were burning everything in their path and were being reinforced by more British, Canadian, Algonquin, and Mohawk troops crossing the Niagara River along the way (Smith 1884).

Residents of towns along the New York side of the Niagara River fled eastward to Batavia and Williamsville and southward to Hamburg and Aurora while Chapin's small militia harassed the advancing British troops in a series of hit-and-run strikes (Letchworth 1874). Chapin's men were desperate to save their homes and, more importantly, their families. With every pause in fighting, a few men left Chapin's unit. Still, Chapin continued his cut-and-run attacks on the marauding British forces. When he encountered fresh British reinforcements who had just landed at Scajaquada Creek, Chapin's men were showered by a crushing volley of musketry that seemed to arise from everywhere in the darkness. Chapin's remaining militia broke ranks, many rushing to Buffalo to gather their families (Hill 1923).

British General Riall continued his march toward Buffalo as reinforcements crossed the Niagara River to join his advance at several points along the New York shore. By the time they reached Buffalo's northern edge, Riall's forces included fifty Canadian militiamen, four hundred American

Indians, and one thousand British regulars. They had burned six villages and every home they encountered along the way, paying little heed to Chapin's assaults or those of other impromptu groups of defenders. The British regulars marched in formation along the portage route that paralleled the Niagara River while their Algonquin mercenaries cleared their advance, spooking everyone with war screams and laying the countryside to waste.

The few men still at his side were Chapin's personal friends and patients. Getting their families to safety became their only priority, and Chapin gave the order for full retreat. Rushing back to Buffalo, his band joined a hurried mass of citizens, ox sleds, wagons, carts, women, children, and dogs clogging every path heading south and east from Buffalo. They joined other fleeing soldiers who earlier resigned to the inevitability of defeat or had reached the limit of their courage. It was an exodus energized by terror, as families sought shelter as far as possible from Buffalo and Black Rock (White 1898).

As he hurried back to Buffalo, Chapin's first stop was the Pratt home. Chapin's close friend Captain Samuel Pratt had died just four months earlier. Chapin burst into the house, shouting an urgent command to leave immediately. Mrs. Pratt later recalled that Chapin's alarm, more emphatic than pious, was awash with expletives (Letchworth 1874).

Chapin's next harried stop was his own home, where he instructed his wife, Sylvia, and his three daughters, nineteen-year-old Sylvia, twelve-year-old Amelia, and nine-year-old Louise, to walk to the Chapin farm in Hamburg. It was one of the season's first bitterly cold days, and snow was falling on not-yet-frozen roads that wagon wheels would soon churn into mud. Chapin ordered his family to use the footpaths that cut through the Buffalo Creek Reservation and directed his apprentice, Samuel Pratt's thirteen-year-old son Hiram, to serve as escort. Hiram's eleven-year-old sister, Mary, joined the Chapin family as they struck out for Hamburg on foot (Letchworth 1874). Mrs. Pratt joined other neighbors traveling by wagon and, after several delays, caught up with her son and the Chapin women at Smoke's Creek. Sylvia climbed aboard the Pratt wagon, but nothing could induce Hiram or the Chapin girls to accept a ride for fear of overburdening the horses and dooming the wagon wheels to the moiled mud (Johnson 1876).

The fleeing Chapins passed piles of discarded possessions. The mud and the strain on their animals had pressed families to cast off furniture, kettles, and heirlooms they had so optimistically loaded on their wagons. Horses were driven to gallops, and oxen felt the persistent application of the whip to keep pace with the panicked flight (Johnson 1876). The extended Chapin family arrived at the Hamburg farmstead just after dawn, their fourteen-mile hike taking most of the night. They had proven themselves to be as tenacious as their father.

※

Back in Buffalo, one man, Job Hoysington, took a position on the corner of Main and Utica Streets to give his family and neighbors several precious minutes to flee. Carrying two small children, with little more than the clothes on her back, his wife fled on foot. Exhaustion quickly overtook Mrs. Hoysington just as two fleeing cavalrymen offered to transport the children on their horses. In the reigning chaos, the planned rendezvous was missed.

It would be spring's thaw before the extent of Job's heroism was revealed. His gunpowder and pellet pouch were empty, and his musket lay by his side. Job had saved his family, but he was finally defeated by a bullet piercing his brain. He was scalped for good measure. Weeks later, his widow found one child being cared for by a family in Clarence and the other with a family near Batavia (Johnson 1876).

※

Earlier that day, General Hall had promoted Dr. Cyrenius Chapin to lieutenant colonel. The promotion was little noticed as the social and military structure dissolved. Chapin's disposition was to assume responsibility anyway, particularly now, with an imminent threat to his home and his adopted village. He had done what he could for his family. As they left for Hamburg, he again turned his attention to fighting the British. Somehow, he found a handful of men and boys willing to make one last stand. One report claims this brave little squad numbered only five. Defending the village was beyond possible, but slowing the British advance could save more lives (White 1898). Chapin retrieved an old nine-pounder cannon, perhaps one he had removed from a British ship the previous year. He and his "boys" set the cannon on a makeshift roadblock near the corner of Main and Niagara Streets, referred to as Black Rock Road in some accounts. The position was next to the Franklin Square Cemetery he and Samuel Pratt had convinced the Holland Land Company to provide for the village in 1807.

From Chapin's hastily drawn line of defense, the British soon emerged out of the forested darkness. Highly disciplined, the British regulars maintained their formation, marching shoulder to shoulder just as the moon peeked out from the clouds, shedding a light that reflected off British bayonets like torches (Johnson 1876).

Chapin lit the fuse and fired his cannon into the British troops. His aim was good and true. The ball opened a sizable hole in the advancing column. His boys immediately reloaded and fired again, but this time, the cannon's makeshift carriage collapsed.

Chapin tore off his white shirt (though some say it was his handkerchief) and tied it to the point of his sword. Mounting a horse, he shouted to his men, "Every man for himself and the devil for us all." According to one member of Chapin's squad, twelve-year-old James Aigin, the doctor rode toward the advancing British Army, alone, as his men and boys raced into the Buffalo village, shouting a final, urgent message to leave.[3]

Chapin later wrote, "A large body of British troops were now within thirty rods of us, and the Indians had nearly surrounded the town. [Some] were in full pursuit of the distressed inhabitants, who had no means of making a rapid retreat, or [able to offer] the least resistance. In this situation, I conceived it my duty to resort to some stratagem to save the people from inevitable destruction" (Ketchum 1865).

Chapin's best hope was further delay. He parleyed with British General Riall in the open at the Franklin Square Cemetery. The doctor offered total surrender of Buffalo and all public property in exchange for protection of private property and an agreement that women and children would not be hurt or molested. Riall's stipulation was that Chapin have all intoxicating liquors destroyed to prevent his English and Indigenous soldiers from getting access (Turner 1849). To seal the deal, Chapin offered himself as a prisoner of war.

Meanwhile, another makeshift unit sent by General Hall was approaching Buffalo. It was led by Lieutenant John Riddle from nearby Williamsville. Riddle yearned to be the hero who saved Buffalo, though he had only forty troops under his command, most of whom had been discharged from a temporary military hospital in Williamsville. Arriving just as Chapin surrendered to the British, Riddle was unaware of Chapin's capitulation. Buffalo's Judge Walden, himself just informed of the surrender, made a wild dash to intercept Riddle and convince him to abandon his advance. Riddle argued

---

3. James Aigin, "Reminiscence of Early Buffalo," 1814, War of 1812 Collection, Buffalo History Museum, New York Heritage Digital Collections, https://nyheritage.contentdm.oclc.org/digital/collection/VTP005/id/240.

that Chapin had no proper authority to capitulate. To Riddle, Chapin's admission of defeat was not only invalid but cowardly. Riddle and Walsh exchanged angry words until finally Riddle agreed to stand down. But as he prepared to retreat, Riddle ordered his one and only cannon to be fired at the British redcoats. His act ended any hope of preventing the burning, pillaging, and raping of Buffalo (Turner 1849).

Riall had all the excuse he needed to claim he had been double-crossed. However, the chaos of the moment made it unlikely that General Riall could have done anything to stop the destruction of Buffalo. His diverse army was intent on plunder and revenge as smoke blanketed the village.

In the early hours of the new day (December 30, 1813), British troops followed their Indigenous mercenaries into Buffalo village proper. Because the British paid tribes, not individuals, the only reward for those who had risked their lives was plunder. Even Riall's regulars joined in looting. Every home was entered, then torched; few prisoners were taken and fewer left alive. The homes of Dr. Chapin and Judge Walden were the last to be torched. One woman, Mrs. Lovejoy, stood in defiant confrontation as troops broke into her house. They stabbed her and threw her body into the street. Judge Walden carried her body back into the house. Within the hour, it too was burned (Turner 1849).

In Black Rock and Buffalo, fires destroyed 104 homes, forty-three barns, and eighteen stores. The British also burned four schooners trapped by ice in Black Rock harbor. They blew up Peter B. Porter's stone mansion and Joseph Palmer's schoolhouse, built in 1808. One eyewitness reported that by three in the afternoon on New Year's Eve, the British had begun loading their boats to return across the river to Canada. They carried with them belongings from most every citizen on the Niagara Frontier.

New Year's Day, 1814, began quietly. Only a few looters roamed the streets. Unworthy to be called Americans, these thieves materialized at a scene of near-total desolation to steal and carry off what little the enemy left behind (Turner 1849). Gradually, several citizens returned to gather the dead. Theirs was a ghastly sight. Most of the bodies were stripped, tomahawked and scalped. Bodies not claimed by friends or family were placed on the frozen ground in the Franklin Square Cemetery and covered with boards for later identification by relatives and friends. Only the walls of two stone buildings broke Buffalo's landscape, the Seneca Street blacksmith shop and the jail on Washington Street.

The British invasion dispossessed twelve thousand inhabitants and depopulated a tract of 160 square miles of Western New York that paralleled the east banks of the Niagara River. Mothers searched for months to reunite with their children or took charge of another mother's orphaned children they found wandering the confusing devastation. The villages of Buffalo, Black Rock, Niagara Falls, Lewiston, and Youngstown and every farmhouse along the way formed a panorama of ruin. In the wilderness, previously abandoned log cabins, barns, and sheds became homes for desperate families. More fortunate refugees moved in with relatives (Turner 1849).

The British took 130 prisoners, including Dr. Chapin. General Riall proudly sent the notorious Dr. Cyrenius Chapin under heavy guard to the British prisoner of war camp in Montreal. The British held him for nine months before his parole in September 1814 (Chapin 1836; Turner 1849).

Throughout the early winter weeks of 1814, there were rumors of another British attack. General Hall assigned soldiers to guard Buffalo's ashes, and twice they repelled British squads crossing the river. The boredom of frigid winter days was occasionally broken by army buglers from rival camps on both sides of the Niagara River, exchanging volleys of bugle calls. A few residents returned to Buffalo, but they were desperate for food, and the army shared what they could from their already stretched commissary. The *Buffalo Gazette* set up publication in a Williamsville print shop, issuing its first post-burn edition on January 18, 1814.

Warmer spring weather eased the desperation somewhat. A traveler passing through Buffalo in May 1814 reported that three taverns, sixteen stores, and over fifty assorted dwellings had risen from the ashes (Turner 1849).

The undermanned United States Army simply could not conduct simultaneous offensive actions from Detroit to the Saint Lawrence and defend the long Atlantic coastline. The army of thirty-five thousand men authorized when Congress declared war in June 1812 never grew beyond 18,500, and those that enlisted were often late in receiving their pay. In July 1814, Buffalo's former congressman Peter Porter, seeing little encouragement from the federal government, stepped up his own recruitment efforts and amassed a sizable state militia that again crossed the Niagara River to capture Canada's Fort Erie.[4]

In July 1814, the Americans attempted to retake Fort George. That effort failed in what many believe to be the most decisive engagement in

---

4. Daniel P. Glenn, "'Savage Barbarities and Petty Depredations': Supply Shortages and Military-Civilian Conflicts in the Niagara Theater, 1812–14," *New York History* 94, nos. 3–4 (2013): 182–204.

the war. Known as the Battle of Lundy's Lane, it was the bloodiest battle ever fought in the Province of Ontario (then Upper Canada; Hickey 2012). Despite several American attempts, the Saint Lawrence River remained firmly under British control.

Sylvia Chapin and her daughters moved in with friends in Canandaigua, where Dr. Chapin found them after his September release. Once his health was restored, he took an appointment as the surgeon at a temporary military hospital in Buffalo. He would later write, "Although I failed in saving the town, still I succeeded in securing the retreat of many inhabitants who would have otherwise fallen victims to savage vengeance" (Assembly 1812; Turner 1849). Meanwhile, back in England, the population was growing tired of continuous wars and the taxes needed to fund them. Parliament pressured the King George III to seek a treaty and end the war known today as the War of 1812. Finally, on Christmas Eve, December 24, 1814, the Treaty of Ghent ended the hostilities. The last battle occurred on January 8, 1815, in New Orleans, before word of the treaty reached all combatants.

The War of 1812 accomplished little strategically, but it matured America's view of the federal government and established the need for the nation to maintain a professional and permanent military organization. It also convinced Americans that they possessed the grit and stubbornness needed to outlast a distant power. Historians have been left to ponder a different outcome had Napoleon not threatened England and ensnared both the British army and navy. The Treaty of Ghent essentially restored prewar boundaries (Pratt 1925).

Former congressman and New York militia general Peter B. Porter received the Congressional Gold Medal for capturing Fort Erie in the summer of 1814. Reflecting on Dr. Chapin's war effort, Porter said "that with the means at his command, none rendered more valuable service to the army and country" (Pratt 1925). For his part, Chapin remained adamant that Buffalo burned because one reckless American commander ordered the unnecessary burning of the Canadian village of Newark.

In hearings before the United States Congress following the war, Dr. Chapin found he needed to defend his militia against detractors who thought the "Forty Thieves" nickname was well-earned. Chapin rationalized that the actions of his militia were essential "for the purpose of clearing the frontier of persons inimical to the States." Chapin believed McClure had failed to do everything possible to win the war, and McClure testified Chapin was an imprudent traitor who did not follow orders. Indeed, there is no evidence that Chapin attempted to rein in the excesses of his militia, suggesting he either endorsed their actions or could not manage his ragtag unit of volunteers. In his testimony, Dr. Chapin bemoaned that "our people [shot] cows, sheep, ducks and poultry of the Canadian farmers." New York Governor Tompkins viewed Chapin as a hero, conferring on him the title "Major of Volunteers" (Ketchum 1865).

When the war ended in the winter of 1814 to 1815, Dr. Chapin moved his family to Geneva, New York, one hundred miles east of Buffalo. There, he worked in the practice of Dr. William Hortson for two years. On April 9, 1816, Cyrenius Chapin again testified before the United States Congress, winning reparations for Buffalo. Congress concluded that the conflagration of Newark by the United States Army provided the enemy with a powerful incentive for retaliation.[5]

In 1818, the government remunerated Dr. Chapin for his unpaid service during the war and awarded him a military pension of $250 annually. The government payments allowed the Chapins to rebuild the drugstore, office, and home complex in Buffalo and contribute toward building a new St. Paul's Episcopal Church (Evans 1903). Chapin also invested $100 to form a company charged with improving navigation of the Buffalo Creek harbor and helped fund the Buffalo and Black Rock Jubilee Water Works Company (Hodge 1885). He was elected to serve as a trustee on the village board. By 1820, Dr. Chapin and his family were living in a brand-new, stately three-floor house on Seneca Street.[6]

The War of 1812 cemented Dr. Cyrenius Chapin's role as a prominent Buffalo citizen. Chapin was widely respected for his sacrifices, and, as age mellowed his brusque nature, his reputation for honesty and practicality prevailed. In 1821, he organized the Erie County Agricultural Society and, with it, the first county fair. He was motivated by a belief that improved farming methods would improve his patients' financial situations. In 1827, Chapin led the formation of an Erie County Medical Society, and he served as its first president.

In 1836, two years before Chapin's death, a committee led by Peter Porter presented Chapin with a silver setting of two massive pitchers and twelve goblets. According to Porter, no one "displayed more patriotic zeal and enthusiasm" or "embark[ed] in almost uninterrupted succession of

---

5. *Property Lost, Captured, or Destroyed by the Enemy 1812–14*, H.R. Rep., 18th Cong., 2d Sess. (1824).

6. K. Burr, "Dr. Cyrenius Chapin," *Buffalo Times*, June 26, 1927.

enterprises against the enemy, involving imminent personal hazard, as well as great fatigue and privation, [and] none [were] more liberal of his purse."[7]

In the late 1830s, when a few disgruntled Canadians conspired to throw off the British yoke, Chapin became an ally of their leader, William Lloyd Mackenzie, providing financial support and encouraging rhetoric advocating for skirmishes that became known as the Patriot Wars. On December 11, 1837, five days after being defeated trying to capture Toronto, Mackenzie showed up as a guest to the Chapin home in Buffalo. Still believing that Canadians wanted to join the United States, Chapin sponsored the planning for an invasion of Canada across a frozen Lake Erie in February 1838. The invasion's illegal staging camp was broken up by United States General Winfield Scott, and, soon after, the sixty-nine-year-old Chapin came down with a fever. He died in his home on February 20, 1838, becoming the last person to be buried in the Franklin Square Cemetery, only a few steps from where he had set up his makeshift cannon to delay the advancing British troops (Rosenthal 2025).

---

7. Pratt, "Biographical Sketch," 6; Kohler, "Colonel Chapin."

4

Clinton's Ditch

The Birth of the Erie Canal, 1825

BRAD L. UTTER WITH THOMAS X. GRASSO

Adapted from Brad L. Utter, with Ashley Hopkins-Benton and Karen E. Quinn, "Enterprising Waters: The History and Art of New York's Erie Canal" (SUNY Press, 2020).

New York's famed Erie Canal, constructed between 1817 and 1825, was revolutionary in many ways. It was planned, financed, constructed, and operated entirely by the state government, the largest state enterprise of the nineteenth century. It was the second-largest human-made canal in the world at the time and the largest in the United States. Project engineers and contractors had little experience with building canals, so construction was a practical school for learning and for developing the engineering profession. For instance, the builders learned to use new equipment and techniques, including hydraulic cement that hardened underwater.

The canal dramatically reduced transportation costs between the Hudson River and the interior of the nation, leading to the development of agriculture, manufacturing, and commerce. The Erie Canal made New York City the nation's most important port and contributed to the growth of New York's canal-side cites, particularly Syracuse, Rochester, and Buffalo. It served as the route for thousands of people moving westward, dramatically spurring population growth.

The Erie Canal was a major factor in the growth of New York and the nation in the nineteenth century.

> No single act—no public measure—except the Declaration of Independence, and the formation of the United States Constitution, has done so much to promote the public prosperity and produce a new era in the history of the country, as the construction of the Erie Canal.
>
> —Jesse Hawley, 1840

To fully appreciate what an extraordinary thing the Erie Canal is, one must understand a good bit about the America that spurred its creation. The canal was built at a time when the United States was not only a young country but an entirely new idea put into practice, an unprecedented experiment in self-governance and civic participation and responsibility. Moreover, the young republic took root on the eastern edge of a vast, unspoiled continent, the realities of which—including a stunningly varied landscape abundant in natural resources—were being actively discovered.

The idea for a cross-state canal in New York came early, decades before its construction, owing to two things: the desire for better access to the rich resources of the North American interior and the unique opportunity New York's natural landscape presented to achieve it. New York is the only state on the Eastern Seaboard that touches both the Atlantic Ocean and the Great Lakes. The Hudson River, flowing from its origin in the Adirondack Mountains down through the Hudson Valley, empties into New York Harbor. The Mohawk River cuts east through a large swath of central New York, joining the Hudson at Cohoes, just north of Albany. Especially significant is the fact that the divide at Rome between the Mohawk River and Wood Creek is the lowest pass in the mountains that form the eastern backbone of North America, stretching from Birmingham, Alabama, to the Saint Lawrence River. All this is to say, New York was the logical place to undertake a human-made navigable connector. Dig a channel from Albany to Buffalo, and you've got a water route—so much easier for transport than overland hauling—between the Atlantic and Lake Erie, and beyond.

But for all this natural potential, the Erie Canal's creation was not preordained, though its economic success was. Human effort—genius, even—was required, and like nearly all things involving humans, there was conflict. The canal's creation required public approval and state support, and not everyone was on board. The anti-canal faction was strong and dismissed a statewide channel as implausible and therefore wasteful to attempt.

Summed up in one allegory, "In the big ditch would be buried the treasury of the state, to be watered by the tears of posterity."

But in 1810, DeWitt Clinton, mayor of New York City, took up the cause. By that time, he had already served as a New York state legislator and US senator, and his political clout elevated the advocacy of earlier ardent canal proponents, leading entrepreneurs and statesmen like Jesse Hawley, Joshua Foreman, and Gouverneur Morris. Their efforts paid off, and in 1817 the state legislature passed a bill authorizing the canal's construction.

DeWitt Clinton became one of the strongest proponents of the Erie Canal, and the success or failure of the project weighed heavily on his reputation; hence the moniker "Clinton's Ditch." Building the canal would prove challenging, both politically and physically. Once completed, it was an immediate success: shipping costs plummeted, and new services and goods became widely available. Cheap, reliable transportation opened new markets to farmers and businesspeople, creating a commercial windfall from New York City to Buffalo. Drawn to new opportunities, settlers moved westward, and forests soon transformed into new communities. "Clinton's Ditch" was no longer used as a derogatory term for the grand Erie Canal.

The Politics and Funding of Internal Improvements

Internal improvements, such as roadways and water-based routes, and their funding were frequent topics of political debate in the early nineteenth century. While many Americans called for improvements, the means to pay for a canal became a divisive issue. A project as ambitious as the proposed canal was deemed too costly for private business to fund and maintain. New Yorkers first sought the help of the federal government and those states who would also benefit from the canal, but no funds were forthcoming. Various plans for federal funding of internal improvements—namely, canals and roads—were not supported by Presidents Thomas Jefferson and James Madison. New York, therefore, decided to raise its own funds to build the canal and embarked on the first large-scale public works projects in the country. In 1817 the New York state legislature established the Canal Act, which created a board of commissioners to oversee the canal's funding and construction.

The planning and operation of New York's canals became a foremost feature in New York politics. Political careers could be made or broken by one's position on the canals. Political parties jockeyed to take credit for successes and to blame opponents for failures. Once the canal proved successful, party lines were usually drawn regarding policies for the management of the canal.

A State-Run Enterprise

The Erie Canal was the first major public works project in the nation and defined government's role in funding and overseeing the improvement of transportation routes. Setting many precedents in the process, the state government had to grow and adapt to manage the operation of the canal system.

The Canal Board, which was made up of the canal commissioners and the commissioners of the canal fund, was the main government arm of the canal system. Among its many duties, it oversaw a large state workforce, the first in the United States. Most employees were politically appointed, and their jobs on the canal were susceptible to political power shifts and corruption. In addition to the laws enacted by the state legislature, the canal commissioners also enacted a set of rules for boaters to follow, including that every boat that operated at night must have a light on its bow, no throwing dead animals in the canal, and no stopping or blocking a lock when it is your boat's turn to go in.

To promote business and increase canal revenues, the state leased the rights to use surplus canal water to generate power for businesses. With the use of a water wheel or water turbine, the excess water could power mills or manufacturing plants. Each year the state would determine the rate of tolls that would be charged for cargo shipped on the canal. Tolls were often calculated to advance certain industries. For example, if the commissioners wanted to help New York cheese makers, they could lower the toll on shipping cheese on the canal.

Myron Holley (1779 to 1841)

An early canal proponent from Canandaigua, Myron Holley served as a canal commissioner and treasurer from 1816 to 1824. As treasurer, he traveled the canal route during construction to pay and negotiate with contractors. He did not officially charge the state for his own expenses for this travel. In 1824 his political opponents induced the legislature to audit the work of Holley and others, and he could not account for some of the funds used for payment. He resigned his position, admitting that he used some of the public money to purchase land, feeling it was owed to him as compensation for his travel expenses. Holley's property was held by the state in penalty, then returned to him in 1828 when his supporters gained control of the legislature. Holley went on to play major roles in the anti-Masonic and antislavery movements in New York state. The village of Holley, in Orleans County, is named after him.

Settling the Land: Acquisition and Dispossession

Before construction of the Erie Canal could take place, the State of New York had to gain ownership of the land needed to build it. When landowners refused to sell, the state enforced eminent domain—the first large-scale use of the practice in United States history.

The value of the land was determined by the state, and then the current owners were paid for the land. Often, the state appraisers would determine that the benefits of the canal increased the value of the land bordering it, so no money was exchanged. Challenges to land values were voluminous. As Carol Sheriff noted in her book *The Artificial River: The Erie Canal and the Paradox of Progress, 1817–1862*, established farmers in the Mohawk Valley quickly found that the legal decisions often ruled in favor of commercial interests over their own.

The triumph of the Erie Canal and the nation's drive to the west—for land, natural resources, and nation building—devastated Native peoples, who were forced off their lands in the name of "progress." National defense, land speculation, and growing populations pushed Native peoples off their ancestral lands across the United States.

Through a series of questionable "treaties," former Haudenosaunee (Iroquois) lands became obtainable to European Americans. Land speculators were quick to purchase the rights to those lands, and Native Americans were sent to reservations. As settlers flooded Western New York, they applied pressure to the government to make more land available, and by 1870 only a few small reservations remained.

An Engineering Marvel

The first shovel of dirt in excavating for the canal was ceremoniously overturned outside of Rome, New York, on July 4, 1817. Over the next eight years, engineers, surveyors, contractors, and laborers with little or no experience overcame immense obstacles to build the Erie Canal.

Canals, locks, aqueducts, and other canal structures had been used for centuries throughout the world. The wonder of New York's canal lay in the enormous size of the project, the landscape that had to be conquered, the structures used to conquer the obstacles, and the lack of experience of the engineers and laborers. Keeping enough water in the canal was no small feat. To maintain the flow of water, very slight declines over miles had to be calculated into the construction of the canal bed, and small feeder canals were built to help supply enough water. For example, a navigable aqueduct connected the canal with the village of Little Falls and a small feeder canal, which drew water from the Mohawk River.

Who Built the Canal?

When the famed English canal engineer William Weston turned down the position of chief engineer for the Erie Canal, New York turned to Benjamin Wright, James Geddes, and others who were not formally trained engineers but had previously surveyed for the canal project. They learned by reading trade books and trial and error, and through experience they became engineers and instructed others on the job. Thereafter, many of the Erie Canal's engineers went on to work on other projects throughout the country, building canals, railroads, bridges, water systems, and roads.

Benjamin Wright (1770 to 1842)

Benjamin Wright is frequently called the "father of American civil engineering." Wright worked on the Western Inland Lock Navigation Company's works, on New York City's expansion, and as chief engineer for the Erie Canal. His leadership and tutelage were crucial to the development of civil engineering in the United States. Wright's early experience and discovery of limestone suitable for stone locks prepared him for his role on the Erie Canal.

James Geddes (1763 to 1838)

James Geddes started on the canal project in 1808, conducting some of its early surveys. By 1816 he was appointed the engineer in charge of survey. He later became chief engineer of the Champlain Canal and went on to work on numerous canals. As an example of learning from experience, in his original plan for the canal crossing of the Genesee River at Rochester in

1817, Geddes called for a dam ten feet high to create a pool for boats to cross. A bridge south of the dam would provide a towpath and the crossing point for the boats. After a few years of experience in actual construction of the canal, it was decided that an aqueduct would be a better solution for crossing the swift current of the Genesee River.

Canvass White (1790 to 1834)

Canvass White served as an assistant to Benjamin Wright and eventually became an engineer in his own right. At the request of DeWitt Clinton, he spent months in Europe studying canals. Like many of the other engineers who got their training on the Erie Canal project, White went on to serve as chief engineer on other canals and railroads. White's patent for an American version of hydraulic cement, which hardens underwater, was made with New York's natural resources. While he was credited with inventing this version of hydraulic cement, recent scholarship suggests he negotiated with the actual inventor, Andrew Bartow, to hold the patent.

The Laborers

The immense scope of the Erie Canal project was split into four main sections: Eastern, Middle, Western, and the Champlain Canal. Each section was divided into smaller parts for contractors to bid on. The contractors in turn hired laborers. The canal commissioners wanted to ensure that the field for bidding was open to all in what was New York's first large-scale use of subcontracting.

During the first few years, construction was completed mostly by local farmers and native-born Americans. In 1819 America experienced its first economic depression. The economic downturn actually helped the canal project; construction costs dropped, and struggling farmers found work as contractors and laborers. As the project grew, it drew laborers from Europe, especially Irish immigrants, who went on to work on the most dangerous sections of the project.

Conquering the Niagara Escarpment

The Niagara Escarpment is a ridge that runs from Wisconsin to Western New York. To complete the canal, engineers and laborers had to conquer this great geological formation, and Lockport was chosen as the best place to traverse the sixty-foot obstacle. At the top of the cliff, a seven-mile channel through solid rock was cut to provide a steady flow of water from Lake Erie. A set of five double locks was built to climb the ridge and enter the deep cut—an engineering feat that made Lockport famous across the country.

On August 24, 1825, a grand ceremony was held to honor the completion of the Lockport flight. Over four hundred Freemasons attended the ceremony, along with an estimated three to four thousand citizens. It was common at the time for Freemasons to dedicate cornerstones of new construction. After a blessing and Masonic ceremony, Jesse Hawley (early projector of the canal), Nathan Roberts (one of the engineers of the flight), and others made toasts to the magnificent canal. The New York State Museum has one of the two capstones that were ceremoniously placed into the structure of the flight that day. It reads, "The Erie Canal 362 miles in length was commenced the 4th of July 1817 and completed in the year 1825 at an expense of about $7,000,000 and was constructed exclusively by the CITIZENS of the STATE of NEW YORK."

Celebrating Early Achievements

On October 23, 1819, Governor DeWitt Clinton, canal commissioners, canal engineers, military leaders, religious leaders, and other dignitaries sailed on the *Chief Engineer of Rome* from Utica to Rome, on the first celebratory canal boat ride. The water had been let into some sections of the canal just two days before. Laborers were stationed at potential trouble spots along the route, and there was one breach that was quickly patched. The boat was welcomed along the route with cheers as the band on board played patriotic tunes. A large banquet was held at Rome, and the boat returned to Utica. This demonstration of the success of the Erie Canal stirred support and enthusiasm for the endeavor and pressure for its completion. In 1823 a grand celebration was held in Albany for the completion of the Champlain Canal and the Erie Canal from Brockport to the capital. Delegates from around the state joined elected officials, military officers, canal commissioners, engineers, contractors, firefighters, members of various societies, and thousands of onlookers for the festivities. The day included performances by bands, parades—on land and in the water—and speeches, and the top stone was laid at Lock 1 (originally called Lock 53). A Masonic ceremony was also held at the entrance of the canal.

Wedding of the Waters

As the deep cut at Lockport neared completion, plans were made for an enormous celebration. The festivities began in Buffalo on October 26, 1825, with speeches and a special cannon "communication" to New York City.

A flotilla left Buffalo on a ten-day voyage to New York City. Aboard the canal boats were elected officials, including Governor DeWitt Clinton, as well as dignitaries and products from the western part of the state and further west, including a Native American canoe from Lake Superior, various animals, lumber, potash, flour, and butter, among other things.

Celebratory cannon fire alerted communities that the grand flotilla had left Buffalo for New York City. Cannons were placed along the route of the canal and the Hudson River from Buffalo to New York City. Once the first cannon was fired, the next within earshot would fire, and the process continued as cannons were fired successively until New York City was reached, going around the harbor and then reversed, returning to Buffalo. The first cannon sounded at ten in the morning on October 26, 1825. The progression reached Albany at 10:57 a.m. and New York City at 11:17 a.m. The message went back up the Hudson and returned to Buffalo just before 1:00 p.m.

Communities along the canal welcomed the flotilla with speeches, artillery salutes, and fireworks, celebrating what New York and American democracy had accomplished. Once in New York City, the celebration included the "wedding of the waters" ceremony, a large parade, and numerous festivities. The wedding of the waters ceremony took place in New York Harbor off Sandy Hook. A choreographed parade of domestic and international vessels formed a circle in the bay while Clinton and others gave speeches and poured water from Lake Erie into the Atlantic.

The canal was already such a boon to the economy of New York City that the common council of the city of New York commissioned medals to celebrate its completion. The medals, designed by Asher B. Durand, who would become best known as a Hudson River School painter, feature both real canal elements, such as locks and aqueducts, and mythical figures, including Pan and Neptune. Lumber from the western part of the state, transported aboard the *Seneca Chief* (part of the October 26, 1825, flotilla), were made into presentation boxes for the medals by leading nineteenth-century American cabinetmaker Duncan Phyfe. Approximately eleven gold medals were made and presented to high-ranking officials, including former presidents, signers of the Declaration of Independence, and the family of Robert Fulton. Federal and state officials as well as other prominent men of the era received silver medals. Medals made of white metal were sent to all invited guests of the grand canal celebration, members of canal committees across the state, and museums.

Not everyone welcomed the flotilla. The new canal bypassed the established communities of Rome and Schenectady. Initially, both communities lost population and commerce because the new canal bypassed the well-established businesses geared around the river trade. To show their dismay with the chosen route, some residents of Rome protested the wedding of the waters ceremony with a mock funeral procession. Using a black barrel containing water from the old Western Inland Lock Navigation canal, they defiantly dumped the water into the Erie in front of the flotilla. Schenectady made no formal celebration plans, and the flotilla's reception was recorded as "rather grave" by William L. Stone, a flotilla participant.

Early Commerce and Industry

The Erie Canal was an immediate success and surpassed all expectations. Dependable and inexpensive transportation opened new markets to farmers and businesspeople, creating a commercial windfall from New York City to Buffalo. Drawn to new opportunities, settlers moved westward, and forests soon gave way to new communities.

INDUSTRIAL GROWTH

> The city of New York, and, indeed, most parts of the State, are now supplied with pails and tubs, and wooden ware of that description, made by turning lathes, and other machinery, moved by water. In our neighboring county of West Chester, there are fields, enclosed by fences, . . . after being transported several hundred miles, were purchased for much less than any other fence, equally good, could be made for, near where they are used.
>
> —Cadwallader D. Colden, 1825

The first half of the nineteenth century saw the rise of both old and new industries that used the canal system for shipping raw materials and large bulk commodities. The Erie Canal opened large regions to commerce and commercial development and opened new markets. Growth in the agriculture, lumber, iron, salt, stoneware, glass-making, furniture, and brewing industries was significant, and New York state grew to become a worldwide industrial and economic leader. Goods of all kinds were shipped on the canal: from live fish to ice to home furnishings, the list of nineteenth-century products that moved along the Erie is almost endless.

Like today, grains formed the base of many of the foods people ate in the nineteenth century. The canal was a cheap and reliable way to transport grains to feed the growing American population. The growing population also needed lumber for fuel and to construct buildings, ships, and wagons. As a result, wheat, flour, and lumber accounted for most of the tonnage on the canal for the entire nineteenth century. To demonstrate the boon, between 1815 and 1825 the cost of shipping wheat from Buffalo to New York City dropped from roughly one hundred dollars to ten dollars per ton.

The state's furniture-making industry expanded rapidly in the years following the Erie Canal's opening. Fine-quality furniture was manufactured in cities and towns all along the canal. This likely also indicates an increased local market for luxury items corresponding to a rise in the socioeconomic conditions of residents in these cities.

The canal provided communities along the route the ability to import and export products that would have been too costly to ship before the canal opened. Farmers who had already lived in the canal corridor went from subsistence farming to cash-crop farming. Well-equipped mills along the route could process agricultural products, store them, and use grain elevators and windlasses (hoists) to help load and unload busy canal boats.

Seventeenth-century Dutch settlers established a brewing center in Albany that continued to thrive into the twentieth century. When the Erie Canal opened, Albany brewers accessed new sources of grains and hops to expand their production and outreach. Most of what became known as "Albany Ale" was shipped to New York City and beyond. Brewer John Taylor took full advantage of the benefits of the transportation revolution taking place on his front doorstep. Taylor purchased grains coming in from the west and placed at least one malt house along the canal. His company partnered in steamboats that would ship his brew south. By 1851, John Taylor & Sons had a global distribution and was among the largest producers of beer in America.

CANAL WAREHOUSES

Warehouses served a vital commercial purpose that benefited local and regional economies. A forwarding agent managed the warehouse and coordinated with businesses and individuals to ship and store goods. Depending on the merchant's needs, products could be stored for long or short term, or until there was enough on hand to fill a boat going to a particular destination.

Canal Stores

As soon as sections of the canal opened, it was clear that boat crews and patrons needed places to buy supplies. Early on, lock tenders opened general stores next to locks, but that practice became prohibited as some lock tenders proved more eager to make money in their stores than tend to their duties "locking boats through."

Soon, privately owned canal stores opened. As boats waited their turn to lock through, passengers and crewmembers could purchase day-to-day necessities. These general stores also had medicines, tools, general boats supplies—almost anything a boater could need while traveling. The stores also served as a social center for boaters and community members.

New Ports and Boomtowns

New communities with nautical names, like Port Byron, Brockport, Gasport, and Lockport, sprung up along the canal and were rich with opportunities. By the time the Erie Canal was completed, the tiny villages had become prosperous towns, and, within a few decades, many became cities.

New Luxuries

> Ours is no longer a western settlement, our children are surrounded by comforts, the blessings and the elegances of life, where their fathers found only hardship, privation and want.
>
> —*Buffalo Commercial Advertiser*, November 14, 1848

As new communities grew out of the forests, the people living within the canal corridor had access to goods and services not previously available. From fresh oysters to high-end furniture, the speed and smooth travel of the canal brought the comforts of eastern society to the west.

Moving Goods: The Boats That Made It Happen

Various types of boats were used from the early days of the canal's operation. The first boats in use were inspired by European designs and Durham boats. As canallers on the Erie gained experience, a few basic styles evolved to best serve the demands of the New York waterways.

Line boats, lake boats, bullhead boats, and the canal schooners carried freight and were designed with their cargo and route in mind. The line boat had space for both freight and passengers. The lake boat, or laker, and bullhead boat were similar, with the exception that a lake boat had multiple hatches across the top deck and the bullhead had one long cover that looked like a cabin covering the deck, each designed to keep its cargo dry. The canal schooner's mast could be removed while in the canal and raised for sailing on the lakes or rivers.

Scow boats had square ends that sloped up from the bottom of the boat at the front and back. These boats were used by state crews to do repairs on the canal and earned the nickname "hurry-up boats" because they hurried to the spots where repairs were needed. Scows were also used to haul lumber, sand, gravel, and other items that could be exposed to the elements.

Line boats were operated by freight-line companies and hauled both freight and passengers. The fee for passengers aboard a line boat was cheaper than a packet, or passenger-only, boat because of the line boat's limited amenities and comparatively slow progress. This was the preferred method of travel for immigrants because they could save on travel expenses and they could bring furniture and luggage with them.

The Packet Boat: A Floating Hotel

In the early days of the canal, people traveled by packet boats, which were often crowded and cramped. Accommodations included a place to sleep, meals, and sometimes entertainment in the form of small onboard libraries or musical instruments. The boats typically carried forty to sixty people, but larger packets held up to one hundred. Whenever the weather allowed, passengers would ride on top of the boats to avoid the stuffy cabin and to view the scenery.

This business thrived until the 1840s, when railroads became competitive in passenger travel. Companies introduced larger, luxurious boats, but by the 1860s they were almost completely gone, superseded by the burgeoning railroads.

The Canal and the Hudson in the Age of Steam

The Hudson River was a vital link in the trade route between the Atlantic Ocean, Lake Champlain, and the Great Lakes. During the 1820s and 1830s, the flat-bottomed canal boats stuck mainly to the canals, while sailing and steam-powered boats cruised the Hudson and the lakes.

By the 1840s canal boats had grown in size, and steam vessels became powerful enough to tow long lines of canal boats and barges between Albany and New York City. By the end of the nineteenth century, as many as 125 boats could make up one long tow. Smaller tugboats were used to help the long tows make turns in the river and to add or remove boats while the tow was moving.

For canallers, the two- or three-day tow between Albany and New York allowed time for boat maintenance, laundry, and to socialize with other crews in the tow. Once in New York City, boats and barges were taken off the tow and steered to designated docks. While unloading, the boat captain might search for his next job. It was not unusual for private barge owners to spend many days at the New York docks looking for the next load to haul north.

One of Albany's earliest African American businessmen, Captain Samuel Schuyler (1781 to 1841), founded the Schuyler Line, a lucrative boat-towing service, and the company grew under the leadership of two of his sons. Captain Schuyler also joined with family members in other business ventures, including real estate, a coal yard, and a flour and feed store.

Life on the Canal

The Erie Canal attracted people from all walks of life. Professional canallers, or "canawlers," had a reputation as rough-and-tough transients who loved to drink and fight, especially when trying to beat another boat into a lock. Although this may have been true of some, there were canallers who did not participate in such activities. In addition to those working on the commercial boats, the state employed workers who kept the canal moving.

Living and working on the canal required the help of many to keep the boats moving and to take care of the needs of the people on board. Canallers had their own set of social rules that deeply challenged the emerging middle-class sense of what was right and wrong. Single women worked on the canal as cooks or in other roles. These women had greater freedom than those who lived a more traditional lifestyle.

The Boat Crew

A typical freight-boat crew consisted of a captain, a steersman, two drivers, and a cook. The captain was in charge of the crew and finances. The steersman would pilot the boat, load and unload, and help with the mules. The drivers were responsible for the mules or horses. Steering and driving were done in six-hour shifts called "a trick"—six hours on and six hours off. The cook was often the wife of the captain or steersman.

Mule Drivers

Canal boats glided along the water behind animal power—a horse or a mule or a team of horses or mules. Horses were the most common early on, but mules slowly became the animal of choice. The canal-boat "driver" was in charge of leading the mule or horse along the towpath. It was a monotonous task that did not require much skill, yet it was essential to the functioning of the canal. The driver was also in charge of feeding and brushing the mule or horse.

Mule drivers sometimes worked for line companies, which owned several boats and barns, each built at the distance it took to travel in a six-hour shift. At the end of a shift, the animals were replaced with a fresh team. While waiting for work, the drivers would stay in the line barns along the route.

Whether seeking adventure or survival, thousands of children, many of them orphans, worked as drivers. It was not uncommon for them to be cheated out of wages or treated miserably by their employers.

Families on the Water

> A captain who had his family on the boats lived a fairly comfortable life, as the woman had the meals on time, did the washing and ironing, kept the cabin clean, and made the beds. She also saw that her husband had a bath occasionally so that he did not get lousy as many other bathless canallers did.
>
> —Richard Garrity, canaller

By the mid-nineteenth century, it was common for captains to operate their boats with their families on board. Similar to life on a rural farm, everyone old enough helped with the family business and household chores. Unless the parents gave lessons on board, children had to wait until the winter to attend school, if they went at all. By the mid-nineteenth century, several thousand families transported products across New York state on the Erie Canal and its adjoining waterways.

SMOOTH OPERATIONS

New York's canals required an intricate system of state and private workers to keep things running efficiently. The wide variety of jobs included lock tenders, bank watchers, "hurry-up boat" crew members, weighlock masters, and longshoremen.

The weighlock masters weighed empty boats at the beginning of the season. The captain received a receipt showing his boat's base weight. Boats were weighed again when loaded to determine the tolls of each trip. Canal tolls were based on the weight of the boat and type of cargo it carried. Weighlock buildings were located at strategic points and equipped with a giant scale and lock to determine the weight of boats and collect tolls. Boats would pull into the lock, and the lock was drained, leaving the boat sitting on the scale. Once weighed, the lock was refilled, and the boat could float back into the canal. The weighlock master oversaw the process and paperwork.

WINTER ON THE CANAL

During the winter, much of the canal was drained, and all traffic came to a standstill. Boats would rush to their port of choice before the canal closed for the season or the onset of an early freeze, sometimes being stuck for the winter before reaching their destination. By the 1840s, commercial transportation was year-round via the railroads in operation.

Travel and Adventure on the Erie Canal

> I cannot conceive a more beautiful combination of verdu[r]e; and as the windings of the canal brought us in sight of fresh vistas, new cultivation, new villages, new bridges, new aqueducts, rose at every moment, mingled up with scattered dwellings, mills, churches, all span new. The scene looked really one of enchantment.
>
> —Captain Basil Hall, 1828

The Erie Canal captured the world's imagination. With travel to the interior now more affordable and accessible, thousands flocked to New York to experience the canal and its natural wonders. Travel guides became widely popular and, in turn, popularized "the Northern tour" from New York City to Niagara Falls, Saratoga Springs, and Montreal via steamboat, canal, and stagecoach.

Tourists frequently visited reservations and purchased souvenirs of Native American handwork. As Native trade networks and landholdings changed, selling to the tourist market became an important source of income, and the forms being sold shifted to reflect demand from non-Native patrons. Popular among tourists at Niagara Falls was the beadwork of Tuscarora women. They produced a variety of objects, including pincushions, purses, and wall hangings.

Trenton Falls was a fourteen-mile carriage ride north of Utica and was a popular destination for tourists. Visitors tested their nerves by walking down the ravine along the falls while holding on to a chain attached to the rock wall along the trail. In 1827 the English writer Frances Milton Trollope (1832, 246) observed, "These [Trenton] falls have become within the last few years only second in fame to Niagara. The West Canada Creek, which in the map shows but as a paltry stream, has found its way through three miles of rock, which, at many points, is 150 feet high. A forest of enormous cedars . . . which droops its branches like the weeping-willow grow in the clefts of the rock, and in some places almost dip their dark foliage in the torrent."

Immigration Corridor

The canal system directly influenced nineteenth- and early-twentieth-century immigration and the settlement of the United States. By connecting the Atlantic Ocean to the Great Lakes, the canal opened access to lands in Western New York and the Midwest that were previously hard to reach. Access to western lands and jobs constructing the various canals helped bring immigrants, along with their cultures and religions, shaping and enriching the character of the nation.

While early migrants were from eastern New York and New England, eventually a large influx of settlers came from Europe. It was common that large groups emigrated from a single community and settled together. A majority of these settlers, although not abolitionists, were opposed to the expansion of slavery into the west, a critical factor leading up to the Civil War.

The Canal's Success and Legacy

The first Erie Canal ran 363 miles, from Albany to Buffalo, and included eighty-three locks and eighteen aqueducts. It was, at the time, the second-longest human-made waterway in the world, second only to the ancient Grand Canal in China. A narrow ribbon of water four feet deep and forty feet wide, it immediately decreased the cost of shipping and transportation, compared to overland wagons, by 90 percent. Boats could carry seventy tons of freight, and the canal became an economic and national wonder. Powered by the income from cargo tolls on the thousands of boats plying the canal, the state paid for its construction and maintenance in just ten years and showed a profit so large that by 1835 it offset the state budget by at least 60 percent. The waterway made New York the "Empire State" and fostered boomtowns beyond New York—big cities like Detroit, Cleveland, and Chicago.

The building of the canal by the State of New York set the precedent for what was possible under the federal and state constitutions. The state raised funds, acquired land, constructed and operated the waterway, in the name of progress for the public good. New York's construction of the Erie Canal helped to inaugurate a philosophy of an expansive role for government that impacted the everyday lives of individual residents in ways that had not previously been envisioned.

The canal also served as an information superhighway, moving not only goods and people along its course but, with them, news and ideas. This influence was so significant and the impact on people's lives so immense that it has been justly compared to the internet and its impact on commerce, society, and culture today.

The Canal Still Exists!

The purpose of the Erie Canal was always commercial, but since the 1980s there has been a new movement focused on the quality of life for canal communities and promoting heritage tourism, bringing canal history to the forefront of the communities' self-expression with festivals, public art projects, and interpretive signage. Today, recreational boaters from around the world use the New York State Canal System for leisure. Visitor centers, public docks, boat rentals, tours, and bike paths line the canals and invite tourists and locals to learn about the past and enjoy the outdoors. The canal continues to be a utility providing a source of irrigation for farms, hydroelectric power, and drinking water for communities along its route. The canal is, in fact, alive and well . . . ready for your next adventure!

5

The Anti-Rent Rebellions, 1839 to 1846

NANCY NEWMAN

Adapted from Nancy Newman, "Songs and Sounds of the Anti-Rent Movement in Upstate New York" (SUNY Press, 2025).

Beginning in 1839, tenants in several mid-Hudson counties staged a sustained rebellion against landlords who held title to millions of acres from land grants dating back to Dutch and English colonial days. The grants continued after the American Revolution. By the 1810s, there were two dozen large estates with about two million acres. The landlords leased individual farms to tenants with tight controls, which varied from one estate to another—for example, the leases were long-term, the landowner set the rent levels, nonpayment could mean eviction, the owner set conditions on tenants' use of the land and often reserved water, mineral, and timber rights. The tenant had to pay land taxes. Tenants could sell their leases with the landlord's permission, but the landlord was owed part of the sale price.

The tenant farmers wanted to be released from these feudal-like obligations and buy the land they were working. The landlords, with a few exceptions, refused to alter the farmers' leases or to sell to the farmers on a fair basis.

The farmers dug in and organized, appealing to the public, the courts, successive governors, and the legislature. They also organized into bands whose members interdicted landlords' agents trying to collect back rents and deputy sheriffs attempting to serve writs of ejectment for nonpayment. There were a few acts of violence and even a few deaths.

New constitutional provisions and state laws ultimately undermined the landlords' privileges, and the rebellion subsided by the Civil War period.

The anti-rent rebellions show the revolutionary power of sustained, organized demand for change.

☙

"New York in the colonial period was like a feudal kingdom," observed Howard Zinn (2015, 48) in *A People's History of the United States*. The patroonships that shaped much of the future state had their origin in the early seventeenth century, when Dutch West India Company cofounder Killiaen Van Rensselaer was granted a vast tract of land lining the Hudson River by the Dutch Republic. This system of perpetual fiefs persisted through the English political takeover of 1664, transforming its patriarchs into manor lords and patent holders. Millions of acres were soon controlled by a small number of interrelated families, including the Dutch Van Rensselaers and Schuylers and the Scots English Livingstons.

The colonial period's hereditary titles were effectively abolished after the American Revolution by the new state constitutions. Patriots and veterans, however, were rewarded well for their loyalty in land grants and retention of certain privileges. Alexander Hamilton, who was married to Elizabeth Schuyler, helped devise a legal instrument so that New York's great landed families could retain their property claims in perpetuity. This arrangement was both sales agreement and lease, making the grantee both owner and tenant. The agreement specified annual payment of rent in wheat, fowl, and labor to about twenty families controlling more than two million acres in the Hudson-Mohawk region. Among other stipulations, if tenants wanted to sell their lease, one-quarter of the sale price was owed to the landlord.

By the 1840s, more than a quarter-million people—approximately one-twelfth of New York state's population—lived under the patroon system. Among its major beneficiaries was Stephen Van Rensselaer III (1764 to 1839), who as Killiaen's descendant claimed upward of 750,000 acres (i.e., about 1,200 square miles). For nearly fifty years, "the Good Patroon" collected annual tribute from his Rensselaerswyck tenants, exerting considerable influence on New York state politics and becoming one of the richest men in America. His death in January 1839 sparked several decades of protest and civil disobedience that coalesced into the "largest and most sustained farmers' movement in American history" prior to the Civil War, according to Reeve Huston (2000, 5).

The movement's initial confrontation occurred in autumn 1839. For several months, Van Rensselaer's heirs had attempted to collect "back rents" from the farmers to pay the family's considerable debt. That September, law officers attempted to serve notice to leaseholders in the Helderberg Mountains west of Albany. "When a deputy arrived in the farming area with writs demanding the rent, farmers suddenly appeared, assembled by the blowing of tin horns. They seized his writs and burned them," describes Zinn (2015, 211). In early December, the sheriff came with a posse comitatus of five hundred from Albany to pursue Van Rensselaer's interests and quell the rebellion. The posse was similarly met by "shrieking tin horns" as the number of resisting farmers approached two thousand. The sheriff's company retreated, but the "Anti-Rent War" had begun. The tin horn, normally used to call folks to dinner, soon became a powerful and practical symbol of the struggle's vicissitudes.

The anti-rent movement persisted as collective resistance until 1846, when the revised state constitution prohibited new perpetual agricultural leases. However, private disputes continued to erupt between the landlords' assignees and tenants for decades. Two thousand lawsuits, initiated by Rensselaerswyck purchaser Walter Church, clogged the courts through the late nineteenth century. Spectacular evictions—the landlords' remaining remedy—occurred periodically. These are just some of the developments that have kept regional memory of the anti-rent movement alive across generations.

A Movement Takes Shape, 1839 to 1844

Stephen Van Rensselaer III's 1839 will divided Rensselaerswyck between the eldest sons of his two wives. Their holdings were neatly bisected by the Hudson River: Stephen Van Rensselaer IV received the land west of the river; his brother William received the land to the east. In order to claim their inheritance, however, the brothers had to settle their father's debts through collection of back rents from the 3,063 farm families residing there.

In spring 1839, Stephen published notices in the Helderberg hilltowns demanding back rents be paid. Farmers held meetings in five townships—Rensselaerville, Knox, Westerlo, New Scotland, and Berne—to formulate a response. Each region selected a representative to meet with the new patroon. They visited the manor office at the Rensselaer mansion in Albany on May 22, but Stephen refused to see them in person. A week later, he rejected their written proposal to modernize the leases and renewed his demand for back rents.

On the Fourth of July, tenants held their first mass meeting and rally in Berne. The gathering, which now included farmers from the township of Guilderland, resulted in the "Anti-Renters' Declaration of Independence." Echoing the spirit of the American Revolution, the authors refused "unconditional submission to the will of one man, elevated by an aristocratic law, [and] emanating from a foreign monarchy." They proposed that Stephen, after proving his title, cast aside "the day's services, fowls, quarter sales, [and] all reservations and restrictions contained in the old leases." The representatives insisted that the wheat rent be converted to a reasonable cash basis and that farmers have the option of purchasing the land they worked with fee simple mortgages.

Undaunted by the tenants' declaration, Stephen Van Rensselaer IV convinced the Albany County sheriff to continue advancing his property claims. Beginning in late August, Sheriff Michael Artcher attempted to serve writs of fieri facias, a prelude to distress and eviction, to dozens of West Manor farmers. The law officers repeatedly encountered collective resistance to the papers' delivery. Intimidation tactics included the threat of tar and feathers and burning official documents. In October, the sheriff and his team were rebuffed by a crowd of nearly one hundred. The officers returned in late November to confront three hundred, many of whom followed the men for miles, blowing their horns and loudly proclaiming, "Down with the rent."

In response, Sheriff Artcher assembled a posse comitatus of five hundred in Albany to quell the resistance. The confrontation that December became the Anti-Rent War's first major conflict. After Artcher's posse was rebuffed, he asked Governor William Seward for the state's assistance. A week later, the sheriff was allowed to summon the military companies of Albany and Rensselaer Counties and have others in readiness. The armed, uniformed troops were met by thousands of anti-renters as they marched into the Helderberg hills. Nevertheless, the state's spectacular show of force led to the tenants' capitulation within a few days. Sheriff Artcher resumed serving papers, which now included arrest warrants. Meanwhile, Governor Seward urged tenant farmers to address their grievances "by application to the Courts of Justice and to the Legislature." Although he had maintained "law and order" as requested, the governor made his sympathies for the anti-renters clear. His annual state address that January advocated for land reform. The ramifications of Governor Seward's position, balancing vested property rights and republican principles, would play out over the next half-dozen years.

The anti-rent conflict became relatively quiet as the participants awaited the consequences of Governor Seward's pledge to address their situation. The legislature, after considerable wrangling between Whigs and Democrats, formed a select committee to study the issues. Its recommendations led to the governor's appointment of a Manor Commission to mediate and negotiate a settlement. Meanwhile, a stay on rent collections benefited tenants and perpetuated their strike.

"Playing . . . Calico Indian"

The Manor Commission was thwarted in its attempts to negotiate a compromise between Stephen Van Rensselaer IV and tenants during the first months of 1841. The patroon's lawyers refused reasonable property valuations and sales without reservations and continued to insist on payment of back rents. With the commission at an impasse, Stephen renewed rent collection. In mid-March, the new Albany County sheriff, Amos Adams, was sent to the Helderberg hills to auction off the possessions of delinquent tenants at distress sales. When the tin horns sounded, Sheriff Adams witnessed something novel. According to Henry Christman (1945, 41), "a party of men gathered round disguised as 'Indians,' in loose pantaloons and tunics of brilliant calico, decked with fur, feathers, and tin ornaments. To prevent recognition, some had painted their faces black or red, and others wore masks of calico or painted sheepskins." No violence ensued, but the sheriff and auction bidders were scared away.

The "Calico Indians" made spectacular appearances again in September 1841 in defiance of Sheriff Adams and his new deputy, Bill Snyder. The conflict resulted in one of the Anti-Rent War's most well-known skirmishes and songs. Snyder had pursued the Rensselaer family's property claims over several weeks with abusive language, stockpiled weapons, and gathered a gang of armed bullies. On September 20, anti-renters in "Indian" disguise managed to isolate Snyder near Rensselaerville, threatening and humiliating him before he was allowed to run off. He returned to Albany indignant, but the encounter concluded his pursuit of the Helderberg farmers.

The practice of Euro-Americans assuming the identity of Indigenous peoples as a form of resistance dates at least to the Boston Tea Party, as Philip Deloria notes in *Playing Indian*. In December 1773, a group of white people purporting to be from the upstate New York Mohawk tribe dumped British tea into the harbor for several hours under cover of night. Deloria (2022, 2) calls this "a catalytic moment" for American national consciousness, "the first drumbeat in the long cadence of rebellion through which Americans redefined themselves as something other than British colonists."

The anti-renters of 1840 were generations removed from being British subjects, but they were keenly aware of the Tea Party's potent symbolism. "We resolved to adopt the same kind of protection that was resorted to by the people of Boston when the tea was thrown overboard," recalled the anti-rent organizer Dr. Smith Boughton. "We then raised in the various counties a large force of men completely disguised to prevent the landlord[s] from executing their threat" (qtd. in Huston 2000, 116).

Without doubt, anti-renter appropriations served their self-interest rather than that of Native Americans. Rensselaerswyck tenants insisted that the patroons' illegal maneuvers with the land's original inhabitants invalidated their property titles. Albany attorney Calvin Pepper challenged the Van Rensselaers' claim that they possessed "Indian deeds" dating from 1630 to 1727 during an 1844 hearing before the New York Assembly Judiciary Committee. "The Patroon then can have no valid Indian deed in his possession," concluded Pepper (1846, 7). And even if the deeds were valid, the maps upon which they were based were highly inaccurate. Finally, the originating deeds would have been made by the Dutch West India Company, not their agent, Killiaen Van Rensselaer.

Another form of identification with—and appropriation of—Native American identity by the anti-renters was the organizational structure of local associations. The first formal anti-rent association beyond Albany County's West Manor was on the forty-thousand-acre Schoharie County Scott Patent, which was claimed by John Livingston's descendants. Current tenants feared the imminent expiration of the leases "in lives" that their forebears had taken. Their choices were to either capitulate to the Livingstons' proposed terms or leave. The Albany and Schoharie associations were imitated in eight more counties by early 1845, representing as many as sixty thousand supporters. The associations had two facets: a public side to plan strategy, create petitions, and host lectures, and a secret side for Calico Indian activities. The latter were neighbor-based cohorts with about a dozen members, led by a "chief" and coordinated regionally. The members' identities were known only to each other, and they were sworn to secrecy. Pseudonyms based on Native American names were adopted. The Blenheim Hill Association, for example, had three chiefs whose namesakes were the prominent Native American leaders Black Hawk, Tecumseh, and Red Jacket. The anti-renters' bodies and personal identities were camouflaged with a subterfuge that—as Deloria has described—was becoming a white American tradition.

During the first months of 1842, West Manor and Schoharie tenants asked the state legislature for redress concerning their respective leases. Their petitions were referred to the judiciary committee, which decided in April that the U.S. Constitution's contract clause prevented the state from intervening. Nothing was to be done. Later that spring, "an armed band of 'Indians' seized the Livingston family agent" in Schoharie, threatening and subjecting him to "some personal indignity," as Charles McCurdy (2001, 95) describes. In another confrontation, a farmer intent on paying his rent to the Livingstons was abducted by Calico Indians. The up-renter was held in a tavern for five hours until he consented to jump three times and shout, "Down with the rent!" Six men were arrested; two were fined and imprisoned for a month. Governor Seward issued a proclamation harshly condemning "unlawful transactions" by "tumultuous bodies of disguised and armed men."

The movement expanded rapidly. By the end of 1843, four thousand tenants on William Van Rensselaer's East Manor established the Anti-Rent Association of Rensselaer County. The Blenheim Hill Association of Schoharie County adopted a seven-point written platform and erected a tall pole with a banner that said, "Down with the Rent." Representatives from the three associations set to work creating a new legal strategy with the assistance of sympathetic lawyers. Using the State of New York's 1787 Act Concerning Tenures as its starting point, the committee drafted an "Act Concerning Tenures by Lease" to address specifics of the manor system. If the bill succeeded, tenants would be able to challenge patroon titles and have their leases converted to outright purchases with the state's assistance. Six thousand anti-renters endorsed the act that summer, and more than 133 petitions were presented in its support to the legislature, which began its consideration in January 1844. The opposition marshaled their resources too.

The Judiciary Committee's report on the "Act Concerning Tenures by Lease" savagely attacked the tenants' cause. The report's endorsement by the state assembly in late April was a devastating defeat for the anti-renters, who had failed to counter the landlords' influence. In addition, two recent court decisions had undermined their proposal. The US Supreme Court had confirmed that title challenges violated the constitution's contract clause, and the

New York Supreme Court disallowed the state from intervening in disputes over private property through eminent domain and related measures. Once again, the tenants' grievances were relegated to individual negotiations rather than collective redress. Predictably, the Van Rensselaer brothers Stephen and William initiated numerous lawsuits against the tenants in response. The anti-renters' next attempt at land reform would be to agitate for revisions to the state constitution.

In spring 1844, the National Reform Association (NRA) in New York City decided to advocate for the tenants. The new organization's founders agreed that individuals' natural rights included an "Equal Right to Land." As the historian Helene Zahler (1941, 22) expressed this ideal, "the natural right to life implied a right to the means of living, that is, to land enough to live on." The NRA's ambitious proposal involved opening public lands to actual settlers, a goal partially realized in the 1862 Homestead Act. Equitable distribution of agricultural land would reduce crowding and competition in urban areas, thus solving the problem of surplus workers and low wages. By September 1845, the NRA was attracting a substantial following, with "land-reform groups in six or eight states and in twelve New York counties" (Zahler 1941, 43).

Fourth of July and More

Celebration of the nation's Independence Day in 1844 allowed the anti-renters to reaffirm their commitment to the cause in response to recent legislative defeats. Their agitation had been underway for five years at this point. From their first gathering in 1839, when Rensselaerswyck tenants created the "Anti-Renters' Declaration of Independence," the annual holiday became a time to express hope and rouse solidarity.

The gatherings proliferated as anti-renters formed associations beyond the three core counties of Albany, Rensselaer, and Schoharie. Notably, a delegation from Schoharie's Blenheim Association began organizing on the Hardenbergh Patent, which covered nearly half of Delaware, Greene, Sullivan, and Ulster Counties, in June 1844. Comprising as many as two million acres in the early eighteenth century, various Hardenbergh parcels were now controlled by the Livingston, Verplanck, and other families. Competing land claims based on imprecise descriptions of the Delaware River's branches, lack of compensation to Native Americans, and other issues were long-standing. Nevertheless, many tenants had become bound by cumbersome leases to those asserting title. Anti-rent organizers encouraged patent farmers to challenge those claims. The Blenheim Association was especially effective in Delaware County, where the movement's climactic episode would take place at a distress auction the following year.

Skirmishes proliferated during summer 1844 as the associations and Calico Indian bands stepped up their activities. The future railroad magnate Jay Gould witnessed his father defend their modest family home in Roxbury, Delaware County. On July 6, five "artificial Indians" confronted Gould's father for defying the anti-renters' restriction on sounding tin horns when he used it to call workers to meals. The defiant up-renter compelled the braves to retreat from the premises "to the tune of the 'old king's arm and shell.'" A larger contingent returned the next day but were similarly rebuffed. The "frightful appearance" of the Indians was agonizing and formative for the eight-year-old Jay. At the age of twenty, he published a lengthy history of Delaware County that criticized the tenants' efforts to "repudiate solemn contracts, and defraud the landlords of their honest dues" (Gould 1856, 255, 260–63).

On the East Manor, William Rensselaer renewed his pursuit of distress for rent, which was once again legal. A late-July standoff with one hundred Calico Indians was quickly followed by two deputies being tarred and feathered. Not infrequently, law officers were coerced to shout "Down with the Rent!" as part of the intimidation. Once again, a county sheriff appealed to the state's highest executive. In August, Governor William Bouck met in West Sand Lake with anti-renters from Rensselaer County's eight townships and agreed that the sheriff would stop serving papers for the time being. A few months later, a new, less sympathetic governor—Silas Wright—was in charge.

Unfortunately, the anti-renters' situation would worsen before it improved. Henry Christman's (1945, 97) estimation is that the landlords, "in a final attempt to destroy public sympathy for the tenants' cause, made a concerted drive to provoke violence." With "The Act Concerning Tenures by Lease" defeated, they pressed sheriffs to serve writs and hold distress sales. The result was a series of hostile confrontations with Calico Indians during autumn 1844. Only the patroon Gerrit Smith, one of the largest landowners in central New York, declared a moratorium on rent collection. Twenty other proprietors, led by John Livingston, Gulian C. Verplanck, and John A. King, formed the Freeholders Committee of Safety in New York City to strategize, raise funds, and promote their interests upstate. By mid-December, they recommended criminalizing the wearing of disguises.

Meanwhile, the anti-rent leader Dr. Boughton led efforts to organize the eight hundred families still under feudal leases on Livingston Manor in Columbia County. Disguised as Big Thunder, he gave speeches during late autumn 1844. County Sheriff Henry Miller became determined to learn the chief's identity after an obstructed distress auction where Big Thunder ordered his papers burned. Through an informant, the sheriff confirmed that Boughton was indeed the Calico leader. "The voice of Dr. Boughton was unmistakable," relates Christman (1945, 109).

On December 18, a pretext was found to arrest Boughton and two others. Tragically, the young William Rifenburg was shot and killed during a meeting of the newly established Columbia County Anti-Rent Association. No one was ever charged with the teenager's death, which the coroner later deemed accidental. But by day's end, Boughton, Mortimer Belden, and Samuel Wheeler were behind bars in the town of Hudson, the county seat. The next day brought another tragedy that stoked the anti-anti-renter fire. On December 19, up-renter Elijah Smith was shot in a confrontation with Calico Indians while cutting timber for William Rensselaer. Fifty men were eventually indicted for rioting or conspiracy to riot.

As protestors assembled at the Hudson jail where Boughton and the others were held, Sheriff Miller appealed to outgoing Governor Bouck for assistance. By New Year's Day, 1845, more than three hundred armed guards, including a contingent from New York City, were assembled to protect the small town. Again, the state's show of force temporarily quieted the situation. Hudson's mayor could happily report "the public burning of many of the masks and dresses" and that Rent Day, January 1, was unusually successful. "Many of the wheat rents were yesterday paid promptly, and by several of the most noisy anti-renters" (McCurdy 2001, 166). Meanwhile, bail requests for Boughton, Belden, and Wheeler were repeatedly denied.

Climax and Denouement, 1845 to 1846

The new year brought a vigorous attempt to suppress Calico Indian activity. Governor Wright's inaugural address to the legislature in January 1845 recommended criminalizing camouflage. Later that month, the state senate and assembly approved "An act to prevent persons appearing disguised and armed," which outlined punishable offenses (*Laws of the State of New-York*, 68th Sess., 1845, ch. 3). Anyone "having his face painted, discolored, covered or concealed" could be charged with vagrancy and held in the county jail for up to six months. Arrests could be made "without process," and any male citizen could be commanded by officials to assist such seizures or risk up to a year imprisonment. Three or more disguised people appearing in a public place without a permit was deemed a misdemeanor; transgressors could be jailed for as much as a year. Facial concealment while carrying a weapon was punishable by up to two years in state prison.

While the governor's recommendation worked its way through the legislature, the anti-renters and their allies held their first political convention. On January 15, 1845, nearly two hundred delegates from eleven counties convened in Berne; delegates were sent from Rensselaer, Schoharie, Delaware, Columbia, Montgomery, Schenectady, Greene, Sullivan, Ulster, and Otsego counties to meet those from Albany. The conventioneers passed resolutions disassociating the movement from masks and violence, a direct rebuttal to Governor Wright's portrayal. They also constructed a petition renewing several demands: abolishment of distress as a remedy for nonpayment of rent, taxation of landlords' rental income, and passage of the "Act Concerning Tenures by Lease." More than twenty-five thousand signed the petition. Nonetheless, its claims were largely rejected by the legislature that spring. Meanwhile, candidates endorsed at the anti-rent convention "swept the local elections" in at least four counties.

Despite the convention's disavowal of violence, tension escalated after the mask law took effect. In mid-February, Delaware County Undersheriff Osman Steele raided the homes of the tenant leader Daniel Squires and several others. The cousin of a patroon land agent, Steele had a reputation for bullying and harassment. His determined pursuit of distress sales and anti-rent resisters in early 1845 foreshadowed the climactic episode leading to his death that summer. Squires, who was suspected of various "Indian" activities, was brought to the county jail in Delhi. Several weeks later, the Calico Indians retaliated by entrapping Osman Steele in an Andes tavern and holding him hostage overnight. Sheriff Green More summoned a posse in Delhi, but Steele's captors ran off before the assembly completed the twelve-mile trek from there to Andes. On March 15, the undersheriff led a contingent that seized about a dozen anti-renters. Various charges and fines were levied, and several were sentenced to the state prison at Sing Sing for two years. Squires was released in May 1845 when a grand jury failed to secure an indictment.

Additional skirmishes took place in Schoharie and Ulster counties; Governor Wright sent munitions to Kingston to quell disorder in the latter. March 1845 also brought Dr. Boughton's trial. Along with Mortimer Belden and Samuel Wheeler, Boughton had been held in the Hudson jail without bail or explicit charges since mid-December. He was finally tried alone for robbing the Columbia County sheriff of papers and conspiracy to obstruct justice. The trial resulted in a deadlocked jury, and Broughton was returned to the Hudson jail. He would remain there until mid-July 1845, when all three prisoners were quietly released on bail.

On August 7, Calico Indians disrupted a distress sale at Moses and Sara Earle's farm on Dingle Hill in Andes. The family's 160-acre plot was part of the sprawling Hardenbergh Patent. The precise boundaries of the patent had been disputed for many years by tenants as well as competing patroon claimants. Charlotte Verplanck, who lived in New York City, controlled about twenty thousand acres. Moses and Sara were not outspoken anti-renters, but their "adopted" daughter had convinced Moses not to pay the two years of rent in arrears until the patroon's title was proved. In response, Verplanck's land agent arranged to auction off the Earle horses and livestock for the sixty-four dollars owed. More than a hundred Calico Indians gathered to prevent the sale. Shots were fired, and Osman Steele was mortally wounded. The Earles took him into their house. Despite a doctor's efforts, he died that evening. Who shot first, and for what reason, has never been ascertained.

Local authorities responded swiftly and harshly to Steele's death. Moses Earle, who was in his sixties, was taken into custody. Multiple posses were assembled to search for others present at the distress sale, and scores of arrests were made. Suspecting that some anti-renters had taken refuge outside Delaware County, officials requested the governor's aid. On August 27, Governor Wright declared a "state of insurrection" in Delaware, Columbia, and Schoharie Counties and sent more than three hundred troops to the region. Recent legislation justified sweeping arrests during the four months the governor's decree remained in effect. The mask law provided "that every fatality arising from the commission of a felony (assembling armed and disguised) constituted murder in the first degree," as McCurdy (2001, 219) observes. Nearly 350 individuals were indicted, about half of them charged with the undersheriff's killing. The great number held at the Delhi jail so exceeded its capacity that the suspects were housed in hastily erected, rough log cabins.

The Delaware County Anti-Renters were not the only ones remanded to state prison. While their fates were being determined, Dr. Boughton's second trial took place in Hudson. Fighting between his lawyer, Ambrose Jordan, and Attorney General John Van Buren was so fierce that the judge charged both with contempt and had them jailed overnight. In late September, Boughton was convicted of highway robbery and received the maximum punishment—a life sentence—while cellmates Belden and Wheeler were released with time served. Boughton met up with about fifteen anti-renters already in Clinton Prison.

The harsh sentences meted out to the anti-renters loomed over the November 1845 elections. Numerous public and private appeals were made to Governor Wright to spare Edward O'Conner and John Van Steenburgh, the two on death row. Horace Greeley argued in the *New-York Tribune* that their execution would exacerbate the societal problems exposed by the anti-rent movement. The governor, whose term ran another year, nevertheless waited until after the election to decide the men's fate. Just one week before their scheduled executions, O'Conner and Van Steenburgh's sentences were commuted to life in prison. They were soon transferred to Sing Sing. Exhortations to pardon them and the other imprisoned anti-renters would not be answered, however, until a new governor was in office.

Final Settlement

The repression of late 1845 had a chilling effect on the movement's visible tactical resistance. The associations again disavowed "Indian" activity, and "crowd actions ceased to be part of the anti-renters' political arsenal," as Huston (2000, 150) notes. With several leaders behind bars, anti-rent efforts focused on the prisoners' fate, pressing for favorable legislation, and revising the state constitution. Their surprising success at the polls that November soon had tangible results; voters approved the constitutional convention that the Anti-Renters had advocated for several months. The Anti-Rent Party resumed the push for title tests, an equitable tax code, and relief from distress actions. The Anti-Renters' increased influence in the legislature helped them attain two goals. The Act to Equalize Taxation and Act to Abolish Distress for Rent were approved and signed by Governor Wright in May 1846. The latter left the landlords' right of repossession for nonpayment of rent intact, but sheriffs were not obligated to auction tenants' household goods on their behalf.

The State of New York's endorsement of anti-rent legislation during the spring seemed to bode well for the state constitutional convention, which met from June 1 to October 9. Most delegates from the leasehold counties were anti-rent sympathizers to various degrees. Although they made up just 10 percent of the total delegates to the state convention, the *Albany Evening Journal* expressed optimism that "whatever of feudalism remains" would be purged from the constitution.

Among those vestigial privileges was that the property of wealthy married women could be protected from seizure for their husbands' debt through prenuptial and other legal agreements. New York's landholders had always been eager to conserve family assets through the designation of "separate property" owned and controlled by wives as if they were femes sole (single women). Less-affluent married women who lacked the means to secure such legal arrangements often had their assets confiscated for their husbands' debt under the prevailing common law. Allowing wives to keep their own property could help insulate households from impoverishment. Anti-rent advocates were at the forefront of proposing constitutional revisions that would extend asset protection to all married women. Although the various relevant proposals were defeated at the convention, the debate "crystallized the issues, placed them in the political arena, and engendered some expectation that passage of a married women's act was merely a question of time," as Norma Basch (1982, 155) observes. In fact, New York's 1848 Married Women's Property Act became a model for other states and was an important step toward woman suffrage and other forms of equity.

The 1846 constitution, which was approved by voters on November 3, achieved certain advances in the democratization of the law. The judicial system was drastically reorganized into its modern form, with the court of appeals as the state's highest court. Judgeships and many state offices were converted from appointed to elected posts, a victory for the anti-renters. Certain progressive measures failed, however. The constitution of 1821 had instated property requirements for Black voters to restrict the increased enfranchisement resulting from the state's gradual abolition of slavery. Challenges to these requirements failed at the 1846 constitutional convention. In response, Liberty Party leader Gerrit Smith offered free forty-acre parcels of Adirondacks land to about three thousand Black men, making them eligible to vote. Smith's role in founding the Black farming community of Timbuctoo and friendship with the abolitionist John Brown have recently received renewed attention.

Most significantly for the anti-renters, the revised New York State Constitution paradoxically relegated manorial leases to the past while allowing part of that past to persist into the present. "All feudal tenures of every description, with all their incidents, are declared to be abolished," stated Article 1. Quarter sales and other reservations on alienation were thereby prohibited. "The entire and absolute property" would be "vested in the owners," giving them clear title and the mineral, timber, and water rights previously reserved to landlords. Nor could leases be perpetual; new contracts for agricultural lands were limited to twelve years. However, the new stipulations applied only to future agreements. While leases for one or multiple lives would be renegotiated on the new terms when they expired, no remedy was available to families holding perpetual leases. The tenant farmers of Rensselaerswyck remained in conflict with the patroons. The anti-rent movement had achieved a major victory in principle, but not entirely in practice. The state's third constitution went into effect January 1, 1847. Although the struggle was not completely over, the constitutional convention and election of 1846 brought its most turbulent chapter to an end.

Coda

To ensure he did not forget his campaign promise, the anti-renters sent a petition to Governor John Young with eleven thousand signatures demanding that the prisoners be pardoned. By February 1847, Dr. Boughton, Edward O'Conner, John Van Steenburgh, and Moses Earle were allowed to return home. Their rights as citizens, which their life sentences precluded, were restored that September. The remaining anti-renters in Clinton Prison were pardoned and released. Homecoming that February included a stop in Clarksville, where they were greeted with a public dinner and "soul-stirring music from the Berne brass band" (Christman 1945, 284).

With the anti-rent prisoners' release, the abolishment of distress, the revised terms of landownership, and a new tax code, the era of collective action came to a close. Private settlement and contractual obligation remained the foundation of property relations in New York, though feudal reservations were now prohibited. Some landlords sold outright or converted the old quarter leases to mortgages. John A. King sold about fifteen thousand acres of the Blenheim Patent in Schoharie County to tenants, clearing his path to congress and the governorship. Approximately half the remaining tenants on Livingston Manor and the Hardenbergh Patent bought out their landlords between 1846 and 1848. Nevertheless, legal battles, financial disputes, and even a few direct confrontations persisted upstate for decades.

The heirs to Rensselaerswyck remained tenacious at first through dizzying circumstances. On the East Manor, William Van Rensselaer challenged Rensselaer County's right to collect tax on rental income until the

New York Supreme Court upheld the assessment in 1850. In 1848, the legislature passed a resolution allowing title tests. Four years later, Judge Ira Harris declared the patroon claim to certain wild lands invalid in *People v. Van Rensselaer*. Also in 1852, Judge Amasa Parker ruled that quarter reservations in leases made after 1787 violated the first state constitution, invalidating a major source of patroon revenue and adding a new challenge to the validity of manorial titles. Harris's decision was reversed by the court of appeals in 1853, but Parker's decision was confirmed, allowing the rent strike to continue with new justification. Meanwhile, Stephen and William had already begun selling parcels of their manors to a distant relative, the land speculator Walter Church, for a fraction of what the tenant farmers had been willing to pay in 1839.

By 1858, Church and his associates possessed what remained of Rensselaerswyck. His engagement of law enforcement and private militias led to multiple bitter confrontations, occasionally arousing the Calico Indians. According to Simon Rosendale, who served as New York's attorney general in the 1890s, Church testified that he had pursued approximately two thousand lawsuits against the tenant farmers. Church made a good living for a time but died in poverty in 1890. The tenth patroon and seventh lord of the manor, Stephen Van Rensselaer IV, died in 1868, and his brother William died four years later.

The historical significance of the anti-rent movement extends well beyond Rensselaerswyck's boundaries. Perhaps this is best encapsulated by a satiric song that appeared in an anti-rent newspaper just as the climactic year of 1846 ended. Titled "The Landlord's Lament," it mocks the patroons' dilemma to the tune of "Oh Dear, What Can the Matter Be?" The satire can also be understood in terms of what L. M. Bogad (2016, 5–10) calls "tactical performance," the use of theatrical elements for political protest. The anti-renters' masks, calico gowns, and tin horns had the immediate practical use of warning and camouflage. But they were also tools for staging disruptive actions, a pioneering use of "sociodrama" for the purpose of effecting change. The songs and sounds of the anti-renters, their allies, onlookers—and even detractors—were the aesthetic expressions of one of the great nineteenth-century reform movements. We would do well to listen closely.

6

The Lemmon Case and Slavery in New York State, 1852 to 1860

ALBERT M. ROSENBLATT

Adapted from Albert M. Rosenblatt, "The Eight: The Lemmon Slave Case and the Fight for Freedom" (SUNY Press, 2023).

New York has been a leader in the long struggle for racial justice and equality in America. We have pioneered in civil rights and campaigns for social justice and have written people's rights into our constitution and our laws. Our state's courts have been exceptionally strong in taking the lead and setting precedents. The courts have been especially notable for asserting and protecting the rights of Black people, a record that dates back to the Lemmon case in the 1850s.

Slavery was abolished in New York in 1827. The Lemmon case, which played out in the New York courts from 1852 to 1860, revolved around the question of whether people brought into New York from Virginia, where slavery was legal, would be free in New York, where it was not legal. This was a high-visibility case. The legal precedents were mixed and inconclusive. The case was important because the divisive issue of slavery would lead to the Civil War in the 1860s.

In a milestone decision in the history of civil rights in the nation, the state supreme court declared formerly enslaved people from other states to be free in New York, and the New York Court of Appeals, in 1860, confirmed that decision.

Editor's note: This chapter uses the term "enslaved people" instead of the term "slaves" to bring the text into alignment with current usage.

☙

Americans celebrate July 4, 1776, as a premier national holiday. It's not possible to find an older American holiday, considering that the date marks our birth—the date we chose to break free from England and to stand on our own feet. It was a break, to be sure, but it was not a total alienation. Despite the separation, the countries share a great deal, such as the English language, culture, and common law—and, over the decades, the two nations have enjoyed a special relationship.

In writing about the history and the background of the era, we can speak of the Revolutionary War, of George Washington, of the inspired founders of our fledgling nation, of Thomas Jefferson, James Madison, John Adams, Benjamin Franklin, John Jay, and others. But it would be a mistake to paint the era in tones so rosy that we hide the darker side of things, particularly slavery. In 1776, slavery had been practiced on American soil for over a century and a half, and it was not only part of the American fabric but so interwoven that it took a civil war to obliterate it.

In parts of the country, not only did slavery thrive during the Revolutionary era, but enslavement was seen as an economic necessity. In other parts of the country, it was abided and lawful. There may have been talk of abolition here and there, but when the states joined together as a union, slavery was widely practiced throughout, to one degree or another. And so, Thomas Jefferson's words "we hold these truths to be self-evident, that all men are created equal, that they are endowed by their Creator with certain unalienable Rights, that among these are Life, Liberty and the pursuit of Happiness" carry an irony. For hundreds of thousands of enslaved people, there was not equality but subordination, in chains. For them, the phrase "life, liberty, and the pursuit of happiness" was an abstraction, applied only to other people.

When our country's founders wrote to the US Constitution, they made provision for slavery. The Constitution's Fugitive Slave Clause required that runaway slaves be delivered up to their owners, and the Constitution's three-fifths clause saw to it that for purposes of representation in the Congress, each slave counted as three-fifths of a person. Those provisions and others were the price the South levied for joining the Union. Both provisions led to woeful practices and federal legislation that we would do well to remember.

In New Netherland (as New York was called when it was a Dutch colony, from 1614 to 1664), the first recorded African slave ship arriving in New Amsterdam (the Dutch name for New York City) was the *Tamandere* (or *Tamandare*), in June 1646. Enslaved people in New Netherland came from a variety of African backgrounds, most from Central African origins. Dutch merchants had established trade relations along the African coasts, and Dutch control of Angola further promoted trade with the Dutch in this region. They purchased African captives from several West African regions a hundred years before the Revolutionary War. In 1644, New Netherland passed a law emancipating enslaved individuals after some nineteen years of service. To protect their settlement, Dutch colonists built a wall (now known as Wall Street). There were surely enough enslaved people in the colony to have been involved in its construction.

At the time, most people took slavery for granted. If any had qualms about keeping humans in bondage, few spoke of it, at least publicly. In 1650, New Netherland had about five hundred enslaved people, outnumbering those in Virginia and Maryland. The number grew after the English took over New Netherland in 1664 and named it New York. By 1698 the number grew to over two thousand, and by 1746, to over nine thousand. There were more enslaved people in Southern states, but New York had the largest enslaved force in any English colony north of Maryland, accounting for over a third of total immigration passing through the Port of New York. The renowned historian George Bancroft remarked that New York was not a slave state like Carolina "due to climate, and not the superior humanity of its founders." Ironically, Massachusetts, which we associate with abolitionism, was the earliest of the colonies to establish slavery, but it never amounted to much, and the Black population never exceed 3 percent of the non-Indigenous inhabitants.

In Dutch New Netherland we find laws as early as the 1640s—two centuries before the infamous United States Fugitive Slave Act of 1850—concerning runaways and penalties prohibiting settlers from "harboring fugitive servants from their masters in New England and Virginia." An August 9, 1640, ordinance lamented that "many servants daily run away from their masters, whereby the latter are put to great inconvenience and expense; the corn and tobacco rot in the field, and the whole harvest is at a standstill, which tends to the serious injury of this country, to their masters' ruin, and to bring the magistracy into contempt."

The British took over the Dutch Colony in the mid-1660s, and, under English rule, slavery grew into an even bigger business, integral to New York's economy. As slavery grew as an established institution, the words *slave* and *slavery* appeared in colonial New York laws, beginning with an April 22, 1684, statute, some twenty years after the English takeover. It baldly stated that

> whosoever shall knowingly Transport or Contrive the Transportation of any Apprentice Servant or Slave or by any ways aideing or assisting or abetting thereunto and be thereof Lawfully convicted shall bee fined for every such offence five pounds Current money of this province for ye use of ye County and make full Satisfaction to the Master or Mistresse of Such Apprentice Servant, or Slave for all Costs Charges and Damages which the said Master or Mistresse can make appear to have Thereby sustained.

According to one commentator, nearly 40 percent of all households in New York City owned slaves in 1698, the year of the first provincial census.

Things began to change toward the end of the seventeenth century. In 1688, as a religious tenet, Quakers invoked the Golden Rule: "These are the reasons why we are against the traffik of men-body. . . . Is there any that would be done or handled at this manner? . . . There is a saying, that we shall doe to all men, like as we will be done our selves: making no difference of what generation, descent, or colour they are. And those who steal or rob men, and those who buy or purchase them, are they not all alike?" In early-eighteenth-century New York, slavery was a working regime, part of the everyday picture. Enslaved people were not allowed to give evidence in any matter, save to testify against each other in cases involving harm to slave owners or their property. In 1702, the colonial New York General Assembly created a slave code authorizing slave owners to punish their slaves, short of taking a slave's "life or Member." The law also provided for a "common whipper" on the public payroll. Special punishment awaited a slave who would "presume to assault or strike any freeman or Woman professing Christianity." In 1708 the New York General Assembly passed an "Act for Suppressing of Immorality," but the lawmakers had a different sort of immorality in mind: requiring that slaves be publicly whipped for talking "impudently" to any Christian. As late as May 14, 1745, New York passed a law to prevent enslaved people from Albany from fleeing to the French in Canada. The offense was punishable by death.

During the Revolutionary War, many slaves gained freedom for fighting for one side or the other. New York offered freedom to any enslaved person who served in the military for three years. The "Act for the Gradual

Abolition of Slavery" passed by the Pennsylvania General Assembly in 1780 was the first such law in America. It begins with an expression of gratitude for deliverance from the "tyranny of Great Britain" and for the opportunity to "extend a portion of that freedom to others." It specified that "every Negro and Mulatto child born within the State after its 1780 passage would be free upon reaching age twenty-eight."

In a Supreme Court decision, *United States v. Stanley*, written after the Civil War, the court summarized some of the disabilities of slave status:

> The long existence of African slavery in this country gave us very distinct notions of what it was, and what were its necessary incidents. Compulsory service of the slave for the benefit of the master, restraint of his movements except by the master's will, disability to hold property, to make contracts, to have a standing in court, to be a witness against a white person, and such like burdens and incapacities, were the inseparable incidents of the institution. Severer punishments for crimes were imposed on the slave than on free persons guilty of the same offences.

New York's road to abolition was a bumpy journey, encumbered by events none more dismaying than those of 1712 and 1741. These are bitter lessons, revealing that a community can become so fearful of slave rebellions as to lose any basic sense of fairness. By 1700, New York had a Black population of well over two thousand. The year before, Governor Bellomont had told the Lords of Trade there were "no other servants in this country but Negroes." By the early 1770s, New York's Black population had increased tenfold, to more than twenty thousand—four times larger than Pennsylvania's.

In 1711 the New York City Common Council established a slave market at the foot of Wall Street, and a year later, on April 6, 1712, the city experienced a slave uprising resulting in trials, convictions, and executions, as the judges were part of the process. The New York legislature seemed not to question the underlying slavery regime but thought only to perpetuate it by passing more repressive laws.

The events of 1741 mark the lowest and most shameful chapter of slavery in New York. After a series of fires, rumored to have been started by slaves in March of 1741, Judge Daniel Horsmanden (1691 to 1778) of the Supreme Judicial Court of New York led an investigation. On the flimsiest proof, he sponsored charges against scores of people, most of whom were enslaved. To make sure the charges would stick, he sat as judge (along with Judges James De Lancey and Frederick Philipse) at the ensuing trials. By the time it all ended, officials had burned thirteen Black men to death at the stake, hanged seventeen more, and sent seventy others to slavery in the Caribbean. Horsmanden published an account of these events that the historian Jill Lepore (2005, xviii) has described as "one of the most startling and vexing documents in early American history." New York's judicial atrocities in 1741 were so notorious that the South, with moral righteousness, would cite them over a hundred years later as evidence of Northern duplicity and cruelty.

The Quakers continued to be a driving force for abolition in New York. As early as 1767, at a Quaker meeting in Purchase, New York, the group questioned whether members could continue to own slaves and yet be faithful to their religious beliefs. They formed committees to visit other Quakers, urging them to manumit their slaves. By 1784, some fifteen years before New York's first stage of abolition, there was only one Quaker slave owner left in New York state.

The 1780s marked one of the early points at which the North and South began to part company over the issue of slavery. Given that the New York State Constitution and the Articles of Confederation said nothing about it, a few prominent New Yorkers were ready to take a stand. In 1785, John Jay, Alexander Hamilton, George Clinton, Melancton Smith, and others formed "The New York Society for the Manumission of Slaves and the Protection of such of them as had been or wanted to be Liberated," better known as the Manumission Society. Jay, as president, and the others wrote a preamble, stating that "the benevolent Creator and Father of men having given to them all an equal right to life, liberty, and property, no sovereign power on earth can justly deprive them of either, but in conformity to impartial government and laws to which they have expressly or tacitly consented." In Jay's words,

> Supported by the public sentiment, [our members] entered upon the discharge of their duties, with the fullest fully confidence in the justice of their cause, tempered with a respectful regard for the long established habits of the community. They were too wise to think of working miracles; too honest to abandon the cause; and too proud of their countrymen not to believe that the time would arrive when history alone should furnish a record that men had lived here—and been slaves.

Governed by these principles and cheered by such hopes, the Society, prosecuting its way through much evil, and no inconsiderable portion of good report, has reached a period, in which its members respectfully solicit the public sanction to the consummation of their great object, the final abolition of slavery in this state.

Among the society's major achievements was the founding of the African Free School in 1787, devoted to the education of Black children as preparation for life as free citizens. The school played a significant role in producing new leadership from within the Black community of New York, before the Manumission Society turned it over to the New York public school system in 1834. The society repeatedly called for outright abolition of slavery in New York, most poignantly in an open letter from Cadwallader Colden to "The Citizens of the State of New York."

By 1799, New York had turned the corner. Under the governorship of John Jay, the state began the gradual process of abolition, ending on July 4, 1827. By this time, other states had done so as well: Vermont in 1777, Massachusetts circa 1783, Ohio in 1802, and New Jersey in 1804, and Connecticut initiated a gradual process of abolition in 1784 that was completed in 1848.

The Lemmon Case

In 1817, during New York's gradual abolition period, the legislature enacted a statute allowing slave owners to sojourn in New York for up to nine months, but in 1827 the legislature struck the allowance—an event that led up to New York's Lemmon Slave Case, one of the most notable antislavery cases in the country's history. All but forgotten today, it was one of the most momentous civil rights cases in American history. There had been cases in which enslaved people had won their freedom after having resided in free states, but the Lemmon case was unique, posing the question of whether an enslaved person can win freedom by merely setting foot on New York soil, when brought there in the keep of an "owner."

The case concerned the fates of eight enslaved people from Virginia, brought through New York in 1852 by their owners, Juliet and Jonathan Lemmon, along with the seven Lemmon children. The group, seventeen in all, had been heading for Texas to take up residence there, but a quirk in their travel plans brought them to New York Harbor. Learning of their arrival in New York, local abolitionists joined in a fight to liberate the Eight on the strength of a New York state law, passed in 1841, that granted liberty to any enslaved person brought into the state. It read,

> On the 6th day of November, 1852, Louis Napoleon, a colored citizen of this State, made application upon a sufficient petition and affidavit to Mr. Justice [Elijah] Paine of the Superior Court of the city of New York, for a writ of habeas corpus to be directed to one Jonathan Lemmon and the keeper of house No. 3 Carlisle street, New York, requiring them to bring before said justice the bodies of eight colored persons, one man, two women and five children, who on the day preceding were confined and restrained of their liberty on board the steamer City of Richmond, in the harbor of New York and were taken therefrom on the night of that day to No. 3 Carlisle street, and there detained under the presence that they were slaves.

Who was Louis Napoleon? What was he doing bringing a petition on behalf of "eight colored persons"? More to the point, the case involved not eight legal entities but eight real people, whose freedom hung in the balance. Who was Judge Elijah Paine? Not one lawyer in a thousand today knows anything of him, and yet he was asked to make an important, unprecedented ruling at that hour: Can the enslaved claim freedom when brought to a free state by their owners? The law was clear on fugitive slaves, who had to be returned to bondage even when captured in free states, but "the Eight" were *brought* to New York by Juliet and Jonathan Lemmon—a situation the courts had yet to rule on.

The case was litigated for eight years in the New York courts, ultimately reaching New York state's highest court, the Court of Appeals, a few months before shots rang out at Fort Sumter, signaling the start of the Civil War.

The case presented a profoundly moving human drama in which eight people fought for their freedom. Any lawsuit might well become more interesting when we pull back the curtain and learn something about the people involved, but the Lemmon case was not like most lawsuits. In this case, the Eight were in court seeking, legally, to *become* people—to change their status under law from objects into human beings. Under the law in Virginia and other slave states, enslaved people were property—chattel—to be treated however their owners saw fit: to be sold; traded; inherited; separated from their spouses, parents, and children; sexually abused; or whipped for trying to read a book.

The story of the Eight reveals, at a powerful personal level, what it was like to try to get out from under a system like that. It includes a remarkable cast of characters. Louis Napoleon, the son of a slave, was an abolitionist activist and a "conductor" of the Underground Railroad who took enormous risks to help others. We count him as part of an antislavery movement in which African Americans played an integral role in the fight for freedom, working actively in the realms of politics, economics, law, and culture. They sometimes collaborated with white abolitionists but often did their work independently.

The case was part of the broader judicial landscape at the time. If a law was morally repugnant but enshrined in the Constitution, what was the duty of the judge? Should there be, as some people advocated, a "higher law"? A "natural law" that transcends the written law? Issues of law and morality abounded. These questions were at the heart of the Lemmon case and of the jurisprudence of the era. They were difficult and important ones in the 1850s—and, more than a century and a half later, we must still grapple with them today.

In Court

By the time the Eight arrived in the courtroom, word of the case had spread rapidly around the country, and press interest was high. Jonathan and Juliet Lemmon were there, of course, as was Erastus Culver, joined by an eminent co-counsel: John Jay II (1817 to 1894).

At thirty-five, Jay was already a well-established lawyer, committed to abolition, and he had the pedigree to go with it. His paternal grandfather was the founder John Jay (1745 to 1829), New York's first chief judge and the first chief justice of the United States Supreme Court. He had also served as the governor of New York. Under his administration, in 1799, the state had begun the gradual abolition of slavery. His son, John Jay II's father, Judge William Jay (1789 to 1858), was also an ardent antislavery advocate in his own right.

Louis Napoleon, the other critical member of the Lemmon team, was in court that day too. The Lemmon case was not the first time Napoleon had asked a court to come to the rescue of a slave, nor was it the first time that he had worked with John Jay II. The two were, in fact, a resourceful pair. In 1846, six years before the Lemmon case, they had gone to court on behalf of twenty-two-year-old George Kirk, a runaway who had secreted himself on a brig out of Savannah. When the brig had docked in New York, Kirk was discovered by the crew, who put him in chains and began beating him. Abolitionists heard Kirk's cries and quickly got word to Napoleon, who, working with Jay, got a writ of habeas corpus ordering Kirk and the brig's captain before Judge John Edmonds.

Once in court, Jay asserted, in a prelude to the Lemmon case, that under the common law of New York a person is no longer a slave when in New York, notwithstanding the law of Georgia. Judge Edmonds chose not to stretch that far. Instead, he simply held that there was no proof that the brig's captain was authorized to act on behalf of Kirk's owner, and he set Kirk free—a superb technicality. A series of twists and turns followed, including New York's Mayor Andrew Mickle rearresting Kirk by invoking a New York statute, under which the state had obligated itself to give stowaway fugitive slaves back to their owners—a concession to the South, as New York was abolishing slavery. After Napoleon and his fellow abolitionists secretly moved Kirk to Vermont, Jay successfully argued for his freedom once again.

Jay had appeared before Judge Edmonds in another case. In December 1848, in broad daylight, on Duane Street in New York, two slave catchers seized Joseph Belt, allegedly a fugitive who had escaped from bondage in Maryland. The slave catchers transported him to Long Island intending to return him to slavery. Rescuers learned of the scheme and, led by Jay, managed to get before Judge Edmonds, who signed a writ of habeas corpus ordering the police to bring Belt and his captors to court.

At the hearing, Belt's owner argued that he had every right, personally or with the help of his slave catchers, to seize Belt in New York for recaption South. He claimed he needed no warrant, adding that those who stood in the way of recaption were "agitating a subject that puts the union in jeopardy." In response, Jay argued that under the federal Fugitive Slave Act of 1793, a fugitive slave could be held in captivity in New York only long enough to be brought before a tribunal for a certificate of removal. Here, however, the captors had concealed and held Belt captive for two days—not to bring him before a court but to spirit him off to bondage in Maryland.

Judge Edmonds agreed, ruling that the slave owner could get no help from the Fugitive Slave Act. If the master or the master's agent, he said, "can do this for two days, he can for two years or twenty." The slave owner then asked Judge Edmonds for an order transferring Belt to the custody of a federal court so he could get a certificate of removal authorized by federal law. Judge Edmond responded with a memorable line: "I must decline your application. My official duty does not require it, and if it is asked on other grounds, it would not be a proceeding to my taste." Belt was free. By hewing *within* the language of the Fugitive Slave Act, the judge was able to blunt its impact and give a measure of protection to alleged fugitive slaves.

Important as it was, the Belt case dealt with alleged *fugitive* slaves. An open question remained concerning slaves who were not fugitives but traveled with their owners: Could they be declared free when their owners' journeys brought them, in transit, through a free state, such as New York? That was left for Judge Paine to decide.

When they arrived that morning to argue the Lemmon case, Culver and Jay were well aware that no judge had ever ruled that enslaved persons in the keep of their owners become free when setting foot in New York. But they knew enough about Judge Paine to expect that at least he would consider their argument with an open mind.

Just before the proceedings began, an extraordinary exchange took place in the courtroom. As Nancy and Emeline, two of the Lemmons' slaves, were nursing their infants, Juliet Lemmon walked over to where they were sitting. She urged them not to "rob" her of their labor.

"Have I ever ill-treated you?" Juliet asked Nancy and Emeline imploringly. "Have you not drank from the same cup, and eat [*sic*] from the same bowl with myself? Have I not taken the same care of your children as if they were my own?" That Juliet could speak these words in apparent earnestness to women she had enslaved says a lot about the country in 1852.

Emeline and Nancy now had to make a life-altering decision. Disobedience for them had always been fraught with peril, never more so than now. Runaway slaves, they knew, were generally greeted with the whip when returned to their owners. Technically, the Eight had not run away—but by taking their case to court and refusing Juliet's pleas, Nancy and Emeline knew they would be doing much the same thing. Emeline and Nancy could only guess how severely the Lemmons would punish them if Judge Paine were to rule against the Eight and keep them enslaved. A favorable ruling, setting them free, was far from a sure thing.

Weeping, and drawing on every ounce of fortitude she could summon, Emeline responded to Juliet. "No," she said. "You sold my husband away from me three years ago, and I have never been able to hear from him since. I don't call that good treatment." In that one instant, Emeline threw off an entire lifetime of abject subservience. She must have felt a dizzying mixture of liberation and fear. She would take her chances with the judge.

To represent them, the Lemmons had engaged two prominent New York attorneys: Henry Dampier Lapaugh (born ca. 1826) and Henry Lauren Clinton (1820 to 1899). Their argument was predictable and straightforward: Because slave ownership was valid under the laws of Virginia and Texas, and because the Lemmons had not intended to bring the Eight to New York except in transit, New York had no right to emancipate them. "The slaves in question, being property," they argued, could readily be brought by their owners from one state to another and pass through New York with no risk of losing ownership. This right, they claimed, was supported not only by the Constitution but by the "law of nations."

Culver and Jay countered, asserting that because New York had no law allowing slavery—and, indeed, had passed a law abolishing it—the common law of liberty must prevail, and the Eight must be freed. They also pointed out that in 1817, during its gradual abolition of slavery, New York, by statute, allowed owners to keep their slaves in New York for up to nine months but that the state legislature had repealed even that exception in 1841. The repeal implied that any slave brought to New York, even for just a moment, should be considered free.

Lapaugh and Clinton countered, arguing that New York had no right to do away with the nine-month exemption. No statute, they said, could deprive an owner of lawfully held "property" merely because the owner had briefly stopped in New York, whether compelled by "necessity or accident." They laid heavy emphasis on the United States Constitution, claiming that it prohibits New York from liberating any slave lawfully owned under the laws of a slave state. Judge Paine appreciated that these constitutional arguments were not empty assertions from uninformed windbags. The claims, advanced by eminent lawyers, were worth debating.

The lawyers on both sides also discussed the importance of England's *Somerset v. Stewart* case, a landmark—perhaps *the* landmark—slavery case under the common law, in 1772. The case concerned James Somerset, an enslaved African, whom Charles Stewart had purchased in Boston. Stewart brought Somerset to England, where he escaped two years later. In Somerset's suit for freedom, the English high court had to decide whether Somerset became free simply by having been brought to the free soil of England. The court freed Somerset, ruling that abolition in England necessarily meant that the country would not recognize a master–slave relationship, even on a transitory basis. The case is associated with the majestic phrase, "the air of

England was too pure to be breathed by a slave." Lemmon's lawyers argued, in substance, that the Somerset case was not binding on the United States and that our Constitution calls for a different result.

Judge Paine allowed the lawyers to go on at length, asking a brief question every now and then. When the slave owners' lawyers contended that "this court cannot go behind the *status* of these people in the state from whence they escaped," Judge Paine posed a three-word question: "Were they escaping?" He was probing the decisive difference between fugitive slaves apprehended in New York and those brought to New York by their owners.

Beyond citing case law and making statutory interpretations, Culver and Jay added another argument based on what they called "natural law." Jay spoke of "the inflexible principles of the common law touching the natural rights of personal liberty." Culver cited Chief Justice John Marshall's writing, in the 1825 *Antelope* case, that slavery is contrary to the law of nature, in that people have a natural right to the fruits of their own labor. Judge Paine surely knew of that case, and that Justice Marshall had also gone on to say that even though slavery was contrary to the law of nature and had its origin in force, "the world has agreed that it is a legitimate result of force, the state of things which is thus produced by general consent, cannot be pronounced unlawful."

Judge Paine did what judges do in these situations: After hearing both sides out, he told the parties that he planned to deliberate for a time and would hand down his decision the following Saturday, November 13, 1852. Pending his decision, he kept the Eight at the Carlisle Street location, in the charge of a police officer, and ordered that Jonathan Lemmon pay for their provision. The judge couldn't make his decision based on how he felt about enslavement. He had to deal with the constitutional issues surrounding the case and New York's own slavery jurisprudence.

By 1852 no one involved in the Lemmon case questioned New York's right to abolish slavery. The issue was of how far New York should continue to go in recognizing Virginia's slavery laws. On that front, some cases were notorious. On April 4, 1837, for example, William Dixon was seized by two New York policemen; Dr. Walter Allender of Baltimore claimed that Dixon was actually Jake Ennis, a slave of his who had escaped in 1832. The newly formed New York Committee of Vigilance, along with the New York Manumission Society, came to Dixon's defense, engaging the attorney Horace Dresser to represent him at a proceeding before New York City Recorder Richard Riker in city hall. Many antislavery people considered Riker unfriendly to their cause. After testimony had begun, and while Dixon was in custody, a crowd of hundreds of people surged forward, freeing Dixon. He was recaptured almost immediately, but his case was never resolved.

The Dixon case says something about New York's mixed attitude toward slavery. On the one hand, we see a crowd of hundreds overcoming police to rescue an alleged fugitive slave. That would have been unimaginable years earlier. On the other hand, those efforts were no match for a knot of unsavory New York officials, whom Jonathan D. Wells, in *The Kidnapping Club* (2020), describes as a confederation bent on circumventing New York's antislavery laws, encouraging racism, and looking the other way as free and fugitive African Americans were kidnapped into slavery.

Another case from that same year reveals the growing reluctance of judges in New York to entertain recaption proceedings. John McPherson of Frederick County, Maryland, claimed that on Clinton Street in New York, he found his slave Nat, who had run away in 1833. The newspaper reports tell of McPherson and his attorney going through a series of judges before the case finally reached Judge Betts, who gave Nat over to his claimant owner.

Communities in upstate New York revealed their abolitionist side. In 1836 the city of Utica experienced a dramatic antislavery event following the arrest of two men at the behest of their alleged owner, John Geyer, of Shenandoah County, Virginia. Brought before Oneida County Judge Chester Hayden, the two alleged fugitives, "Harry Bird and George," represented by the attorney Alvan Stewart, were in the judge's office when a crowd assembled, overcame the captors, and rescued the two, who were never heard from again.

In 1840, the New York legislature added another layer of difficulty for slave owners, granting a jury trial and appointing the district attorney as counsel for alleged fugitives. It also authorized the governor to appoint agents to help restore liberty to persons kidnapped and to help return them to New York state. Southern slave owners, of course, were not happy having their claims adjudicated by Northern jurors, many of whom had no stomach for returning someone who had escaped from slavery. But how far could Northern states like New York go in resisting the easy recaption procedures of the Fugitive Slave Act of 1793?

The United States Supreme Court provided the answer just two years later, in 1842, in *Prigg v. Pennsylvania*. In that case, the court decided that a state law that conflicted with the federal Fugitive Slave Law was unconstitutional. It was a case that would have been on Judge Paine's mind a decade later, when he began to consider the Lemmon case.

Just a week after having heard arguments in the Lemmon case, Judge Paine had his decision ready. It was a tour de force of judicial writing and reasoning, one that in other hands might have taken months to prepare. Paine had announced he would be giving his decision in court late in the morning of Saturday, November 13, 1852. A crowd, mostly Black, began to form at city hall very early in the morning. Soon the room was full, with overflowing crowds in the adjacent hallways. With everyone in attendance, Judge Paine brought the courtroom to order and, before a rapt audience, began reading his decision aloud.

He began by addressing three cases, decided by courts in Indiana, Illinois, and Massachusetts, cited as precedent by Jonathan Lemmon's lawyer. These cases had been offered to support the proposition that slave owners from slave states may take their slaves with them from one slave state to another slave state and pass freely through a free state with the slaves with no risk of the slaves gaining freedom.

No one knew better than Judge Paine that the three decisions, being from out-of-state courts, were not binding on him. He found the Aves case (1836) to be the most pertinent of the three. In *Commonwealth v. Aves*, the Massachusetts high court had freed a slave who had *resided* for a time in Massachusetts. Paine noted that the Massachusetts court had gone out of its way to say that it was leaving open the question of freedom for slaves who merely passed through Massachusetts with their owners, in transit to another state—the very question that needed to be decided in this case.

Paine then turned to one of the slave owners' postulates: namely, that the Eight, "being property," by "the law of nations" could be brought by their owners from one slave state to another slave state, free of any risk that they could be confiscated in New York. Paine argued that this was based on a misunderstanding of the law. He noted an important fact: "The property which the writers on the law of nations speak of is merchandise or inanimate things that by the law of nature belong to their owners." Nowhere, he wrote, did authorities on the law of nations—and, by extension, the law of nature—"speak of a right to pass through a foreign country with slaves as *property*." This in fact was impossible, he continued, because the authorities had all agreed on one fundamental principle: "that by the law of nations alone, *no one can have property in slaves*." As soon as Judge Paine uttered those words, many of the people of color in the courtroom shed tears.

Lawyers and judges today rarely speak of "natural law," but almost everybody would agree that some kind of higher principle should stand in the way of laws that are immoral or crazy. Today we might call such laws "unconstitutional," often on due process or equal-protection grounds. But that was not possible in the case of slavery. Given that it was contemplated in the Constitution, how could judges call slavery unconstitutional? As Judge Paine knew when he was considering the Lemmon case, he could not. He supported his decision, in part, by turning to natural law.

By the time Judge Paine set out to write his Lemmon decision, the concept of natural law had gone through several incarnations. He understood the many resonances of the term and used it or its equivalent more than twenty times in his Lemmon decision, in each instance making the same point: that freedom, not slavery, is our natural condition. But that didn't mean that slavery couldn't exist. Judge Paine acknowledged that slavery could still be imposed and sustained through statutes that explicitly allow slavery—enactments that amounted to "positive law" rather than natural law. Liberty may be our natural condition, but a state or country was free to pass statutes (positive laws) authorizing slavery, as the Southern states had done, and as the Constitution had recognized.

But in the absence of such positive laws, the condition of liberty subsisted, because it is our default condition. This applied to the Lemmons, he reasoned. They had brought their slaves into the state of New York, a jurisdiction with no laws allowing slavery. When New York had abolished slavery in 1827, Judge Paine noted, slavery's platform in the state had collapsed, creating a void—and all that was left was natural law, which on its own does not support slavery. For good measure, he continued, emphasizing that New York had even gone a step further, filling the void with a positive prohibition *against* slavery. Anybody and everybody in New York, therefore, had to be considered free, except fugitive slaves.

But what of the laws of Virginia? The Lemmons claimed they acquired good and legal title to the slaves, as recognized by Virginia. Paine acknowledged that under Virginia law, the Lemmons were lawfully free to own human property in Virginia. New York could do nothing about that. Nevertheless, he said, Virginia could not impose its concepts of human ownership on New York, a free state. Virginia residents could not bring Virginia laws with them wherever they went. To do so, Paine continued, would create "a perfect confusion of laws."

Wisely, Judge Paine did not base his decision entirely on the lofty grounds of natural law. A superb legal technician, he supported his ruling with a strong pillar, a New York statute. When originally passed in 1817, New York's abolition law had included certain exemptions, one of which allowed out-of-state slave owners to bring their slaves into New York for up to nine months. It was a concession that allowed Southerners to visit and vacation in the state—and bring their slaves with them. This exception, Judge Paine noted, would have applied to the Lemmons and the Eight, but it was no longer in force, because the exception had been repealed eleven years earlier, in 1841. Any law repealing an exemption implies total, not partial, repeal. So in the aftermath of the repeal of the nine-month exemption, Judge Paine did not see how he could allow slave owners to bring enslaved people into New York for *any* period of time—not even a two-day sojourn, a one-hour travel tour, or a five-minute stopover. Stripped of the exemption, he wrote, the law removed all ambiguity: The moment that people enslaved in other states set foot anywhere on New York soil, they were free.

And with that, it was time at last for Judge Paine to read out his verdict. "My judgment," he concluded, "is that the eight colored persons mentioned in the writ be discharged."

Exultation followed. "Scarcely had his Honor pronounced the concluding words, which decide the fate of the women and the children, than there arose a wild hubbub, and cries of 'good, good,' and other expressions of approbation. The crowd outside and inside the room, appeared to be intoxicated with joy, and it was some minutes before order could be restored."

Despite their jubilation at the outcome of the case, everyone in the courtroom knew that the ultimate fate of the Eight, now free, remained uncertain. What lay in store for them now, with their connection to the Lemmons—and life as they had known it since birth—severed? Judge Paine remarked that no one would be more desirous than he to see some means provided for the temporary maintenance for the Eight. "I must confess," he said, "that I feel much distress, in regard to the decision, that these persons may not be very happily situated thereafter."

Henry Lapaugh, the attorney for Julia and Jonathan Lemmon, seems to have hoped in this moment that the Eight, as they contemplated the upheaval their lives were about to go through, might have second thoughts. So he approached them one last time and asked if they would not prefer to return to the familiar life—of bondage!—they had always known with the Lemmons. The Eight, predictably, declined. The court discharged the slaves, who immediately went to Canada, as they would not be safe in New York, given federal slavecatchers who were determined to capture slaves, or supposed slaves, and send them south into servitude.

The case worked its way through the New York appellate system, and in 1860 New Yok's high court, the New York Court of Appeals, affirmed Judge Paine's ruling. Several months later, South Carolina seceded from the union, the first state to do so. Not long after that, shots were fired at Fort Sumter, marking the beginning of the Civil War.

After the war, the United States promulgated the Thirteenth, Fourteenth, and Fifteenth Amendments, ending slavery and declaring that the "right of citizens of the United States to vote shall not be denied or abridged by the United States or by any State on account of race, color, or previous condition of servitude." It was a ringing endorsement of the promises of the Declaration of Independence of 1776 and a major step toward what we hope will eventually be full equality for all, under the law.

7

Welcome to the Club

Louise Blanchard Bethune, Breaking Barriers for Women in Architecture, 1885

Kelly Hayes McAlonie

Adapted from Kelly Hayes McAlonie, "Louise Blanchard Bethune: Every Woman Her Own Architect" (SUNY Press, 2023).

New York has always been a state of opportunity for people to advance. Its history includes many examples of pioneering women who defied conventional expectations, pushed back on restrictive norms of what women should and could do, and broke barriers. The famous Seneca Falls Women's Rights Convention of 1848 and New York women's success in achieving the right to vote in 1917 are outstanding examples.

But there are many other, less-well-known instances of New York women breaking barriers and making notable achievements in their fields. In the nineteenth century, women eventually gained entry to and slowly expanded their presence in professions such teaching, law, and medicine.

But some male-dominated professions were harder to breach. Buffalo's Louise Blanchard Bethune (1856 to 1913), through grit and determination, became the nation's first woman architect. She opened her own architectural firm, another breakthrough. Bethune merits recognition for her achievements in designing and overseeing the construction of several buildings, some still in use today. But she went further, demanding and achieving membership in the leading national professional (all-male) associations of the day (at a time when being admitted to such organizations was tantamount to an endorsement of an individual's professionalism). Not content with that, she led in the establishment of a new professional architects' association in Western New York.

Bethune also insisted that women architects should be paid the same amount as men for comparable work. Her against-the-odds achievement served as a model for other women, though in the field of architecture change through expansion of women's membership came slowly as the professional associations themselves evolved.

☙

It was June 1876 in Buffalo, New York. Richard Waite, the most prominent architect in the city, was very busy. The construction of the Pierce Palace Hotel was about to begin, and there were other significant projects on the boards in his office. Waite's exciting new projects promised to elevate his firm's reputation beyond the confines of Western New York.

Summer is warm and pleasant in Buffalo, a welcome respite from the long and snow-filled days of wintertime for the Queen City of the Great Lakes. During one of these warm and busy days, nineteen-year-old Louise Blanchard entered Waite's office in the German Insurance Building at Lafayette Square, looking for employment. This was most unusual because there were no woman architects practicing at the time in the United States, or anywhere else for that matter. Architects were expected to do more than just draw plans for a building; they had to oversee construction, negotiate rates, maintain budgets—to manage the entire process that goes into successfully completing a project. According to the sentiment of the time, women just didn't seem to have the required capabilities to be successful architects. For starters, they were thought to lack the physical stamina to work on construction sites. Why, even their clothing—which included tight corsets and long skirts with bustles—precluded this kind of work. The idea of a woman performing the many duties of an architect was hardly thinkable.

Blanchard told Waite that she had wanted to be an architect since childhood. She said her friends mocked her in grade school, but she persevered in her ambition to pursue her dream. She graduated from Buffalo High School in 1874 and continued in its two-year college-preparatory program with the intention of enrolling in Cornell University's newly opened architectural department. She took advanced courses, tutored other students, and traveled in preparation for her continued studies. She hoped Waite would hire her for the summer until her program began. Despite the common prejudice against women working in the profession, Waite hired her in June 1876, enabling Louise to fulfill her dream and become an architect.

Louise Blanchard Bethune was the first professional woman architect in the United States. She was raised and practiced in Buffalo, New York, while the city was experiencing unprecedented growth and wealth. She was accepted in the professional associations by the most well-respected architects of the time; Daniel Burnham, Louis Sullivan, and especially John Root were her colleagues and champions. Louise was not only admitted into the "boys' club" of professional associations—the American Institute of Architects (AIA)—but she also became one of its leaders during a crucial period in architecture's maturation from a craft and gentleman's pastime to a serious profession.

After winning an apprenticeship with Waite, she chose to forgo college training and then founded her own firm, confronting potential prejudice from male colleagues and builders and winning architectural commissions from (mostly male) clients. Yet Louise Blanchard Bethune's story is very familiar to contemporary women. She went into business with her spouse, and theirs was very much a partnership of equals. She balanced the conflicting demands of managing a firm, caring for her family, and pursuing personal interests with her friends. She believed that women should be treated equally in business and fought for pay equity, and she managed to fit a regular exercise regime in her busy day.

Louise faced more opposition within the profession than she admitted. Publicly, she stated that her male colleagues, clients, and contractors had been nothing but respectful of her and her opinions. However, we know that some AIA members were hesitant about admitting her to their ranks and only did so at the lowest level, and her firm fell out of favor with the City of Buffalo when it became apparent that Louise was a partner and not just an employee.

While she had close women friends, Louise was not the beneficiary of a women's network in support of her practice. While the women architects who followed Louise received commissions from women of means, she did not find support among Buffalo's newly wealthy women, despite her fame. She was unable or unwilling to court favor from potential upper-class female clients as other women architects did and would do in the future.

Louise lived during a time of profound changes in the architectural business as well as broader social forces that would greatly impact society. She worked in an industry that was maturing into a profession from a craft and technologically advancing in its use of building materials and new systems. Throughout her life, the women's movement increased in intensity, as advocates sought reform on many fronts. She also lived in a city that was quickly growing in population and wealth, just like the country at large. The society in which she navigated was moving from a rural economy to an urban, industrial one, accompanied by social upheaval and ethnic and class discrimination along the way. How this remarkable Gilded Age woman charted her own course by navigating these currents is the story I will tell.

Fighting for Acceptance

During the early to mid-1880s, Louise Blanchard Bethune made history three times: when she opened her own office and then was elected into the two leading American professional architectural associations. In 1881, she became the first professional woman architect to open an office, which led to some notoriety regionally. However, her acceptance into the two architectural associations signified her status as an architect nationally. In 1885, she successfully applied to the newly formed Western Association of Architects, the first woman to do so. Her admission placed her on the national stage and profoundly impacted her male counterparts' view of women as architects and the very notion of professionalism. Then, two years later, she was admitted to the AIA—the first woman to be accepted in that national organization.

Defining an area of expertise was—and still is—an important strategy for architects to develop and maintain credibility and ensure the long-term health of the business. Another form of establishing credibility is obtaining licensure or certification. However, in the 1880s, no licensure law existed for architects in the US, and so admission into professional associations provided the only vital recognition that an architect was a professional with high ethical standards.

Throughout much of the 1800s, members of the architectural profession fought for the credibility that other occupations, such as law and medicine, enjoyed. For architecture, as an occupation that was founded upon the craft of construction and the arts, the aura of professionalism was hard-fought in the United States and in the Western world in general. Because there were no schools of architecture in the US until later in the nineteenth century and no licensure until the early twentieth century, architects needed to create their credibility through membership in a professional association.

The First Professional Association and the Founding of the AIA

The first society of architects was likely the Brethren of the Workshop of Vitruvius Society, which was founded in 1803 in New York. However, this was a short-lived society composed of men who worked in the art, craft, and construction side of the profession. The first true American organization for professional architects was the American Institution of Architecture. Founded in New York in 1836, the association was concerned with improving architectural education and the public recognition of architects. It was one of many professional associations to be founded in the 1820s and 1830s. The two leaders of the eleven-person organization were Alexander Jackson Davis and Thomas U. Walter. While the organization strived for national influence, the members were active only in New York City and Philadelphia. According to the architectural historian Mary Woods (1999), the confluence of a competition between the members from Philadelphia and New York, the lack of engagement with the general public, the juxtaposition of exclusivity in its membership during an age of egalitarianism, and the financial panic of 1837 all led to the demise of the association.

Twenty years later, architects tried again to organize. On February 23, 1857, the architect Richard Upjohn convened a group of twelve New York colleagues, including Thomas Walter, to discuss the creation of a professional association. The original name proposed was the New York Society of Architects. Walter suggested the "American Institute of Architects" in the hopes it would become national in its reach. The first few years of the AIA were productive ones, as the membership steadily grew. Sadly, this momentum began to wane with the outbreak of the Civil War, but it was revived again in the mid-1860s after the war ended. In the 1860s to 1870s, the AIA primarily focused on architectural education, setting rules for design competitions, establishing standard professional fees, and growing its national membership by creating chapters in cities around the country.

The AIA's focus on establishing standard fees and rejecting design competitions that relied on submissions of unpaid work was part of their mission to elevate the profession in the mind of the general public. Its members advocated for standardized professional fees commensurate with the construction costs of a building. This was in contrast to the daily wage paid to artisans or mechanics and was an effort to differentiate that work from professional architectural service. They adopted a rate of 5 percent of a project's cost in 1866. However, this could not be mandated to the membership and certainly not to the clients. According to Woods (1999), most architects in the late 1890s were charging a far lower percentage for their services. As such, the fee schedule was a suggested rate of charges.

The AIA encouraged cities and regions to establish local chapters. Nonetheless, there was concern that the AIA was elitist. While it was a national organization, the institute was still largely based in the Northeast. In 1882, twenty-five years after the founding of the AIA, membership had grown to 362, of whom 65 percent were from the Northeastern chapters and over 21 percent practiced in New York City.

Given the imbalance of the membership favoring the Northeast, it was likely inevitable that architects in the growing western regions of the country would establish their own professional association. In 1884, the Western Association of Architects was established, and its first convention took place November 12 to 15 of that year. By this time, the WAA had already enlisted 126 members, all from western cities, including seventy-two members from Chicago as well as members from St. Louis, Minneapolis, Kansas City, and Des Moines.

The Western Association of Architects

The WAA was led by architects—some of whom were also members of the AIA—who thought the AIA was too focused on its Northeastern membership, denying leadership roles for its western members. The true force behind the WAA was Daniel Burnham (not an AIA member), who served in a leadership position throughout most of the existence of the association. In his address at that first convention, Burnham spoke of the evolution of the architect from master builder to contemporary professional. He stressed the unique challenges of the western American architects as torchbearers for the design excellence and quality of the monuments of the Old World, without mentors on hand to guide their practice. He saw them as pioneers in a pioneering land. Therefore, he actively encouraged the "restoration of the spirit of brotherhood" to overcome their isolation.

Despite any competition between them, the WAA and AIA shared many areas of concern. They immediately established standing committees to work on resolutions on design competitions and professional fees. They also created a committee on the revision of state statutes regarding building laws. Yet there were several topics on which the AIA and the WAA differed. The WAA sought a certification process that would endorse the architect as a professional working for the public good. The AIA strongly opposed licensure, because it would be based on the technical skills of the architect rather than artistry, which they viewed as the foundation of the profession. A second point on which the WAA and the AIA differed was governance. WAA members believed in a more democratic process in decision-making, while the AIA formed a board of directors to represent its membership as a more efficient and robust method of conducting business.

The most contentious disagreement between the two organizations was their philosophy regarding membership, including the admission process and members' standing. The AIA was just far too selective and elitist to advance the profession amid the industrial era in the aftermath of the Civil War and as the US was blossoming into an international economic powerhouse. It had two levels of membership: the associate and the fellow. The thought was that junior members would join as associates and would be elevated to fellows as they developed in stature within the profession. The AIA contended that the dual membership levels would ultimately provide the association with the ability to increase its numbers by having multiple entry points for admission, based on experience and stature within the profession.

When initially formed, the WAA had been quite liberal in its admission of members, including members who came from the building trades in addition to those with professional training or education. However, they retracted this practice after complaints from the more professional membership. By 1886 the WAA had created the Committee on Professional Membership to address its previous admission of builders. Nonetheless, the WAA strenuously opposed the AIA's two-tiered membership policy. They believed that members should be equal, period.

The WAA leadership immediately knew that a large organization would provide the association with the strength to influence the public perception of the profession. They also understood the power it would possess to lobby legislators who had the authority to develop procurement standards for awarding public work. However, this obvious open-door admissions policy attracted architects who would otherwise have no vehicle to effect change in their profession. One of these individuals was the first woman architect, Louise Blanchard Bethune.

Enter the Lady Architect

In 1885, just one year after the WAA was established, Louise applied for membership. Despite the WAA being considered more progressive than the AIA, admission was not automatic, and neither the WAA nor the AIA had a woman member. In 1885, Louise and her husband, Robert Bethune, traveled to Chicago and conferred with WAA leadership—including Daniel Burnham, Louis Sullivan, and John Root—regarding their applications. During this meeting, the parties developed the strategy for Louise's unprecedented admission.

Initially, both Louise and Robert submitted their applications for membership to the WAA. However, Robert withdrew his nomination before his application was reviewed, presumably at the advice of the WAA leadership and in anticipation of a charge that the Bethune firm's work was his alone. With her application, Louise submitted a portfolio of her work to demonstrate her abilities as an architect. She had previously intended to attend the WAA convention but decided against the appropriateness of such a gesture, given the fact that she was not a member and the potential embarrassment of not being admitted while present. The yearly membership was reviewed at the WAA national convention in St. Louis in November. Burnham chose to separate Louise's nomination from that of the other members, to ensure the association would be prepared to include the admission of women as members in their constitution. This was a carefully orchestrated action to yield a positive outcome to the board's intention of opening their membership to women. The meeting's proceedings capture the drama of the moment:

> The president called the meeting to order and said: There is a bit of unfinished business before we can proceed. All the members recommended by the directors for admission were voted in except one, and nothing was done on that subject.
> Mr. Burnham: That was with reference to a lady.
> The President: Now I will ask if the committee are prepared to recommend that party in all respects except the fact that she is a lady?
> Mr. Sullivan: Yes, sir.
> The President: What shall be done with this question?
> Mr. Burnham, of the Board of Directors: May I say that what the board desires is to be instructed upon the principle of admitting women as members of the association. That is the thing. If the decision is given us to admit women, we will make the recommendation. We would like the decision, now, of the convention, as to whether it desires to admit women as members of the association. We want the By-Laws interpreted.

A member: I would like to know what the opinion of the Board of Directors is.

Mr. Burnham: We are all agreed; we are very much in favor of it.

Mr. Cochrane: Then I would recommend that the secretary cast the ballot for the lady.

A member: Is the lady practicing?

The President: Yes, sir.

Mr. Cochrane: Let the secretary cast the ballot as he did for the others.

The motion was seconded.

Mr. Sullivan: What we desired was a vote of instructions as to the admission of women as a general thing.

A member: It seems to me that if you carry the motion as made by Mr. Cochrane, that it will suggest a precedent for future consideration. If the lady is practicing architecture, and is in good standing, there is no reason why she should not be one of us.

The President: The motion is made and seconded that this lady applicant be admitted to membership. All in favor of this will say aye.

Motion was adopted.

The President: Mrs. Louisa [sic] Bethune is the applicant. . . . She has done work by herself and been very successful. She is unanimously elected a member.

While the board members were seeking direction from the membership, they were signaling their strong support for the candidate. Sullivan, Burnham, and Root were particularly supportive of Louise's candidacy. Even more importantly, they used the opportunity to address the broader issue of the admission of women to the WAA.

While she was an ideal candidate to champion the admission of women in the association—given her experience and body of work—Louise's submission was somewhat complicated because she was in partnership with her husband. A skeptic could easily argue that she was riding on the coattails of her husband's work. With Robert's retraction of his submission, Louise was able to submit her application based on her own merit. (Robert successfully applied for membership to the WAA in 1887.)

Not all members were comfortable with expansion of the WAA's membership to include women. Once again, their concern was that women could not supervise construction. After this historic vote, the WAA established its official definition of an architect in the organization's constitution as the following: "a professional person [as opposed to 'man,' which was originally suggested] whose sole occupation is to supply all data preliminary to the material, construction and competition of a building and to exercise administrative control over contracts stipulating terms of obligation and fulfillment between proprietor and contractor."

Louise was deeply touched by the careful stewardship that the WAA leadership took to forward her candidacy. She understood her submission could make her the object of ridicule in architectural circles, and she appreciated the orchestrated approach by the board. Following the convention, Louise wrote to John Root:

> My sincere thanks are certainly due to you and thro' you to all members of your society for the cordiality of the welcome you have accorded me and also for the extreme delicacy and adroit work with which the nomination and election were arranged . . . I am particularly sensible of the kindness the association has rendered me, and the honor it has done itself in preserving admission from any taint of ridicule or notoriety. If the society's new member is no great acquisition, its new measure is certainly credible and progressive.

Louise's admission to the WAA made national news in newspapers throughout the country, from Nashville to New Orleans, and especially in the Midwest. Most stories were positive about her breaking this barrier, although some just neutrally reported the fact. The *Buffalo Courier* and the *Woman's Exponent* in Salt Lake City took exception that the *Woman's Journal* referred to Louise as "a practicing architect of Chicago," saying, "It is hard that Chicago should have the credit of the woman architect of whom Buffalo has such reason to feel proud."

As might have been expected, Louise's acceptance by the WAA led to more general articles on the best and least appropriate areas for women architects to practice. Edward Godwin, a "distinguished English architect," as the newspapers described him, was quoted at length on the subject. He asserted that women would be most useful in "designs in architecture, including furniture and decorations, illustrations of old work, cabinet work, metal work, monuments, carpets and hangings, painting on cabinets, wall paper designs, tiles, private and public buildings." Godwin was a progressive and leader in the English Queen Anne Revival movement, so he was probably very supportive of women becoming architects. Whether intended or not, his emphasis on the decorative and ornamental tasks of the profession, as opposed to the functional and structural, only reinforced a preexisting bias. Godwin also noted that "many young women possessed all the requisite talents to become architectural workers . . . [however,] an impulsive, gay, free-as-air, lightsome sort of girl is not the stuff for an architect." Here, again, we encounter his obviously sexist attitude, demonstrating a prevailing attitude about women professionals that early women architects needed to counter head-on.

Following her admission to the WAA, Louise enjoyed the status of being the first and leading female architect. As a trailblazer, she was called upon frequently to speak about women in architecture, women professionals, and women's education. In 1889 she was part of a panel of professional women speaking to the Graduate Association in Buffalo, which also included the writer Mary Lee Perkins; Dr. Mary Moody, the first woman to graduate from the University of Buffalo Medical College; and Dr. Mary Wetmore, also a graduate from UB. In her comments, Louise agreed with Godwin's commentary on the hard work involved in becoming an architect and that not every woman would be suited to or interested in its study. However, she was unequivocal about a woman's ability to oversee construction:

> Women are entirely competent to become architects, but I do not believe the profession will ever be crowded, as it requires too much application and hard work. Unless a woman has a love and decided aptitude for the preparatory work she will tire of it quickly. This idea that a woman cannot superintend the erection of buildings is all nonsense. Any woman with a moderate amount of physical endurance can do it. As for dealing with carpenters and builders, there is no trouble at all. I have always found them an accommodating, agreeable class of men in all business transactions.

The Struggle to Join the AIA

In February 1888, Louise applied for the highest level of membership of the AIA, the fellow. By this time, she had been a member of the WAA for over two years. However, longtime AIA Secretary Alfred Bloor advised her instead to apply for the associate level. Bloor reflected the view of many members when he told her that the associate level was "largely an educational & probationary term, which may very properly be regarded by its incumbents as simply a stepping stone to the higher grade of Fellowship." The AIA required two or more sponsors from the organization. Bloor agreed to sponsor her, along with AIA member G. W. Rapp, and he waived the requirement for a third, possibly because of her WAA membership and standing within that organization and the profession at large. In addition to the recommendation letters from her AIA sponsors, the package included a letter of support from Sydney Smith, the 1888 president of the WAA, and John Root, who recommended her to be a fellow. She also submitted drawings for several of her projects.

At the 1888 AIA convention, the group admitted seven members at the associate level, elevated four members from associate to fellow, and admitted thirteen new members at the fellowship level. In other words, more than half of the applicants were admitted at the higher level. The thirteen new fellows' years of experience ranged from eight to thirty; W. W. Carlin was an outlier with only four years (although this was probably an error in the written meeting minutes because he was six years older than Louise). Louise applied with twelve years of experience. However, after "some discussion," the board admitted Louise as an associate member. Given her years of experience and the endorsement of the WAA leadership, she could have made a compelling case for fellowship. We don't know why Bloor recommended to Bethune that she apply as an associate, but he did so with the consent of the AIA board, and they could have elevated her if they accepted Root's suggestion.

The difference in Bethune's admission process between the WAA and the AIA underlines the very different philosophies between the two organizations about their membership and women's role in architecture in general. The WAA was composed of progressive members who strongly supported women entering the profession and prospering. They actively worked to change professional norms by collaborating with potential trailblazers like Louise to present her application in a manner that supported a successful outcome. The WAA admission process was more democratic in nature, which also favored Louise. New members were voted upon in the open forum of the annual convention by all members. Members were initially vetted by the executive committee and then brought to the membership, with the expectation that they would be accepted. The convention forum allowed for an open dialogue, but it also inhibited discrete sidebar conversations where dissenting voices might gain traction. Because Burnham, Root, and Sullivan orchestrated Louise's membership vote, a dissenting member would have had to had to openly challenge the judgment of the executive committee to oppose Louise's application.

The AIA was much more conservative. They were focused on elevating the profession to be on par with law, medicine, and engineering. They had been working to establish this status for several decades and were at the cusp of a breakthrough, given the obvious need for expertise in the built environment, which was underscored by the maturation of the Industrial Revolution, the need for new building types, and the passage of additional laws addressing building safety. The AIA admitted its members through its board of directors, at its own discretion, and reported the admissions at the convention, as opposed to holding a membership vote in that forum.

Louise applied for membership in the AIA at a very auspicious time in its history. She was already the first woman admitted to a professional association, by more than two years. She was a proven leader, because—as we shall see—she had established the Buffalo Society of Architects. By this time her firm had built significant factories, residential projects, and schools. Louise's nomination for the AIA was stronger than her WAA application because she had more important projects in her portfolio. To be clear, there is no indication that the AIA was opposed to a woman becoming a member. However, it is striking that the first woman to apply was admitted at the entry level, given Louise's compelling application.

Another factor that probably influenced the AIA's decision to admit Louise as a member was that by 1887 there were serious conversations underway regarding the merger of the AIA and WAA. Daniel Burnham, now a member of both organizations, originally suggested the idea at the 1887 AIA convention. Both organizations agreed that one larger entity advocating for the profession would benefit all members. These negotiations advanced in October 1888 at the AIA National Convention in Buffalo, where Bethune, as a new member, served on the host committee.

Just after the AIA convention in Buffalo, the WAA held its annual convention in Chicago in November 1888. In an unexpected term, Louise Bethune was elected second vice president of the board of directors, beating the other six candidates and becoming the first woman to be elected to the association's executive committee. While Louise was active in WAA committee work, she had not yet assumed a leadership role within the association. Her election demonstrated the confidence her colleagues had in her work and stands in sharp contrast to her admission process to the AIA. One may wonder if the WAA members' personal interaction with Louise in Buffalo the prior month contributed to her election.

The consolidation of the two organizations took place at the AIA convention, which was held November 20 to 21, 1889, in Cincinnati, Ohio. Some of the long-standing philosophical differences between their members had not been resolved. To assuage the WAA concern about membership levels, all current WAA and AIA members were raised to fellows upon consolidation—so Louise's tenure as merely an associate was very brief. To address the concern about geographic diversity among the new association's leadership, the newly elected executive committee included positions filled by former AIA and WAA members. Several WAA members refused to join the newly consolidated AIA until much later, if at all. One of these was Robert Bethune, who remained very active in the local AIA Buffalo/Western New York (WNY) chapter but did not join the national AIA until 1902. And although Louise remained a member of both the local and national AIA organization, she was never involved nationally with the group after the consolidation. Indeed, she did not attend the 1901 AIA convention that was held in Buffalo, although Robert was there.

The Buffalo Society of Architects

Immediately upon her admission to the WAA in 1885, Louise joined the membership committee with the charge of establishing a presence in New York state. On March 10, 1886, she organized the first meeting of the Buffalo Society of Architects, with twelve members. The Buffalo Society of Architects steadily grew and was very active by the time it received its charter from the AIA and became AIA Buffalo/WNY, in March 1890. Much of the work of the society was in concert with the advocacy of the national associations, in particular lobbying for paid design competitions with educated jurors and actively and financially supporting the passage of a professional licensing bill for architects in New York state.

The Buffalo association was active in other areas, too. In 1888 it successfully worked with the city on the passage of the Building Laws as a revision of the charter of the city. The society also successfully protested to the federal government against the original design of Buffalo's new post office building in 1893 and unsuccessfully opposed the Buffalo Public Schools regarding the terms of the design competition for a new high school in 1901. The Buffalo Society of Architects was also instrumental in forming the Western New York Association of Architects in October 1886, the only regional component of the AIA until the creation of AIA New York State in 1931. This organization encompassed Buffalo, Rochester, Syracuse, Ithaca, and Binghamton, and extended to Albany.

While a vibrant and active national association was vital in promoting the profession to the general public and the federal government, the state and regional chapters would be on the front lines in advocating for professional licensing, increased architectural education opportunities, and other state legislative issues. The Western New York Association of Architects was particularly focused on passing a professional licensing bill for architects calling for the creation of a board of architects to oversee the regulation of the architect profession. The association worked with the AIA New York chapter to jointly lobby for the passage of the bill in the 1892 state legislature session. The bill was passed by both houses, giving Governor Flower thirty days to sign, which he never did, apparently due to opposition from select architects in New York City who had access to the governor. Also, it was reported that the governor considered the legislation an opportunity for organizing a trade union. Ultimately, Illinois became the first state to legislate an architectural professional licensing bill, in 1897, through the advocacy of Dankmar Adler and N. Clifford Ricker, director of the architecture department at the University of Illinois. The loss of this tremendous effort dampened the enthusiasm of the Western New York membership, as was demonstrated in the relative inactivity of their annual reports. Licensure in New York state was finally passed in 1915. The Western New York Association of Architects did, however, also work hard to build enduring bridges between professional architects and schools of architecture, conducting regular visits and meetings at the schools of architecture at Syracuse and Cornell Universities. Professors from both schools were also very active in the organization.

However, the geographic region of the Western New York Association of Architects eventually became too large to maintain a vibrant engagement model. The executive committee recommended merging with the very active AIA Buffalo/WNY chapter, which the members outside of Buffalo resoundingly rejected. Ultimately, the regional association became the Central New York chapter of the AIA in 1897. And while gender issues were never part of the regular discourse of this or any architectural association, Louise, by her mere presence, forced the issue. In the opening address by the WAA president to the Western New York Association of Architects in 1888, the issue was raised—somewhat obliquely: "Gentlemen—I wish I could add ladies, but I hope the day is not very far distant when I can add that to it . . ."

This comment reflects WAA's optimistic attitude about the future of women in architecture. However, despite Louise's early success, she was not followed by large numbers of women pursuing the profession in the region. Because the Bethune, Bethune & Fuchs office records do not survive, there is no record that she hired women as interns. The first woman architect to succeed Louise in Buffalo as a firm owner was Bonnie Foit Albert, who established her office in 1977, ninety-six years after Louise established her firm. In upstate New York, following Louise, twelve women became members of the AIA before 1970. Helen Cittenden Gillespie of Syracuse was the first of these women, whose AIA membership began in 1943.

Describing Louise as a "trailblazer" within the AIA could be said to be inaccurate because women did not immediately follow her into the organization, and the institutional memory regarding her historic admission was lost when they started to apply. Instead, she was a lone warrior who benefitted from good timing, progressive advocates within the profession, and, most importantly, unfailing strength and perseverance. She refused to be a victim and never outwardly criticized her AIA colleagues. However, she did note that women professionals were not treated equally to their male counterparts. And she chose not to be involved in the national AIA after the merger. Her inactivity, as someone who had been so very active just two years earlier, demonstrates her attitude toward the association. Ultimately, Louise would deeply impact her women successors, but it would be those who entered the profession one hundred years after her, among the baby boom and the generations that followed, who rediscovered her story and celebrated it.

The Women Who Followed . . . Eventually

Once Louise won her hard-earned positions with both the WAA and AIA, it would seem that the issue would have been settled for future generations. However, reviewing Louise's successors provides additional context to the continuing sexism that women architects experienced and the opposition they encountered from their male counterparts within the AIA.

Sallie T. Smith was the second professional woman architect in the United States, but her career is not well-documented. Born in Columbus, Mississippi, she attended Verona College in that state and then studied architecture with her father, W. S. Smith. He made Sallie a junior member of his firm, which moved to Birmingham, Alabama, in 1886. In March 1887, daughter and father were among a group of architects to form the

Association of Alabama Architects, which was associated with the WAA. Sallie was elected to the Alabama association to solicit new members throughout the state. At its 1887 convention, Sallie and W. S. Smith were admitted to the WAA. However, neither Sallie nor her father joined the AIA after its consolidation with the WAA, and her name is not found in subsequent AIA member lists.

While the WAA admitted its second woman member only two years after the first, it took the AIA thirteen years. The next woman to be admitted to the AIA was Lois Howe (1864 to 1964) in 1901. According to Boston architect and AIA member C. H. Blackall, "Miss Howe came in to the Institute . . . because most of the members who voted on her thought Lois was a man's name." However, she did not become a member of her local AIA chapter, the Boston Society of Architects, until 1916 and was not made a fellow until 1931, the first woman after Louise Bethune to be given this status. Henrietta Dozier (1872 to 1947) was admitted shortly after Howe, in 1905. A graduate of the Massachusetts Institute of Technology in 1899, Dozier worked in Atlanta from 1900 to 1913 and served as the secretary of AIA Atlanta from 1910 to 1912, then opened a practice in Orlando.

Ida Annah Ryan's (1873 to 1950) story demonstrates the struggle of early women architects for equality among their male counterparts. Before applying for AIA membership in 1907, Ryan wrote to the organization asking whether she could be considered for membership even though she was not a member of her local chapter, the Boston Society of Architects, because it was "positively closed to women," citing Lois Howe's failed attempt to join it. The AIA's reply must have given her the confidence to apply. However, her application was rejected by the board of directors on a ballot vote; her application garnered nine letters of opposition. Of the three that survive, two opposed her because of her gender and stated they did not know her. Seth Temple wrote that "I have never known a woman who pretended to practice Architecture who was worthy to be included in so distinguished body." And C. H. Blackall asked "the Directors to consider whether it is wise to admit women at all unless they have achieved some signal [sic] distinction in the profession." A third member, D. Austin, from Boston, objected to admitting Ryan on the grounds that she was not a member of her home chapter. The fact that her application was rejected almost twenty years after Bethune's admission is astounding. Ryan was finally successful in joining the AIA in 1921, when women were more welcome.

In 1918, the AIA admitted two women: Marcia Mead (1879 to 1967) and Theodate Pope (1868 to 1946). Mead was the first woman to graduate from Columbia University's architecture program. She had practiced with

Anna Pendleton Schenck until Schneck's death in 1915 and then continued as a sole practitioner, mentoring Esther Hill, one of the first woman Canadian architects, from 1923 to 1924. Theodate Pope was born into a wealthy Ohio family. While Princeton University did not accept women, she hired a Princeton professor for private lessons and designed the family estate in Connecticut under the tutelage of Charles McKim. In the 1920s, after women got the right to vote with the passage of the Nineteenth Amendment, the AIA admitted more women; ten new women members were admitted in the 1920s alone, starting with Julia Morgan (1872 to 1957) in 1921.

Louise's story is remarkable when compared with her initial successors because her admission to two professional organizations was so early; she was not succeeded by another female member for thirteen years. Despite the best intentions of the early WAA leaders to encourage women to join the profession and the perseverance of her successors, there was a concerted effort to limit the architectural profession to men only by a significant portion of the AIA's membership. This broke down somewhat in the 1920s, but it was not until the 1970s, after the beginning of the second wave of feminism, that the AIA began to address the fact that its women members made up just 1 percent of its total roster. Louise was correct that women had entered the architectural profession far earlier in its development than was the case in other professions, and initially there were promising signs that they would be welcomed as equals long before they would receive that status in other aspects of society. However, after that initial wave, the profession closed ranks, and women would struggle to achieve the equal status that Louise experienced until well into the twentieth century.

Unlike several female architects who followed her, Louise did not benefit from the patronage of women, which could have been available to her in such an affluent industrial city as Buffalo. Other women architects were hired by women patrons, such as Minerva Parker Nichols in Philadelphia. However, there is no evidence that Nichols applied for membership in the AIA; she may have questioned whether she would be admitted. She also may not have felt the need for its endorsement, given her status with her largely female clientele. Throughout her career, Louise could never rely on women patrons; instead, she relied on public work and industrial and commercial clients.

8

The Triangle Fire and the Velvet Revolution in Workplace Safety, 1911

DANIEL KORNSTEIN

New York has led the way in enacting legislation to benefit working people. Sometimes progress came after crucial needs were demonstrated through tragedy. The Triangle Shirtwaist Factory fire in New York City in 1911 is perhaps the best example. It resulted in 146 deaths but led to an unprecedented public demand for state government action.

The legislature responded by creating the Factory Investigating Commission later that year, which studied safety needs and proposed legislation. Over the next four years, it carried out the broadest, most thorough study of workers' safety and health done up to that point. The commission proposed sweeping factory safety and health regulations. The legislature soon passed three dozen laws the commission formulated. The laws gave New York the most advanced industrial code in the nation.

☙

Revolutions come in different varieties. Some, like our American Revolution, are violent overthrows of hated or oppressive governments. Others, like the Darwinian revolution, are transformations in fundamental thought. Some are economic and social revolutions caused by new inventions (the cotton gin and the computer chip, for example) or new means of production (the Industrial Revolution). Still others are quiet—or "velvet"—revolutions, like the transition of power in Czechoslovakia in 1989, that profoundly alter oppressive social, economic, and political structures without widespread violence.

One such velvet revolution was the significant and beneficial change in workplace safety and working conditions following a tragically fatal 1911 fire in the Triangle Shirtwaist Factory in Manhattan. That great but quiet revolution in labor law should be commemorated as part of the 250th celebration of the American Revolution.

That terrible fire, which caused 146 deaths, still haunts New Yorkers. The sting of memory has not lessened, and with good reason. The fire was a pivotal event in the city's history and in the history of America. A city remembers the dates of deadly tragedies. New York, for example, will never forget September 11, 2001, and what happened that day when terrorists flew two jet planes full of passengers into the Twin Towers at the World Trade Center, destroying the buildings and killing thousands of New Yorkers. Likewise, New York will always remember, as it should, what happened at the Triangle factory ninety years earlier, on March 25, 1911.

Every year on March 25 people gather in front of the Triangle factory building near Washington Square Park in Manhattan's Greenwich Village to remember. Like Memorial Day each May and September 11 each year, March 25 is an emotional day of remembrance. On that day, at the site where it happened, the gathering remembers those who died and were injured over a century ago in the deadliest workplace accident in New York City's four-hundred-year history.

It is a day worth remembering not only for the many unfortunate victims but also for the much needed and overdue reforms in workplace safety that resulted from the tragedy. For out of this traumatic event came lasting, dramatic, long-delayed beneficial change spearheaded by New York state. Within a few months of the fire, outraged and concerned private citizens prevailed on sympathetic New York politicians to start investigating workplace hazards and then pass tough, comprehensive new laws to improve the safety of workers. Other states soon copied New York's new laws, which contributed greatly to the later torrent of New Deal labor legislation during the hardships of the Great Depression.

It was a revolution, albeit a quiet, nonviolent one (except for the innocent victims of the fire).

This seeming paradox of disaster and reform as two contrasting sides of the same coin and how one reform-minded state can lead the rest of the country by example deserves another look, especially on the 250th anniversary of the American Revolution. No matter how many times the heartrending story is told, the grisly Triangle Shirtwaist Fire, like a classic literary work upon rereading, continues to yield new meanings, insights, warnings, and lessons.

Saturday, March 25, 1911, started out as a fine early-spring day in New York City. It was the sort of morning that kept at bay all unpleasant thoughts, especially of death and disaster.

That Saturday was a 9:00 a.m. to 4:45 p.m. workday for employees, mostly impoverished young Jewish and Italian immigrant women and teenage girls, at the Triangle Shirtwaist Company. Those Saturday hours were about three hours less than the arduous normal weekday work schedule of 7:30 a.m. to 5:45 p.m. Located at the corner of Washington Place and Greene Street, just a block east of Washington Square Park, the Triangle factory was where these employees made fashionable, popular light-cotton women's blouses (called shirtwaists) styled like men's shirts.

As those employees—seamstresses, pressers, finishers, and drapers—left their tenements and walked or rode on the Third Avenue El or trolleys to the factory early that morning, they saw and felt the disparities in living conditions and opportunities amid the rich tapestry of life in their city. They passed with envy the beautiful homes they would never live in on lower Fifth Avenue and Washington Square North while they no doubt thought with pleasure about the next day, Sunday, their one day off each week. They enjoyed the meager pleasures available to them. Perhaps they happily planned in their minds how they might relax, spend time with family or friends, or go dancing.

Little did they expect that by the end of that Saturday, 146 of them would be dead and scores of others seriously injured because of a furious flash fire in their factory that lasted only eighteen minutes. Many of them died trying to flee the fierce flames and acrid, deadly smoke by jumping out of windows nine floors up because they could not otherwise avoid being burnt alive. They did not expect to be the victims of one of the worst workplace tragedies in American history. Nor did they expect their suffering to produce vast and permanent legal reforms for workplace safety and to become a milestone on the still-unfinished road to social and economic justice.

We thus have the apparent paradox, that seeming contradiction, the mysterious hidden truth of the same traumatic event—a fire, so emblematic of disaster—being both a tragedy and a powerful catalyst for change.

In this historical episode, we see how a disastrous and deadly fire seared the conscience of the public and yet ignited a powerful reform movement to make working conditions safer forever after. It is a story about a crucial event from America's past with important meaning for America's present and future. It is an example of how democracy and the law can respond effectively to improve life for ordinary people. It is a key lesson learned about the long and continuing struggle between capital and labor, about the potential for politics and government to remedy society's problems, and about the complicated, sometimes tortured relationship among capitalism, liberal democracy, and social welfare.

It illustrates how the law in one state—New York—can be a pioneer, a beacon that lights the way for the rest of the country, like Lady Liberty's torch in New York Harbor. New York became a "laboratory for democracy" in which a "single courageous State," as Supreme Court Justice Louis Brandeis once famously said, "may, if its citizens choose, serve as a laboratory, and try novel and economic experiments without risk to the rest of society."

A tragedy can be a change agent, an inflection point that alters public attitudes and incites and precipitates crucial and overdue reforms. Sometimes it takes a tragedy to move the needle of progress, to shake us out of our complacency. Disasters may be terrible events that bring about, as a secondary or incidental consequence, good and welcome change that might otherwise not happen or only happen much later. If necessity is the mother of invention, then disaster is the father of reform.

Coming to terms with this Triangle Fire paradox is crucial to any understanding of the Triangle Fire, and understanding the Triangle Fire and its aftermath is essential to learning how a traumatic event can produce beneficial change, even a legal revolution of sorts.

Some stories should be told again and again, lest we forget. All cultures have such stories, be they origin stories, independence stories, war stories, breakthroughs, or other stories of importance, that contain lessons, examples, morals, and insights about the ability to adapt and cope with challenges and adversity. Such generational storytelling is ancient and goes back to the dawn of history. The Triangle Fire is such a story.

Time aids perspective as well. Each generation interprets past events by its own lights, emotions, and needs. Turning the pages of the calendar provides distance, new experience, calmer feelings, and different ways to think about long-ago events. More than a century has passed since the 1911 Triangle Fire. To the extent they know about that 1911 tragedy at all, many today see it and its surrounding events as faded and dim, like a half-remembered book read long ago. The passage of time gives us more to reflect on.

What happened before the fire provides context. After the Civil War, the Industrial Revolution and almost unbridled capitalism fueled America and quickly brought tremendous growth in the United States economy. Factories using many workers sprang up in American cities. Large corporations began to dominate the economy. A few individuals accumulated great wealth.

Yet the underside of the era's development was apparent. With profits as their primary if not only goal, and few labor unions to offer countervailing bargaining power to workers, business owners and managers kept wages as low as possible and employed children and young immigrants who would work under harsh conditions for little pay. One result was that owners spent little or nothing on worker safety. The age-old, sometimes violent struggle between capital and labor gripped America. Bitter, sometimes violent strikes occurred, and employers were aided by politicians and even a predominantly anti-labor judicial system.

These various forces converged and picked up speed and energy in the first decade of the twentieth century. Anti-union attitudes, low pay, long hours, and horrible and unsafe working conditions led to a strike at Triangle in September 1909.

The Triangle strike focused the public attention on the problems of garment-factory employees. The owners brought in other women to start fights with the strikers and thugs to beat up the striking women workers. Police clubbed and arrested the strikers, not the thugs or the prostitutes. Every day for six weeks, the women walked their picket lines in front of the Triangle building.

By November 1909, the situation boiled over. The protests and arrests attracted support from middle- and upper-class women, the so-called "mink brigade," which included the daughter of J. Pierpont Morgan and other wealthy women. Two young unions, the International Ladies Garment Workers Union (ILGWU) and the Women's Trade Union League, called for a general meeting of all garment workers. Three thousand garment workers came; it was standing room only. Speakers, including Samuel Gompers, founder and leader of the American Federation of Labor, talked for two hours about the need for solidarity and preparedness, but their caution made the audience restive.

Suddenly, a twenty-two-year-old garment worker named Clara Lemlich, an ILGWU organizer, rose from the audience without an invitation and spoke. "I have listened to all the speakers," Lemlich said in her native Yiddish, "and I have no further patience for talk. . . . I am tired of listening to speakers who talk in generalities." Then came a clarion call to action: "What we are here for is to decide whether or not to strike. I make a motion that we go out in a general strike—*now!*"

Lemlich's few, impassioned Yiddish words stirred the crowd like nothing they had heard before. Hearing one of their own speak in their native tongue, the garment workers were ready to march and responded with five minutes of loud applause and wild, roaring cries of support. The overflow crowd immediately and unanimously agreed to go on strike the next day.

The next morning, fifteen thousand garment workers throughout the city walked off their jobs, and another five thousand joined them the next day. This mass walkout became known ever after as the "Uprising of the Twenty Thousand." The largest single strike by women up until then, it brought the shirtwaist industry to a halt.

Feminism and sisterhood drew strength from the events. Similar strikes involving tens of thousands of garment workers soon broke out in other major cities such as Philadelphia and Chicago.

By late January 1910, after some seven hundred arrests of women workers, many factories—but not Triangle—settled and agreed to recognize the ILGWU. The stubborn anti-union Triangle owners held out. In February 1910, the ILGWU officially ended the strike. Triangle agreed to some wage increases and shorter hours but continued to resist unionization. The Triangle strikers returned to work.

If the striking garment workers had not achieved complete success, they had nevertheless won a lot. The public was moved and impressed. The young women workers had advanced the cause of feminism. Uniting women as never before, the strike helped the fundamental cause of women's suffrage. The intrepid strikers were in effect shouting "I am woman, hear me roar!" more than six decades before the words became a popular and powerful song lyric.

On the picket lines, the women strikers stepped forward into history, into the life of their time; they mounted history's stage to try to make the era better, a force for social justice. Years later, Frances Perkins, a future secretary of labor who would play a leading role in improving workers' lives, said the strike "was a true example of an angry, emotional outburst such as fiction writers often depict as the beginning of a revolution."

And then, thirteen months later, came the fire. In the Triangle factory's tinder-filled environment littered with flammable cloth and thin paper patterns, the flames and smoke spread everywhere almost immediately. Many of the workers on two of the three floors escaped and survived by using elevators that worked briefly during the fire and stairs to the street and roof that were passable for a short time. But hundreds of workers on one floor were not told of the fire until it reached them, and by then it was too late for most of them.

Elevator cables were melting from the heat, the one inadequate fire escape collapsed, and one of the two staircases was unusable due to fire and smoke. The other stairway immediately became controversial as many survivors said the door to that stairway was locked and could not be opened, thus causing many deaths, while other survivors said that door could be opened. Like some of the unfortunate office workers ninety years later in the Twin Towers on 9/11, sixty-two scared Triangle employees jumped to their death nine floors below rather than burn to death. The huge number of fatalities—146 young people, some only fourteen years old—still numbs the mind even after all these years.

The fire and its death toll stunned, saddened, and angered the public. Shock, bewilderment, and grief were the immediate responses. Unions promptly called for a huge funeral procession by workers, which took place on a dark, rainy day in Manhattan, weather that matched the march's mood. Four hundred thousand people saw the procession, and 120,000 marched in it. It was the largest demonstration ever made in New York up to then by working people.

People wanted to know whom to blame. But public officials all said it was not their fault. Two weeks after the fire, a lawyer-activist said, "We want to put somebody in jail, but when the dead bodies of girls are found piled up against the locked doors leading to the exits after a factory fire . . . what we want to do is start a revolution." Popular fury focused on the owners of the Triangle factory.

A grand jury quickly returned seven indictments against the owners. Each indictment contained seven counts of manslaughter, all identical except that the names of the victims differed, and carried a maximum sentence of twenty years in prison. Amid courthouse shrieks from relatives calling for revenge against the "murderers," a celebrated three-week trial on one indictment ended in acquittal on all counts, a highly controversial and unpopular verdict that maddened many. When one of the other indictments with a different victim came on for trial months later, another judge told that jury, before hearing any witnesses, that they must acquit based on double jeopardy grounds. This second acquittal led to more anger and frustration.

Simultaneously, reaction to the Triangle Fire started to move in another, more far-reaching and positive direction: constructive change. Instead of looking back, people began to look forward. This shift was a major and long-lasting beneficial development that touched the future.

The Triangle Fire altered many lives, including that of Frances Perkins, a thirty-one-year-old eyewitness to the fire. Perkins, a social worker active in the Consumers' League, grasped that it might be possible to capitalize on the outrage the city felt to get substantive reforms made. It was a magical moment, as if New Yorkers found a philosopher's stone that through some strange, helpful alchemy transmutes not base metal into gold but disaster into much-needed reforms.

The horror of the fire, which everyone knew about due to widespread and emotional press coverage, startled the entire country, especially New Yorkers, and cried out for change. The tragedy unified a city usually riven by differences and tensions. The unsafe conditions that led to so many deaths of young people shocked and embarrassed everyone else and made them feel guilty. If no individuals were responsible, then all were. It was as if the weeping Jewish and Italian mothers of the many dead young victims quietly, and the press not so quietly, had laid a massive guilt trip on the rest of a society that had previously ignored and overlooked the plight of workers. Shame and guilt can be great motivators for changes in behavior.

Change does not usually happen by itself. It needs people to bring it about. And so it was with the change that eventually followed the Triangle Fire. Those reforms owe their existence to some extraordinary, energetic, far-seeing, committed, passionate, and compassionate human beings.

In the weeks after the fire, several organizations met to discuss it, the main topic being "Now what is going to be done about it?" Framing the question in those words may, or may not, have been a subconscious echo of Lenin's 1902 revolutionary pamphlet entitled "What Is to Be Done? Burning Questions of Our Movement." Many immigrants from Eastern Europe did hold socialist views, and some of the most outspoken union activists became ardent communists.

That threatening tone persisted. At one meeting a few days after the fire for thousands of relatives and friends of the victims, Abraham Cahan, editor of the *Jewish Daily Forward*, told the audience that a worker upset over the fire had come into Cahan's office and told him that "only the placing of a few bombs in the camp of the capitalists would bring redress to the working classes." The meeting hall then filled with similar shouts: "Throw a bomb under city hall." "Blow the place up."

Later the same week, another speaker at another meeting declared, "Something's got to be done to the law." She added, "And if it's not constitutional to protect the lives of workers then we've got to smash the constitution! It's our 'instrument,' and if it doesn't work, we've got to get a new one!" The audience cheered.

On Sunday, April 2, a mass public meeting drew thirty-five hundred people to the Metropolitan Opera House. The purpose of the meeting was to protest the lack of safety and the inhuman conditions in the factories. The goal was to make sure something like the Triangle Fire could never happen again.

Those in charge proposed various resolutions. Regarding such steps as too weak and fed up with the talk of more committees and more resolutions, the turbulent workers seated and standing in the galleries booed and hissed.

On the brink of dissolving amid disagreement, the meeting heard a young speaker who gripped the audience and held them spellbound, just as Clara Lemlich had done in November 1909. The mesmerizing speaker was Rose Schneiderman, who had been a leader in the 1909 to 1910 Triangle strike.

Schneiderman's speech, like Churchill's speeches during World War II, mobilized both the English language and her listeners for battle. She said in a soft voice, "I would be a traitor to these poor burned bodies," she began, "if I came here to talk of good fellowship." Then came the accusation: "We have tried you good people of the public and we have found you wanting." She explained, "The old Inquisition had its rack and its thumbscrews and its instruments of torture with iron teeth. We know what these things are today: the iron teeth are our necessities, the thumbscrews are the high-powered and swift machinery close to which we must work, and the rack is here in the firetrap structures that will destroy us the minute they catch fire."

She went on to the hushed listeners. "This is not the first time girls have been burned alive in this city. Every week I must learn of the untimely death of one of my sister workers. Every year thousands of us are maimed. The life of men and women is so cheap and property is so sacred! There are so many of us for one job, it matters little if one hundred forty-six are burned to death."

Then came more impassioned accusations. "We have tried you, citizens; we are trying you now, and you have a couple of dollars [more than $100,000 had been collected for relief] for the sorrowing mothers and daughters and sisters by way of a charity gift. But every time the workers come out in the only way they know to protest against conditions which are unbearable, the strong hand of the law is allowed to press down heavily upon us. Public officials have only words of warning to us—warning that we must be intensely orderly and must be intensely peaceable, and they have the workhouse just back of all their warnings. The strong hand of the law beats us back when we rise. . . . I can't talk fellowship to you who are gathered here. Too much blood has been spilled. I know from experience it is up to the working people to save themselves. And the only way is through a strong working-class movement."

Schneiderman's angry speech, her *j'accuse*, had quieted the well-heeled audience. Like Émile Zola with the Dreyfus Affair, Schneiderman had made her listeners feel embarrassed and guilty about the Triangle Fire and implicitly threatened them with militant action. With her impromptu little speech, she showed how angry people were and challenged those in authority to change, to make the necessary reforms. Her speech shows the power of words, words that live in the mind.

Galvanized by Schneiderman's tongue-lashing, shamed by her accusations of inaction, and worried what would happen if they failed to act, the mass meeting got into gear. The Triangle Fire became a rallying cry for political change. Before then, workplace reforms seemed a faraway hope or mirage. The Triangle Fire inspired hundreds of activists across New York state and the nation to push for fundamental reform.

Reformers also must have been concerned about the possibility of violence if changes were not made. Some saw the Triangle Fire, with its huge death toll, as a form of industrial warfare. The fire's 146 fatalities were far more than the seven civilians killed by British soldiers in the 1770 Boston Massacre that helped spark the American Revolution. Bomb throwing and the word *revolution* had already been bandied about. Bitter class antagonisms festered. Government response up to that point had been ineffective. The Progressive movement showed that intellectuals were transferring their allegiance away from social Darwinism and laissez-faire capitalism. The seeds of revolution were planted and growing in fertile soil.

With unions and employers unable to resolve health and safety issues, serious reformers had to overcome their dislike of practical politics and turn to government. The opera house meeting decided to urge then-Governor John Dix to form a Bureau of Fire Prevention and to appoint a permanent nonpolitical committee made up of distinguished citizens to propose and obtain new factory safety laws. The governor told them to see Al Smith and Robert Wagner, the leaders of the state legislature.

Frances Perkins, as secretary and chief lobbyist of the newly formed Committee on Public Safety, then went with two other committee members to meet with Al Smith, a meeting that made all the difference. To counteract the power imbalance between employers and employees, Perkins and her colleagues would soon discover how to use the levers of government to accomplish her goals. They would be taught by a master of the legislative process.

In 1911, Al Smith, thirty-eight years old, was already an influential member of the New York State Assembly. That year, Democrats obtained a majority of seats in the assembly, and Smith became majority leader. Smith had a personal connection to the Triangle victims. Many of them lived in the same Lower East Side district he lived in and represented. Right after the fire, Smith went to the places where the victims lived, the tenements, and consoled the families, telling them how sorry he was. It was an experience Smith never forgot.

Smith told Perkins and her two colleagues to form a legislative commission. "If you want to get anything done," Smith said, "you got to have this, a legislative commission. If the legislature does it, the legislature will be proud of it, the legislature will listen to their report, and the legislature will do something about it. But if the governor appoints the commission, they will just give it the cold shoulder; they won't pay any attention to it."

The next stop was Robert Wagner, thirty-three-year-old majority leader of the state senate. Wagner, who also grew up poor, agreed with the idea of a legislative commission. Together, Smith and Wagner submitted a resolution to the legislature to appropriate funds for an investigative commission. On June 30, 1911, only three months after the fire, the resolution offered by Smith and Wagner passed, and the legislature approved an appropriation for establishing the Factory Investigating Commission (FIC). Governor Dix signed off on it.

The FIC consisted of nine members appointed by the senate, assembly, and the governor, although in reality Governor Dix allowed Perkins to pick many members of the FIC. The members included Smith, Wagner, and the labor union leader Samuel Gompers, among others. Smith had himself appointed to the FIC so he could see with his own eyes what was going on. Such personal involvement had a profound impact on both Smith and Wagner and in time the whole country.

Of the elected officials on the FIC, half were Democrats and half Republicans. "That is the way to do it," Smith told Perkins, "because you can't get these laws through unless you have, you know, the support of both of them."

Being members of the FIC gave Smith and Wagner their education in achieving social justice by legislation. They got a firsthand look at industrial and labor conditions from which they never recovered. Politicians and other members of the FIC accompanied investigators on unscheduled surprise visits to factories so they could see for themselves what was going on. As a result, they realized something could be done about such unsafe working conditions.

Wagner became chairman, and Smith vice-chairman. With such powerful legislators in those positions, the chances rose that laws proposed by the FIC would be enacted. It was one of the most important positive consequences of the Triangle tragedy.

The scope of the FIC's work was broad and unprecedented. It was not limited only to fire safety in the New York City garment industry. On the contrary, the FIC studied the whole state, a vast range of trades, and a number of issues including low wages, long hours, child labor, and unsanitary conditions. They were also charged with recommending "such new legislation as might be found necessary to remedy defects in existing legislation, and to provide for conditions at present unregulated."

In a word, the FIC was unique. It was both a fact-finding and law-making body. It could investigate, hold hearings, and report on a wide range of conditions. Because of the influential legislators on the FIC, the new laws it recommended stood an excellent chance of being enacted, which gave the FIC a de facto legislative function.

The extreme breadth of the FIC's investigation broke new ground. As the FIC noted in its Preliminary Report, New York became the first state to authorize a general investigation of the conditions in manufacturing establishments within its borders. Other states had appointed commissions more limited in scope. In this sense, New York led the way.

The FIC's Preliminary Report found that "In the matter of industrial production, we are still under the sway of the old 'laissez-faire' policy." Although the country had made "great strides" in industrial organization, our industrial system had "practically neglected . . . the human factor." This "utter neglect" jeopardized the "care, health and safety" of employees.

The FIC operated for four years. In the first year, the commission heard 222 witnesses, including factory workers, public officials, union leaders, and civic leaders. It drafted fifteen bills, all of which were eventually passed into law. The new laws included banning smoking in factories, requiring mandatory fire drills, requiring automatic sprinklers in buildings above seven stories, and requiring factories to register so inspectors could check them.

After giving special attention to the problem of fire hazards, the FIC recommended the formation of a Bureau of Fire Prevention to investigate whether proper safety measures were in place, such as functioning smoke alarms, fireproofed materials and stairwells, automatic sprinklers, and fire drills. After its first year, the FIC issued a three-volume preliminary report that included transcripts of testimony on safety and working conditions.

During its second year of operation, the FIC proposed twenty-eight bills. They concentrated on mandating more stringent requirements for new and old buildings as well and requiring all factory doors to be unlocked during working hours. The new laws required fire escapes, improved building exits, occupancy limits, adequate washing facilities, clean drinking water, sanitary and ventilated restrooms, and a doctor's certification that a child laborer was over the age of fourteen. In the next year, the FIC spent more time on working conditions, fireproofing requirements, fire extinguishers, alarm systems, better eating facilities, and limited hours of work for women and children.

In 1915, after four years of work, the FIC ended its investigations. It produced thirteen volumes of reports and recommendations, including drafts of bills. All told, thirty-six of the bills it proposed were enacted into law by the state legislature. In its final report, the FIC said the new laws "marked a new era in labor legislation in the State of New York. It placed New York in the lead in legislation for the protection of wage earners."

These laws served as models for other states and ushered in what is known as "the golden age of remedial factory legislation." In 1911, ten states passed mandatory workers' compensation laws. The New York reformers earned a well-deserved reputation as progressives toiling on behalf of the working class. In Frances Perkins's words, "The extent to which this legislation in New York marked a change in American political attitudes and policies toward social responsibility can scarcely be overrated."

The turning point also involved a more subtle and less recognized but no less important aspect of the transformation that took place: the beginning of the welfare state. More clearly in retrospect, turning to government to solve labor problems was a new approach. Previously, workers (through unions) and employers dealt with their issues themselves without government being part of the process (except when employers called on the government to use force or the courts). Progressive reformers had brought about this change, taking power away from the parties themselves. Now it was the duty of a strong state, not just the union, to protect innocent workers. The FIC brought in the state and significantly reduced the role of laissez-faire economics in labor relations.

Another part of this shift to a welfare state can be seen in the two stages of the FIC's work. In the first phase, the FIC focused on workplace safety issues such as fire safety, hygiene, sanitation, and accidents. The FIC's second stage concerned social welfare issues such as minimum wages, maximum hours, old-age benefits, and disability and accident insurance. As a result, one might say the welfare state was born in New York.

The Triangle Fire transformed politics and the law. The result of these changes made New York into a beacon of labor reform, a big bright light in the darkness. New York became an example, an inspiration, and an encouragement to labor reform.

Smith and Wagner became popular liberal heroes. Smith's role in creating the FIC helped propel him a few years later to the governorship. Judicial rulings more favorable to labor and its regulation started to be handed down. Wagner became a US senator and leader of the New Deal.

Publicity surrounding the Triangle Fire and the changes in New York law even pushed workplace safety issues onto the national stage. In 1911 the American Society for Safety Professionals came into existence. In 1913 the National Safety Council was formed. In the same year, Congress and President Woodrow Wilson established the US Department of Labor, whose mission was, among other things, "to foster, promote, and develop the welfare of the wage earners of the United States, to improve their working conditions."

Meanwhile, as a result of her energy, commitment, and good judgment following the Triangle Fire, Frances Perkins was herself moving onto bigger stages. In 1918, Al Smith, by then New York's governor, appointed Perkins as the first female member of the New York State Industrial Commission. In 1926, she became chair of that commission. In 1929, Governor Franklin Roosevelt appointed Perkins as New York State Industrial Commissioner. In 1933, Roosevelt, who was by then president, appointed her as secretary of labor. She was in a position, with the help of some of the same people who midwifed the new laws growing out of the FIC, to generate similar laws during the New Deal.

Frances Perkins was a little like Moses at the biblical burning bush. According to Exodus, Moses saw a "bush that burned with fire, and the bush was not consumed." "I will now turn aside," said Moses, "and see this great sight, why the bush is not burnt." The Bible says God told Moses, "I have seen the affliction of my people . . . and have heard their cry by reason of their taskmasters, for I know their pain and I have come down to deliver them." It was a transformative moment for Moses, one of personal growth and spiritual rebirth, calling him to a special purpose, that is, leading the Israelites out of Egypt and lessening their afflictions.

The Triangle Fire was Frances Perkins's burning-bush moment. The Triangle building burnt but was not consumed. It still stands and today houses the biology and chemistry departments of New York University. Like Moses, Perkins "turned aside" to see this "sight," and it inspired her to devote the rest of her life to lessening the afflictions of American workers. In a sense, we are all Moses and should turn and look at the Triangle Fire with new interest and new eyes.

March 25, 1911, the day of the Triangle Fire, was, according to Perkins, "the day the New Deal was born." She went on to say the New Deal "was based really upon the experiences that we had in New York State and upon the sacrifices of those . . . who died in that terrible fire on March 25, 1911." That terrible March day is often referred to, and not just by Perkins, as a decisive "turning point" in a long struggle to reform working conditions and workplace safety.

From her catbird seat in Roosevelt's cabinet, she led the charge on a national level to bring about the reforms needed as a result of the Triangle Fire and the workers' struggles that preceded it. Her fingerprints are on all the pieces of New Deal legislation that helped working people.

In 1932, even before Roosevelt was president, Congress passed the Norris–La Guardia Act, which has three main parts. First, it made yellow-dog contracts, in which employees agree as a condition of employment not to join a labor union, unenforceable in federal courts. Second, the act stopped federal courts from enjoining nonviolent labor disputes. And third, the Norris–La Guardia Act gave employees "full freedom of association" to form unions without employer interference.

In June 1933, after Roosevelt entered the White House, Congress passed the National Industrial Recovery Act (NIRA). It allowed the executive branch to regulate prices and wages to avoid unrestrained economic competition, which many thought produced the Great Depression.

Section 7(a) of the act, drafted by Wagner, stated, first, that "employees shall have the right to organize and bargain collectively through representatives of their own choosing, and shall be free from the interference, restraint, or coercion of employers." Then section 7(a) banned yellow-dog contracts outright. Although the Supreme Court ruled the NIRA unconstitutional in 1935, section 7(a) was unaffected.

Barely forty days after the Supreme Court's decision, Congress passed, and President Roosevelt signed, the statute that has become the premise for United States labor law, the National Labor Relations Act, also known as the Wagner Act for the senator most responsible for its passage. Robert Wagner's experiences with the FIC and constant reminders from Frances Perkins kept Wagner focused on the lives of working people.

The animating idea behind Wagner's statute was to correct the inequality of bargaining power between employers and employees. Unlike employers, employees did not have full freedom of association or true liberty of contract. To accomplish this goal of correcting the inherent imbalance, the statute in essence allows labor to create countervailing power to deal more fairly and effectively with employers. Thus section 7 of the Wagner Act reaffirmed that employees have the right to join a union, engage in collective bargaining, and engage in other collective action, such as strikes. The new law also finally banned "company unions," which had been used by employers for decades to frustrate union organizing and workers' hopes. The Wagner Act also established the National Labor Relations Board to define unfair labor practices, to create rules for collective bargaining, and to pursue labor violations.

Also in 1935, Congress passed the Social Security Act, which provides unemployment insurance, social security taxes on payrolls, and paychecks for the elderly. In 1938, Congress passed the Fair Labor Standards Act. This law included the familiar eight-hour day and forty-hour work week and a national minimum wage with time and a half for overtime, and it also banned oppressive child labor.

In 1970, Congress created a new agency, the Occupational Safety and Health Administration (OSHA). OSHA's mission is to "assure safe and healthy working conditions for working men and women." In 2021, on the anniversary of the Triangle Fire, OSHA acknowledged its linkage to that fire by issuing a statement saying its "mission and the safety of every worker are more important now than ever. We can't wait for another workplace crisis to remind us of the important work that needs to be done now. OSHA works hard every day to assure that no worker has to face the same terrible working conditions or tragic end as in that garment factory."

Despite the great progress that has been made in improving workplace safety since the Triangle Fire, problems remain. The velvet revolution accomplished much, but it is incomplete. Marginalized groups still exist. Poverty-stricken men, women, children, and immigrants are still vulnerable to bad working conditions. Occasional workplace fires still occur.

The Triangle Fire is an example of how tragedy can be a beneficial change agent. Traumatic, disruptive events—such as the Triangle Fire—can make people think society has stopped working properly. When that happens, cultural change occurs, and culture shapes action. Before disasters occur, societies generally resist change. Before societies will abandon their usual preference for the familiar, a sufficiently dramatic event must occur that forcefully demonstrates the need for change. A disaster is such an event. Disasters threaten order and stability, which societies value highly. After a disaster, opportunities for reform exist. People, organizations, and legislatures can bring about pioneering change or reform in a fraction of the time normally required to pass similar legislation.

The story of the Triangle Fire is an enlightening, powerful, and inspirational true story about how a disaster can help to create a more just society. Those who died in the Triangle Fire are still remembered as martyrs in the cause of workplace safety. The Triangle Fire was a central moment, a hinge in the history of the labor movement. It was a catalyst for decisive, revolutionary change.

March 25 is American labor's Memorial Day in honor of those who died in the Triangle Fire. More than a hundred years later, the story of the Triangle Fire still resonates and draws people together.

The Triangle building still stands, and its victims live on in both memory and the raft of workplace safety laws prompted by their sacrifice. The impact of the Triangle Fire has grown; the ghosts of those victims rose, phoenix-like, to goad their fellow New Yorkers to address the woes of factory workers and to lobby successfully for better working conditions. The Triangle Fire burns forever in people's hearts and minds as a symbol and a transformative event that called the people of New York and their elected representatives to the special purpose of improving workplace safety.

In this sense, we should now try to understand the great importance as well as the paradox of how the disastrous Triangle Fire had a revolutionary impact that benefitted society in the long run. It was a quiet revolution that brought America closer to realizing the pursuit of happiness envisioned for each American in the Declaration of Independence.

9

Black New Yorkers in World War I
The Extraordinary Achievements of the 369th US Infantry, the Famous "Hellfighters," 1916 to 1918

Anthony F. Gero

Adapted from Anthony F. Gero, "Black Soldiers of New York State: A Proud Legacy" (SUNY Press, 2009).
  For many years, Black people experienced prejudice and discrimination even in New York. A regiment of Black New York soldiers, informally called the "Harlem Hellfighters," proved their courage and determination in World War I but experienced prejudice even after returning home. As the afterglow of their wartime service faded, they were relegated to second-class status as soldiers and confined to segregated units even in New York. New York eventually did better. It became a leader in combatting prejudice, enacting a civil rights law in 1945, making it the first state in the country to adopt legislation prohibiting discrimination in employment based on race, creed, color, and national origin. The armed forces were desegregated at the federal level in 1948. But the story of the "Harlem Hellfighters" is a reminder that sometimes revolutionary-scale change is slow to arrive.

☙

The year 1916 would be monumental for Black New Yorkers' participation in the state's National Guard. The United States was a racially charged nation, primed to explode in violence against African Americans. For example, in 1916 a Black man had been publicly burned to death in Waco, Texas, while in South Carolina a mob had killed another African American. In Mexico, due to United States intervention, twenty-two troopers of the US Army's famous Black Tenth Cavalry had been killed in action. Meanwhile, the European war threatened a neutral America, especially Imperial Germany's use of the U-boats in the Atlantic Ocean. When the United States Congress finally declared war in April 1917, many African Americans believed that this new conflict provided a chance to finally end the color line.

After war was declared, wild rumors swept the South of a German plot to set the country ablaze with Black insurrections, helping to fuel a new round of lynching and terrorism. Yet, despite this increased violence at home, many in the African American communities felt that a foreign war was "a God-sent blessing" that would allow them to earn the respect of white Americans through valiant wartime service. As a result, the Central Committee of Negro College Men was formed and met with President Wilson to establish special officer-training camps for Black officers for the proposed Black regiments then being raised in the expanded federal army.

In April 1917 there had been only 750,000 men in the Regular Army and National Guard, of whom approximately ten thousand were African American. Segregated National Guard units existed in Illinois, Ohio, Maryland, Connecticut, Massachusetts, Tennessee, the District of Columbia, and now New York, but many Southern states had eliminated their former Black National Guard units, which had been created in the 1870s and maintained into the 1890s. Black Americans could not join the United States Marine Corps, and their role in the US Navy was limited, although by war's end thirty Black women served as naval yeomanettes. Other Black women served in the American Expeditionary Forces (AEF) as secretaries or YMCA workers; some women of color even served as nurses.

When the national draft was instituted, although 10 percent of the total population was Black, 13 percent of the draftees were men of color. One out of five African Americans who were sent to France saw combat, while in the AEF, as a whole, two out of three white soldiers took part in battle. Although drafted in greater numbers in proportion to the general population, Black soldiers would see limited combat because of racial attitudes in the army.

Commissioned Black officers experienced discrimination also because, traditionally, officers are viewed as "officers and gentlemen," so elevating

African Americans to such rank ran against segregationist practices. In the years before the war, Black Americans had been barred from officer-training programs; however, pressure from the Black community help set up a segregated officers' school in Des Moines, Iowa, from June to October 1917, from which at least eighteen New Yorkers graduated. Regrettably, this school commissioned few senior officers above the rank of captain, which would impact the 367th and 369th Infantry Regiments from New York state.

The AEF's commander, General John J. Pershing, had experience with Black soldiers in the American Indian Wars and the Spanish-American War and generally favored their valor. In his memoirs, Pershing stated, "My earlier service with colored troops in the Regular Army had left a favorable impression on my mind. In the field, on the frontier and elsewhere they were reliable and courageous. . . . Under capable white officers and with sufficient training, negro soldiers have always acquitted themselves creditably." While hardly a ringing endorsement of Black soldiers, nonetheless, it does show Pershing's willingness to use African American soldiers, whose reliability and courage he did not question. The latent prejudice of the caveat—if led by "capable white officers and with sufficient training"—would grow even stronger in the United States Army from 1917 into 1918.

As units for the AEF were shipped overseas, the governments of Great Britain, France, and Italy put enormous pressure on the United States to fill out their hugely depleted forces by using American soldiers as replacements in their armies. Neither did the Allies desire to have a separate United States Army on the Western Front. Although some individual Black New Yorkers did enlist in the British Army, the British, although wanting American soldiers, were not receptive to African American troops. The French, meanwhile, had had good experiences with their Black West African troops so were more positive toward American Black soldiers. As a result, a compromise was brokered wherein four regiments of African American soldiers would be "temporarily" assigned to the French. One of these regiments was the Fifteenth, now redesignated the 369th United States Infantry.

At the same time, German propaganda was directed toward Black Americans. According to John Hope Franklin, the "Germans made the most of these unfortunate incidents in their efforts to spread anti-war sentiment among the Negroes. They kept a careful record of lynchings and the attacks of whites on Negroes and urged Negroes to desert the struggle out of which they were gaining nothing." German efforts to create disloyalty among the Empire State's Black citizens had grown so bad that on March 15, 1918, a New York citizen, Trumbull White, wrote George Creel, federal director of the Committee on Public Information, that rumors in circulation in Harlem among the families of Black servicemen then in France were creating morale problems. German agents had promised that if Germany won the war, a Southern state would be set aside as a Black colony, exclusively for African Americans' use as "a Black Republic."

Overseas, German propaganda was directed toward Black soldiers as well. Leaflets were dropped trying to convince them not to fight. One "captured" leaflet's message was very direct:

> To the Colored Soldiers of the United States Army
> Hello boys, what are you doing over here? Fighting the Germans? Why? Have they ever done you any harm? Of course some white folks and the lying English-American papers told you that the Germans ought to be wiped out for the sake of humanity and Democracy. What is Democracy? Personal freedom; all citizens enjoying the same rights as the white people do in America, . . . or are you not rather treated over there as second class citizens? Can you get into a restaurant where white people dine? Can you get a seat in a theatre where white people sit? . . . And how about the law? Is lynching . . . a lawful proceeding in a Democratic country?

Amazingly, despite all of these efforts to disrupt the loyalty of America's Black soldiers, their morale stayed high and their service to the war effort did not slacken. Although it would be hard to ignore the racial discrimination of the period, Black New Yorkers remained loyal and served with distinction in France.

Prior to World War I, an African American New York City resident, Charles W. Fillmore, had attempted to have a Black National Guard unit raised in the Empire State. Legislation was authorized on June 2, 1913, but no unit was formed. By 1916, in part due to the exploits of the Regular Army's Tenth Cavalry in Mexico, and with the election of New York Governor Charles S. Whitman, the Fifteenth Infantry (Colored) Regiment was created, and William Hayward was appointed colonel. Two hundred New York City residents, many with previous military service in the United States Regulars, immediately joined and provided the nucleus of the regiment's enlisted men.

Hayward, son of United States Senator Monroe L. Hayward (Nebraska), had been a colonel in the Second Regiment of Infantry, Nebraska National

Guard, and a Republican Party leader by 1908. He moved to New York in 1910, opened a law office, and became active in politics. In 1914 and 1916 he had managed Whitman's campaign for governor and, during Whitman's second term, was public service commissioner, when he was invited by the governor to organize the Fifteenth Regiment.

White and Black men made up the Fifteenth Regiment's officer corps. Many of the white officers were from National Guard units, eager to serve with this new Black regiment. Some were Ivy Leaguers from Harvard, Yale, and Princeton, and one, Captain Hamilton Fish Jr., was the son of Hamilton Fish II, speaker of the New York State Assembly, and grandson of President Grant's secretary of state, Hamilton Fish. Some paid the ultimate sacrifice in war, such as Second Lieutenant Ernest H. Holden, killed in action while serving with the regiment in France.

The African American officers were from the "intellectual minority" of New York's Black community. Lieutenant James Reese Europe organized the regiment's band and was the only Black officer left in the regiment by 1919. Another was Captain Napoleon Bonaparte Marshall, in civilian life a lawyer, seriously wounded in fighting at Metz, and transferred out of the unit in March of 1919, under AEF directives against Black officers. The others were Captain Charles W. Fillmore, First Lieutenant George W. Lacey, and Second Lieutenant D. Lincoln Reid.

From its formation, the Fifteenth had a regimental élan. Several nicknames attached themselves in those early days, such as the "15th Heavy Foot" and "The Traveling 15th." Major Little referred to the men of his battalion as his "men of bronze."

In 1917 the Fifteenth was low in the ratio of officers to enlisted men, usually numbering two officers per company, instead of the six called for. It had supply problems with a shortage of uniforms, equipment, and weapons, although this was not an uncommon problem in America's expanding military forces. The regiment had no armory to drill in either, which hindered its training. Lastly, no Regular Army noncommissioned officers from the Twenty-Fourth or Twenty-Fifth Infantry Regiments were transferred to train the Fifteenth; neither were any Regular Army officers assigned until after the Armistice in 1918.

The regiment went into camp at Peekskill, New York, in May 1917, where the men were given additional rifle practice while also assuming guard duty at various military and civilian sites in New York and New Jersey. It was at this time that the regiment suffered its first war casualty when one of its soldiers was killed by a pro-German sympathizer. In another incident, guards of the Fifteenth captured a German spy for whom "the secret service men had been looking for some time" (Little 1936, 46).

While the regiment chafed at performing guard duty, other units from New York state were being sent off for further training, before being sent overseas. Formed from infantry regiments of New York's National Guard, the newly created Twenty-Seventh Division left to go to South Carolina, after a grand parade down Fifth Avenue, but the Fifteenth was not allowed to go with them. When the Sixty-Ninth Infantry of the New York National Guard paraded in New York City as a part of the Forty-Second Division, nicknamed the Rainbow Division, the Fifteenth was not allowed to join in. Colonel Hayward was informed that the reason why his regiment was not being sent with the Rainbow Division was because black was not a color of the rainbow. His response reportedly was "Damn their going-away parade! We'll have a parade of our own when we come home—those of us who do come home—and it will be a parade that will make history!" (Little 1936, 47). Hayward kept this promise, in grand style, when the regiment returned in February of 1919.

Colonel Hayward now made the rounds of the military authorities, determined to get his regiment sent for more training. Ultimately, his efforts resulted in a directive that ordered the unit to Spartanburg, South Carolina, "to be attached to the 27th Division, for training" (Little 1936, 47).

At Spartanburg, several incidents illustrate what lost opportunities the service of the Fifteenth with the Twenty-Seventh Division could have provided. While the regiment tried to be cordial with the local community, racial incidents developed. One of the more potentially dangerous involved Lieutenant Europe and Noble Sissle of the Fifteenth Regiment, who had been turned away by a local hotel manager as they tried to buy a newspaper. When several white soldiers tried to intervene on behalf of these two soldiers, Europe commanded that all soldiers present should leave before violence broke out. Since other merchants near the Twenty-Seventh Division's training camp also refused to sell goods to men from the Fifteenth, in a dramatic show of support, men from the Twelfth and Seventy-First Regiments confronted those merchants and demanded that they either serve these Black New Yorkers or close up their shops since "they're our buddies. And we won't buy from the men who treat them unfairly" (Little 1936, 57).

Unfortunately, local tensions would not subside. On October 24, 1917, the Fifteenth Regiment was ordered shipped to France and was detached from the Twenty-Seventh Division. As the regiment headed out of camp to the train station, a spontaneous event happened that, if depicted in a movie, might be seen as a Hollywood moment. As Major Little (1936, 71) wrote, "as we swung along through the camps of the Twelfth, Seventy-first and Seventh Regiments, in the course of our hike, thousands of brave New York lads of the 27th Division lined the sides of the road-way, and sang us through, to the tune of *Over There*."

What a grand sight that must have been, and what a lost opportunity it was, since the Fifteenth was no longer attached to the Twenty-Seventh Division. What might have been achieved socially if the Fifteenth, as a National Guard regiment, had stayed with the Twenty-Seventh Division? Would their service in combat in France with the Twenty-Seventh Division have helped to create a "band of brothers" that would have had profound influence in the postwar years? I believe it would have, but the opportunity was lost.

With the Fifteenth now headed for France, the question was what to do with them once there. General Pershing had three Black National Guard regiments available to him then, but he could not, or would not, integrate them into any white divisions. Therefore, he formed these three regiments into the Ninety-Third (Provisional) Division and attached a regiment of drafted Black soldiers to complete its infantry structure. At first, Pershing wanted to use this division as Service of Supply troops or Pioneer Infantry, but under pressure from the Allied governments for American combat soldiers, he assigned all four Black infantry regiments to the French Army.

The assignment of these regiments let Pershing resolve two problems. First, it allowed him to placate an Allied power; second, it helped remove a potential racial problem in the AEF. In his postwar memoirs, Pershing (1931, 1:291) stated, "Very naturally, the four infantry regiments of the 93rd Division (colored) which had been assigned to the four French Divisions, were anxious to serve with our armies, and I made application for the organization and shipment of the rest of the division, but to no purpose and these regiments remained with the French to the end." When the Fifteenth arrived in France, it was redesignated as the 369th United States Infantry and would not serve with the American AEF in combat. Rather, the regiment would be assigned to the French Army, but not right away. At first, the 369th spent months on fatigue duty at Saint-Nazaire, at times harassed by army officials who had "the spirit of the South," as one Black officer put it (Barbeau and Henri 1974, 106).

Local French authorities were different in their attitudes toward these African American soldiers, however. As one Black officer of the 369th wrote, "I have never before experienced what it meant to be really free, to taste real liberty, in a phrase to be a man." The humane reception by the French toward the 369th and other Black American troops would eventually bring about a secret and infamous AEF memo to the French government to stop such civil and humanitarian fraternization.

With regard to the regiment's history in France, several other events must be considered. The first deals with the band tour, ordered by General Pershing as a morale booster for American servicemen, which helped make the 369th's band world famous but which showed the latent discrimination in the AEF. Originally raised by Lieutenant Europe, the band had recruited musicians all across the nation and had obtained thousands of dollars in donations; even John D. Rockefeller had given $500. Before it was ordered on tour, it was rumored Lieutenant Europe was not going to be allowed to command because a white officer had to be in charge. Colonel Hayward would have no part of this indignity and managed, somehow, to have Europe stay in command during the tour.

The second event involves the regiment's élan, as seen by the actions of the regimental color bearer Sergeant Cox of Major Dayton's battalion. As recounted in Little's history (1936, 183–84), the regiment had entered the Zone of the Advance in April 1918. When enemy planes were sighted on the march to Remicourt, the unit was ordered to halt, fall out, and lie down, which was promptly carried out, except for by Sergeant Cox, who bore the colors and who stood on the road. When questioned as to why he refused cover, he stated that he had promised Governor Whitman, back at the Union League Club presentation of the regiment's colors, never to let the flag droop in the dust.

On March 13, 1918, the 369th moved from Saint-Nazaire and went to Givry-en-Argonne to become a part of the Sixteenth Division, Eighth Corps, Fourth French Army, commanded by General Gouraud. In April 1918 the regiment's reserve battalion was paraded before French General Gouraud, a Battle of Gallipoli veteran. On this day, Sergeant Cox, without orders, dipped the National Standard in salute to General Gouraud, feeling that George Washington would have done the same. Like the Fifty-Fourth Massachusetts Regiment in the Civil War, the actions of the 369th would be reported in the press, which only heightened the 369th's élan. In mid-April the regiment was given responsibility for a 4.5 kilometer sector of the front. Although the 369th was less than 1 percent of the American troops then in France, at this time it held 20 percent of all territory assigned to American combat forces.

Late in May an event happened that would gain the regiment a combat reputation. While on observation-post duty in the frontline trenches, Henry Johnson and Needham Roberts were attacked by enemy trench raiders. Despite suffering severe wounds, Johnson, a former railroad porter from Albany, drove off the Germans in fierce hand-to-hand combat. In the process he killed at least four of the raiders and may have wounded upward of thirty more. For his brave deed, the French would award him the Croix de Guerre with golden palm, signifying extraordinary valor.

After the action, Major Little and a group of others explored the site. From their inspection, it was obvious that Johnson had killed one of the raiders by thrusting his bolo knife through the man's pillbox cap and into his skull. Major Little retrieved this grisly souvenir, and when French General Le Gallaes, chief of training, asked for the cap, it was sent to him. The general then had it framed and hung on his office wall as an example of a "*bon soldat.*"

The American press also reported on this fight. In *The Saturday Evening Post*, Irwin Cobb curiously wrote, "Because we had grown accustomed to thinking of our negroes as members of labor battalions working along the lines of communication-unloading ships . . . but that the heroism of Johnson and Roberts would mean that n-i-g-g-e-r will merely be another way of spelling the word American" (qtd. in Barbeau and Henri 1974, 117). *The Boston Post*, in an article entitled, "No Color Line There," stated, "In the service of democracy there is no such distinction. General Pershing's late report places in the roll of honor the names of two soldiers of one of our colored regiments, Privates Johnson and Roberts. . . . This is the true ideal of service. No matter what the color of skin, we all recognize it."

In Pittsburgh, the *Chronicle Telegraph* quoted General Grant on the positive fighting ability of the Civil War Black soldiers and then made note of their service in the American Indian Wars and Spanish-American War. The *Chronicle Telegraph* went on to say, "And now in France they are living up to the reputation they have won on other far distant fields." The exploits of Johnson and Roberts were also favorably reported on in the *Buffalo Evening News*, *Brooklyn Times*, *The New York Times*, and the *New York Tribune*.

Others of the 369th proved equally as valiant. In June 1918 the Germans launched their last great Western Front offensive. Helping to stop that enemy drive was Sergeant Bob Collins, who earned his Croix de Guerre for effective handling of his machine gun during heavy enemy action. Private

Jefferson Jones, who manned an observation post during the same assault, sent a message back to his company officer, "I am being fired upon heavily from the left. I await your instructions. Trusting these few lines will find you the same, I remain yours truly, Jefferson Jones" (Barbeau and Henri 1974, 117).

By July, the 369th was attached to the French 161st Division, Fourth French Army, and was assigned to the front-facing Butte de Mesnil, near Minancourt. After coming under heavy enemy fire while advancing more than six miles, the regiment got a newly coined motto, "God Damn, Let's Go." When ordered by French General Foch to attack an enemy bulge at the Marne, a Black officer of the 369th, Captain Charles Fillmore, was officially commended in this attack for his calm leadership under fire.

As a final example of the regiment's bravery and the cost of modern warfare in human terms, the Distinguished Service Cross was won by Corporal Elmer Earl of Company K and Private Elmer McCowin, also of Company K. In describing how he won his medal, Corporal Earl stated, "We had taken a hill Sept. 26 in the Argonne. We came to the edge of a swamp when enemy machine guns opened fire. It was so bad that of the 58 of us who went into a particular strip, only 8 came out without being killed or wounded. I made a number of trips out there and brought back about a dozen wounded men" (Sweeney 1919, 152).

As a result of these and other brave deeds, the Germans began referring to the soldiers of the Ninety-Third Division as "*blutlustige schwartze Manner*," or "bloodthirsty black men." The enemy also referred to the Black American soldiers as "Hellfighters," which pleased the French, who had nothing but praise for these American regiments assigned to their formations.

Regrettably, AEF policies toward the 369th between May and November 1918 are hurtful to review. Combat soldiers were pulled out of the unit to serve as orderlies to General Pershing; pay was stopped to the entire regiment, except Company C, in May; and even special holiday rations at Thanksgiving and Christmas were not sent. Fortunately, the regimental officers did supply, from their own resources, special treats for their men on both holidays.

The greatest slight was directed, I believe, toward the five Black officers who had originally come over with the regiment. Eventually, these officers were transferred to the Ninety-Second Division (Colored) AEF, despite Colonel Hayward's valiant efforts to keep them. He wrote,

> In August, 1918, the American Expeditionary Force adopted the policy of having either all white or all colored officers with

Negro regiments, and so ours were shifted away (though Lieut. Europe was later returned to us as bandmaster, whereas he had been in the machine gun force before). Our colored officers were in the July fighting and did good work, and I felt then and feel now, that if colored officers are available and capable, they, and not white officers, should command colored troops. . . . There is splendid material there. I sent away forty-two sergeants in France who were commissioned officers in other units. I would have sent others, but they declared they'd rather be sergeants in the Fifteenth than lieutenants or captains in other regiments. (Scott 1919, 213)

When the Armistice came, *The Stars and Stripes* had this to say about the 369th: "The farthest north at 11 o'clock (when the armistice went into effect) on the front of the two armies was held at the extreme American left, up Sedan way, by the troops of the 77th New York Division. The farthest east—the nearest to the Rhine—was held by those New York soldiers who used to make up the 'old 15th New York' and have long been brigaded with the French. They were in Alsace and their line ran through Thann and across the railway that leads to Colmar" (Scott 1919, 279).

In summary, the regiment's record was outstanding. It had remained under enemy fire for 191 days, without relief, and suffered fifteen hundred men killed and wounded. Within its ranks, 171 officers and men got either the Legion of Honor or the Croix de Guerre. Several were awarded the American Distinguished Service Cross. The regiment never lost a man through capture, or lost a trench, or a foot of ground to the enemy. It had been "first to the Rhine" and was deserving of its title of "Hellfighters."

Back home, newspapers gave the regiment glowing praise. For example, *The Literary Digest*, on January 18, 1919, in an article entitled "Croix de Guerre and Rare Praise for American Negro Troops," pointed out the 369th's valiant efforts, while the New York *Evening Sun* stated that America's Black soldiers had "proved their valor on countless occasions, and it was one of the common stories that Jerry feared the 'Smoked Yankees' more than any other troops he met."

Unfortunately, despite the 369th Regiment's great combat record, the discriminatory practices of the United States Army would not go away. No amount of blood spilled or medals won would earn these proud Black New Yorkers the equality they had hoped to gain from their service. As a final affront, when the regiment left France, Colonel Hayward did not feel it was safe for the regimental band to play as the 369th paraded down to the transport ship waiting to take them home. Only at the urging of the French port authorities and once the regiment was safely aboard did Colonel Hayward let the band give a final musical send off. In Colonel Hayward's defense, he would not let this last indignity be repeated when the regiment got home.

Once in New York City, the regiment had a parade of epic proportions. Passing by the reviewing stand on Fifth Avenue, where Governor Al Smith stood, the regiment marched in massed formation. Playing French military music that rebounded off the buildings, Lieutenant Europe's band heralded the 369th's return. When the regiment turned up Lenox Avenue at 130th Street, the band struck up the song *Here Comes My Daddy*, to the shouts of thousands of joyous Harlem spectators. Let Major Little (1936, 19) have the last word on the 369th's history:

> The 15th Heavy Foot was a self-made regiment of the American Army. It started without traditions, without education, and without friends. In all its career it never had even one thoroughly equipped first class officer as a member of the regiment. It never had an American Army instructor come from the outside to try to teach it anything, until about two months after the armistice had been signed, when, while waiting for a ship to take us home, . . . a young officer from a military school who had never heard a hostile shot, lectured the regiment upon . . . the open sight in battle.

The year 1919 was one that started with bright expectations for New York's Black community but tragically evolved into an infamous summer of nationwide racial violence. On February 17, 1919, the 369th Infantry had left Camp Upton and made its famous parade before New York City crowds, estimated at more than one million spectators. The regimental band played many French military tunes that day, such as the stirring *Marche du Regiment de Sabre et Meuse* and the *Salute to the 85th*. This music was made even more appropriate as the drum line was using four captured German instruments to help sound the cadence.

A New Yorker who witnessed this monumental parade wrote,

> I was strolling up Fifth Avenue on February 17, 1919, during lunchtime, with a lot of my buddies from school, when we heard the fanfare of bugles and the booming of drums. . . . Even before the troops appeared, the sidewalks were jammed from building

to curbs with spectators, for there was something odd about this parade right from the start. Most of the other parades came down Fifth Avenue—this was moving uptown!

We soon saw why. Back from the Rhine to get the applause of their city and of Harlem were the troops known in France as the 369th U.S. Infantry, but known in New York as the Harlem Hell Fighters.

Not till many years later would I understand the reason for the great impression of steel-helmeted power, those of us on the sidelines got that day. Shoulder to shoulder, from curb to curb, they stretched in great massed squares [and] they tramped far up the Avenue in an endless mass of dark-skinned, grim-faced, heavy booted veterans of many a French battlefield.

Then we heard the music! Somewhere in the line of march was Jim Europe and his band that the French had heard before we ever did.

On February 18, *The New York Times* commented on the regimental parade that "New York's Negro soldiers, bringing with them from France one of the bravest records achieved by any organization in the war, marched amid waving flags." Nicolas Murray Butler, president of Columbia University, praised the 369th and proclaimed, "When fighting was to be done, this regiment was there." *The Independent and Harper's Weekly* of March 1 felt that the 369th's band was one of the four best in the world, ranking with the British Grenadiers, the Garde Républicaine, and the Royal Italian Band.

A lead editorial in the *New York Tribune* of February 14 expressed words of hopeful insight on what the 369th's arrival home should have meant:

> The bas-relief of the Shaw Memorial became a living thing as the dusky heroes of the 15th cheered the Liberty statue and happily swarmed down the gangplank. Appropriately the arrival was on the birthday of "revered Lincoln," and never was the young and martyred idealist of Massachusetts filled with greater pride than swelled in Colonel Hayward as he talked of his men the best regiment, he said, with pardonable emphasis, "of all engaged in the great war."
>
> These were men of the Champagne and the Argonne whose step was always forward; who held a trench ninety days without relief [and] who won 171 medals for conspicuous bravery First

class fighting men. Hats off to them! The tribunal of grace does not regard skin color when assessing souls.

A large faith possesses the Negro. He has such confidence in justice, the flow of which he believes will yet soften hard hearts. We have a wonderful example of patience that defies discouragement; the "Soul of Black Folks!" When values are truly measured some things will be different in this country.

These contemporary samplings make clear that a mood of optimism and pride cut across the city's ethnic groups. For many, it was hope that the service of the 369th would make a difference in the Empire State in civil rights for years to come. At least that was the mood in February 1919.

The spirit of that February was not just confined to New York City. In Buffalo, similar parades to honor returning Black veterans took place, and when the Ninety-Second Division landed in Hoboken in March 1919, New York City did not forget that command for another grand parade was held to honor these Black servicemen. In Chicago, the famous 370th Regiment (the old Eighth Illinois, National Guard, an all–African American regiment) paraded before jubilant crowds downtown and into the South Side. Yet, once the parades were over, Black veterans, like their white counterparts, had to try and adjust to civilian life. It soon became obvious, in the next few months, that the Black veterans of the Great War had come home to a nation that, in many regions, still drew the color line as hard as it had ever been drawn before.

While the normalcy of civilian life tried to return to the nation, as the Black poet and writer James Weldon Johnson wrote, for African Americans those summer days turned into "The Red Summer." Many cases of racial attacks, lynchings, mob violence, and major riots, especially in Washington, DC, and Chicago, broke out, many specifically directed toward Black veterans. Seventy lynchings were recorded in that summer, and more than ten victims were ex-servicemen. These atrocities motivated President Wilson to speak out. The president condemned these horrendous acts, especially toward Black veterans, since "our Negro troops are but just back from no little share in carrying our flag to victory."

In New York state these racial attacks, along with the national resurgence of the Ku Klux Klan, were especially condemned by the Black media. For instance, in the *New York World*, an editorial writer commented on the issue of war, race, and nationalism with words of such poignancy that they bear careful reading:

War has sinister markings of its own, won in all sufficiency. There is no room for the color line across its torrid front. Such is the thought that suggests itself afresh, for there have been other events calling to mind the gallantry of our colored troops. The Negro has WON his decorations in France on "soldierly merit." He has WON at the same time by the manifestations of his courage, and his devotion and his loyalty, a more even chance in American life. And the victory should be made sure. We do not intend now that we have served the Nation in every war of the Republic [but] to further accept the indignities heaped upon us as a race without a solemn protest to every sense of conscience and right in America.

There is one thing this World War had done. It has lifted the Negro problem out of the provincialism of America into the circumspection of the civilized world. We purpose to carry our cause into the open forum of the world. We purpose to let the world know that the soldiers that brought glory to the American flag in the fields of France are denied common courtesies in too many cases when they return home. . . . We make this appeal to the world in no sense of disloyalty to our Nation. We do it because we are loyal. We will be heard. We will not be lynched and robbed and hedged about without a solemn protest. We do not plead for pity or sympathy. We want what we have earned by every rule of the game.

However, the "rules of the game" had not been changed substantially by the dedicated service of Black soldiers in World War I. In Washington, DC, a weakening Wilson Administration could not stop Congress from discouraging new Black immigrants to the city, bills to segregate its streetcars were introduced, and even prestigious Howard University was threatened to have its appropriations cut. Outside government, the newly formed American Legion, at its 1919 national convention, set no nationwide standards for the admissions of Black veterans. Instead, it permitted each state group to make its own rules, which generally excluded Black veterans from Legion posts. As a result, Black veterans formed the League for Democracy to protest this side-stepping act of the American Legion and its Jim Crow attitudes. In 1924 the Lincoln Legion was formed, headed by George W. Lee and Charles P. Howard, graduates from the Fort Des Moines officer-training school, to help promote the record of Black servicemen in World War I and to fight for the inclusion of African Americans in the armed services and related organizations.

Internationally, the secret AEF Headquarters wartime memo, which had directed the French not to treat American Black soldiers with more fairness and equality than they experienced at home, was exposed to the French Assembly. In July 1919 an indignant member of the French National Assembly, René Boisneuf, read the AEF document to the French legislature. The French Assembly promptly passed a resolution condemning this AEF memo and expressed confidence that any infraction committed within French territory against Black US troops would be punished, no matter who the perpetrators or who the victims were. Just to what extent this reaction exemplifies the values of liberty, equality, and fraternity or represents wounded French pride need not be discussed, but it is interesting to note that when the French war painting *Le Pantheon de la Guerre*, by Pierre Carrier-Belluse and Auguste Francois Gorguet, was unveiled, troops of all the Allied countries were represented, except for one notable exception—the omission of America's Black soldiers.

Two other examples typify what transpired in this era. In 1924 a federal bureau decided to dedicate a plaque inscribed with the names of its servicemen killed during the war. Unfortunately, when unveiled, there were two tablets, one for the white soldiers and a separate one for the Black servicemen. In 1930 Congress approved funding to send Gold Star mothers to Europe who wanted to visit their sons' graves. Thousands accepted, but when Black mothers who wished to join were told they were to be assigned segregated quarters, trains, and hotels, several refused, saying they wished "to remain at home and retain our honor and self-respect." Others did go, but they went under segregated arrangements.

In June 1925, letters began to appear in New York City papers defending the Black soldier, especially the Black veterans of New York. On June 12, Republican Congressman Hamilton Fish Jr., formerly a major in the 369th, sent a letter to the *New York Tribune* defending the Black soldier. On June 14, Captain L. Edward Shaw, also of the 369th, wrote the *Tribune*. In his correspondence, he stated, "Since the war I have been answering constantly one question: 'What do you really think of the colored soldier?' My answer has always been, and still is, 'If there were another war tomorrow I should try to go with the colored troops.'"

Captain Shaw, in that same letter, went on to note one of those events in history that gives us much insight into life, but, if not recorded by a contemporary, can be lost. Shaw stated that on June 14, 1925, at three o'clock, on Edgecomb Avenue and 136th Street, a square would be dedicated for a soldier born and raised in New York City: Private Dorrance Brooks, 369th Infantry. Private Brooks had been killed in action in the Argonne-Meuse while leading forward remnants of the Third Machine Gun Company after its four white officers, two Black sergeants, and two corporals had been killed or wounded. Shaw felt that Dorrance's act of bravery from "a humble colored soldier from New York city honored the valor of the American colored soldier and stand as a permanent answer to all uniformed or prejudiced critics of the colored soldiers." Today, this historic square is maintained as part of the Greenstreets program in New York City.

Despite the "Red Summer" of 1919 and the designs of the Regular Army in the early 1920s, the 369th Infantry was still active in the Empire State. On September 6, 1924, the regiment was reorganized and federally recognized, with headquarters in New York City. Between 1924 and 1934, a regimental armory was built and expanded, and by War Department General Order 11, issued in 1924, the 369th was allowed the following decorations: "French Croix de Guerre with Silver Star, World War I, Streamer embroidered Meuse-Argone." As a result, after 1924 the Empire State would not degenerate into its former exclusiveness, and the 369th would be maintained in the military structure of the state.

As to the hopes for African Americans' World War I service ending segregation and racial attacks in the United States, by 1930 not much had been accomplished. As Emmett Scott stated in 1933, "as one who recalls the assurances of 1917 and 1918 . . . I confess personally a deep sense of disappointment, of poignant pain that a great country in time of need should promise so much and afterwards perform so little." During the last half of the 1920s and into the early 1930s, the 369th was, apparently, the only National Guard regiment of African Americans allowed in the Empire State. Other segregated units were not created in places like Buffalo or Syracuse, which might have been able to maintain such units. The 369th Regiment's continuation did provide some military opportunities for Black New Yorkers, especially when it went to the State Camp at Peekskill, but the regiment was watched carefully by Regular Army authorities, and its existence was tenuous. On one level, the Empire State was one of only two states, the other being Illinois, that had complete regimental-size African American National Guard units in the period. More could have been accomplished on the national and state levels for African Americans to join the National Guard, but it was not to be.

10

How New York Women Won the Vote, 1917

Susan Ingalls Lewis

Adapted from Kathleen M. Dowley, Susan Ingalls Lewis, and Meg Devlin O'Sullivan, editors, "Suffrage and Its Limits: The New York Story" (SUNY Press, 2020).

The struggle for woman suffrage in New York state began in 1846, when six women from Jefferson County signed a petition to the men participating in the state constitutional convention that year asking for inclusion of women's right to vote in the revised constitution. It gathered momentum at the famous Seneca Falls convention in 1848. Elizabeth Cady Stanton, Susan B. Anthony, and other leaders kept campaigning for suffrage for the rest of the nineteenth century and the opening years of the twentieth.

But the struggle did not conclude with success in New York until 1917 and at the national level until 1920. It was a new generation of twentieth-century leaders who got New York and national woman suffrage accomplished. Carrie Chapman Catt was the most prominent and effective suffragist of the time. She led the two-million-strong organization National American Woman Suffrage Association and key organizations in New York.

In 1917, the successful campaign used tactics from earlier years but also took to the streets with massive suffrage parades and appeals customized to various neighborhoods and language and ethnic groups in New York City and emphasized women's work for the war effort in World War I. Catt's tactics paid off—the legislature approved woman suffrage in 1917, and, as Catt had *predicted, the victory in New York in turn helped lead to national victory three years later.*

☙

What part did New York state play in the national woman suffrage victory of 1920? Why was New York (rather than another eastern state) the first to confirm voting as a woman's right? Which individuals, organizations, and tactics were most responsible for the New York suffrage victory, and why did the New York referendum to give women equal suffrage pass in 1917, not earlier or later?

With the centennial of the woman suffrage victory behind us, we are in a good position to reevaluate both the movement and its interpretation. Numerous commemorations, new research, and an explosion of publications celebrated the hundred-year milestone of this major political achievement. What can we conclude from this wide range of efforts?

For many years, the most common characterization of this long-sought, dramatic expansion of voting rights in New York and across the nation was that women had been "given" or "granted" the vote. Men, in their beneficence, it seemed, had suddenly decided that half the population should be included in the great American experiment of democracy. Reality, as revealed by scholarly research, was quite different—women (and their male supporters) made a huge effort, lasting over seventy years, to "win" the vote. Yet it is not true, as advertised on the cover of an otherwise excellent PBS documentary, *The Vote* (2023), that women "took" the vote. They had no legal means to do so. In order to attain this basic right, male voters had to be convinced that women actually wanted the elective franchise and that they deserved it. This was the essential struggle.

The woman suffrage victory in New York represents a vital turning point in national as well as state history. Many Americans still assume that all women in the United States were given suffrage at the same time in 1920, as the result of the Nineteenth Amendment to the US Constitution. Actually, women achieved voting rights across the nation in an irregular, piecemeal fashion. As early as 1869, the territory of Wyoming allowed women to vote, and, when it became a state in 1890, it was the first state where women could vote in all elections. By the time the federal suffrage amendment passed, fifteen states (including New York) already had full suffrage, and many others had partial suffrage—that is, women could vote in some but not all elections. (For example, in some states or localities women could vote in presidential elections, primaries, municipal elections, or school board elections.)

Unfortunately for our understanding of how the suffrage movement finally reached its goal, public events, reading lists, and press coverage often continue to focus on the period before 1917—hailing the contributions of Susan B. Anthony, Elizabeth Cady Stanton, Sojourner Truth, and Matilda Joslyn Gage (all of whom were dead for more than a decade before 1917). To understand the who, what, when, why, and how of the New York state suffrage victory, we must analyze the successful tactics of 1917 and the individuals who shaped that triumph.

Anthony, Stanton, Truth, and Gage were all important leaders who ultimately failed to see their dreams fulfilled—not for lack of energy or compelling arguments, but because they were unable to convince most male legislators and voters of their period that women needed, wanted, or deserved the vote. Instead of retracing old ground and reinscribing former myths, we now have an opportunity to stress the importance of those who were truly central to New York's final suffrage victory, individuals like Alva Vanderbilt Belmont, Harriot Stanton Blatch (Elizabeth Cady Stanton's daughter), Carrie Chapman Catt, Mary Garret Hay, Rose Schneiderman, Mary Burnett Talbert, Vira Boarman Whitehouse, and many, many more. This essay proposes to delve into recent historical material and complicate arguments that remain underexplored in public and political discourse.

Background: The Progressive Era and the "New Woman"

The period from 1848 to 1920 is commonly known as the "first wave" of the feminist movement, but that term gives a false impression of unity. What was called the "woman movement" by its participants changed over time in both focus and tactics, and within each period members often differed about which goals to pursue and how to accomplish them. The Progressive Era (1890 to 1920) was a pivotal period for many reform movements. The suffrage victory was clearly a product of this historical moment, which was distinguished by remarkable female activism and major changes in American women's roles and expectations as well as dramatic developments in the women's movement itself.

In 1890, the two major women's rights organizations (the National Woman Suffrage Association and the American Woman Suffrage Association), which had split the movement after the Civil War, united to form the National American Woman Suffrage Association (NAWSA). Under the leadership of Susan B. Anthony, NAWSA became the major US organization promoting women's voting rights. At the same time, woman suffrage also gained support from other reform groups, most notably the Women's Christian Temperance Union (WCTU) under Frances Willard. Temperance, a movement devoted to limiting or abolishing the consumption of alcohol in the United States, was supported by many women because male alcoholism was associated with spousal abuse and the neglect of family responsibilities. The support of the WCTU was a huge advantage for NAWSA in terms of membership (far more women had been committed to temperance than to suffrage), but it stiffened the resistance of liquor manufacturers and immigrant communities to women's voting rights, and it alienated suffragists committed to the separation between church and state, like Matilda Joslyn Gage.

Another vital development of the 1890s was the emergence of a new model of ideal womanhood, the so-called "New Woman." In direct contrast to the archetypical Victorian maiden or matron, the "New Woman" was independent, educated, self-supporting, and often professional (Patterson 2005, 2008). The typical "New Woman" fought for suffrage but also for many other causes. She might live and work in a settlement house (like Jane Addams), serve as a factory inspector and expose the plight of child laborers (like Florence Kelley), advocate for birth control (like Margaret Sanger), campaign against lynching (like Ida B. Wells), organize women workers (like Rose Schneiderman), head a woman's association dedicated to racial uplift (like Mary Church Terrell), invent the field of public health nursing (like Lillian Wald), or simply work as a journalist, writer, artist, teacher, lawyer, doctor, or minister. "New Women" (who included those of diverse races, religions, classes, and national origins) were at the heart of the Progressive movement, in New York state as well as across the country. As the first generation of women's rights trailblazers reached the end of their lives, leadership of the suffrage movement passed to such "New Women," born shortly before, during, and after the Civil War and often college-educated professionals.

Interestingly, the argument for women's voting rights also changed somewhat between the mid-nineteenth and early twentieth centuries. Anthony, Stanton, and Gage, as well as Truth and other suffragists of color like Frances Harper, had argued that women deserved the vote as a human right. The "New Women" of the early twentieth century added the justification that women deserved the vote not just because they were like men but also because they were different and represented different ideals that would benefit society and the state. These women argued that females were by nature more caring, more peaceful, more nurturing, and more selfless than men and that they would bring better values into the political process, reforming government for men, women, and children alike. Yet suffragists never abandoned the issue of equality; instead of seeing these arguments as contradictory, they saw them as mutually supportive.

This generation of suffrage activists not only brought fresh energy to the movement but devised tactics that were more public, dramatic, and commercial than the speeches, petition drives, and educational efforts of the past. Unafraid of "displaying themselves" (despite public criticism) on street corners and in parades, they harnessed the power of the mass media and advertising to support their cause.

Analysis of the 1917 Victory: Who Was Responsible?

Historical interpretations of the 1917 New York state referendum victory depend largely on one's understanding of how social movements succeed. Emphasizing Stanton's and Anthony's leadership, for example, suggests that the most important aspect of any movement is its beginning, giving the greatest credit to the pioneers. Another way to understand a movement is by giving credit to "baby steps," assuming that each and every tiny step on the road to woman suffrage was equally vital. A third school of interpretation focuses on major turning points that pushed the movement forward at a particular time. Still other analyses stress underlying factors, big changes in society and economics that made progress possible. And, of course, within each interpretative framework historians may disagree about which pioneer, which small step, which factor, or which turning point was most decisive.

Even historians focusing on the 1917 victory rather than the early battles of the mid-nineteenth century differ in their interpretations. In their meticulously researched and well-argued *Women Will Vote: Winning Suffrage in New York State* (2017), Susan Goodier and Karen Pastorello stress that the New York state victory required contributions from a wide variety of individuals and groups. Women in upstate rural New York, African American women, immigrants, and suffragist men, they believe, must be considered alongside the more famous white, middle- and upper-class activists in New York City. Goodier has depicted the coalition of activists in the movement as a "rich beautiful fabric that comes together that takes decades, and all kinds of people—black, white, Italian, Jewish, you name it." In *Suffrage and the City: New York Women Battle for the Ballot* (2019), Lauren Santangelo has argued that it was votes from the city, particularly from immigrant men, and most strongly Jewish socialist men, that made the difference in 1917.

Happily, the last decade has produced several intriguing, though differing, analyses. Johanna Neuman, author of *Gilded Age Suffragists: The New York Socialites Who Fought for Women's Right to Vote* (2017), gives credit to elite, stylish women who took suffrage from "frumpy to fashionable." Neuman reasons that such wealthy and influential women provided the first celebrity endorsement of a political campaign in the twentieth century, sparking renewed interest in the cause. In *Funding Feminism: Monied Women, Philanthropy, and the Women's Movement, 1870–1967*, Joan Marie Johnson (2017) stresses the importance of money to support all the apparatus (travel, publicity, staffing, communications) required by a modern movement. Brooke Kroeger's 2017 monograph *The Suffragents: How Women Used Men to Get the Vote* argues that the New York–based Men's League for Woman Suffrage played a vital role in the suffrage victory, both in New York state and nationally. Others, including Ann F. Lewis, an experienced political strategist and major collector of suffrage memorabilia, insist that the New York leaders of NAWSA, particularly Carrie Chapman Catt and Mary Garrett Hay, deserve credit for the political campaign that delivered the vote. Some historians prefer to highlight the contributions of little-known figures like Maud Malone, "General" Rosalie Jones, Mabel Lee, Gertrude Bustill Mossell, and Sarah J. S. Tompkins Garnet, believing that credit for a movement that depended on diverse contributions must be shared among many. This position certainly has merit as a corrective to an exaggerated focus on leaders alone—but the press, politicians, and public hardly seem aware of Catt or other major suffrage leaders of 1917 (with the possible exception of Alice Paul). In classrooms and public talks, one rarely finds anyone who has ever even heard Catt's name.

THE ARGUMENT FOR CARRIE CHAPMAN CATT

The debate over who deserves credit for the suffrage victories is not new. Even at the time of the suffrage victories in New York state (1917) and nationally (1920), suffragists themselves disagreed about who deserved recognition. Naturally, most felt that their own organization, tactics, and leaders were most responsible. For example, according to Neuman (2017, 141), Vira Boarman Whitehouse (president of the New York Suffrage Association from 1915 to 1917) "was widely credited with the win" and was hailed at the time as "the brilliant field-general of the New York State Suffrage army." Whitehouse was one of the wealthy socialites whose importance Neuman argues has been neglected in histories of the movement. Yet, as Neuman notes, Catt gave "no credit" to Whitehouse in her own 1923 memoir, insisting instead that Mary Garrett Hay was responsible for the victory in New York City, which swung the state. Neuman suggests that it was her personal relationship with Hay that made Catt neglect Whitehouse's contributions (after Catt's second husband's death, she and Hay lived together as partners and are even buried together). But "Mollie" Hay did head the New York City Suffrage Party and was even known by reporters as "The Big Boss."

Of course, this was a mass movement, and every individual's story is valuable. Yet to allow the name of Catt, the most prominent suffragist of the time—and leader of an organization (NAWSA) two million strong—to be forgotten, ignored, or even downplayed in our analysis seems counterproductive. If we are to learn from the ultimate success of this movement, we should look closely at its political campaigns, strategies, and tactics as well as the individuals who developed and enacted them.

Catt's return to the United States in 1913 (from working for woman suffrage abroad) marked a turning point in both the New York state and the national movement. No eastern states allowed women to vote in statewide or federal elections. In 1914, Miriam Leslie, a businesswoman and publisher, bequeathed to Catt a million dollars for the woman suffrage cause. Although the terms of the will were disputed, and Catt received only part of the original bequest, this infusion of funds greatly assisted the campaigns that followed.

1915: The Road to Victory Begins with Loss

The background to the 1917 New York state victory includes a heartbreaking 1915 loss in four eastern states: New York, Massachusetts, New Jersey, and Pennsylvania. The Empire State Campaign of 1913 to 1915 had been spearheaded by a unified committee with Catt as its chair, coordinating the efforts of the New York State Suffrage Association, the Woman Suffrage Party (WSP) in New York City with Hay as chair, and other groups. The Political Equality Association, headed by the multimillionaire Alva Vanderbilt Belmont, and Harriot Stanton Blatch's Women's Political Union (an organization that focused on working women) organized separately. African

American women organized and advocated in their communities through groups such as the Colored Woman's Suffrage Club of New York City, led by Annie K. Lewis, Brooklyn's Equal Suffrage League with Verina Morton-Jones as president, and the Empire State Federation of Women's Clubs, founded and presided over by Maria Coles Perkins Lawton of Harlem.

Under Catt's Empire State Campaign, the state was divided into twelve regional districts, 150 assembly districts, and 5,524 election districts, each with its own chair, leader, or captain. According to Elisabeth Israels Perry's (2019, 29) *After the Vote: Feminist Politics in La Guardia's New York*, "the WSP under Hay's direction [in New York City] held 60 district conventions, 170 canvassing suppers, 4 mass meetings, 27 canvassing conferences, and a Carnegie Hall convention," and by Election Day it had "held over 5,000 outdoor meetings, 660 indoor meetings, and 93 mass meetings." The campaign engaged both paid organizers and as many as two hundred thousand volunteers. Goodier and Pastorello (2017, 165) discovered that over ten thousand New York City public school teachers joined the Empire State Campaign, some giving up their summer vacations to "get down into the trenches."

According to the suffragist Gertrude Foster Brown's retrospective analysis "A Decisive Victory Won" of 1940, the campaign was organized around the insight that "it was useless to invite men to come to suffrage meetings. Where they were not opposed, they were indifferent, or considered the whole business a joke. Since they would not come to women, suffragists had to go to them wherever they were" (NAWSA 1940, 109). An estimated seven million leaflets went out in twenty-four languages. Whitehouse chaired the publicity committee and raised money to fund its efforts. Stamps, posters, playing cards, pins, paper cups, and fans were produced and distributed around the state. Suffrage workers "approached letter carriers, conductors, motormen, subway workers, elevated guards, street sweepers, ticket sellers, firemen, and police" (Goodier and Pastorello 2017, 164). Hay "directed her followers to identify voters in every possible profession, craft, or job—from barbers to firemen, street cleaners to bankers, factory workers to clergy—and to create special days for each group" (Perry 2019, 29). Catt urged her volunteers to reach out to members of all religious affiliations, including Catholics and Jews. When Lyda D. Newman, an African American hairdresser and inventor, opened a suffrage headquarters in Manhattan, Hay sent representatives to coordinate activities with the WSP. Press and publicity departments not only spread the news of suffrage activities but "undertook the task of creating news . . . and of seeing that anti-suffrage articles and editorials were adequately answered" (NAWSA 1940, 111). Meanwhile, Blatch and her independent Women's Political Union ran a separate campaign with its own speakers, meetings, and events.

The 1915 campaign culminated in a massive "Banner Parade" in New York City led by Catt and an international delegation of suffragists. More than a million spectators watched tens of thousands of women, who all wore white but marched amid a rainbow display of banners. Women "from every class and walk of life, and from every kind of employment were in line . . . all united for a common cause" (NAWSA 1940, 110). On the day of the vote, six thousand women were on hand as poll watchers, having been carefully prepared for this work by training schools.

Yet despite all the organizing, publicity, speeches, meetings, parades, rallies, and mementos distributed, regardless of the anticipation experienced by the suffragists themselves, woman suffrage was defeated in all four eastern states, even losing in New York City by more than eighty thousand votes. Two nights after the defeat, Mary Garrett Hay chaired a meeting at Cooper Union to kick off a new campaign. The women immediately raised $100,000 in pledges and transformed the multiple organizations that had made up the Empire State Campaign into the New York State Woman Suffrage Party. Catt was chosen as its chair. Because suffragists aligned with Catt refused to accept defeat, the failed campaign of 1915 actually provided a strong starting point for the successful battle of 1917. In contrast, this loss caused Blatch to give up on the New York campaign, merge her organization (the Women's Political Union) with Alice Paul's Congressional Union, and focus solely on the federal amendment. Neither Blatch nor Paul was active in New York's 1917 drive, as both were working from Washington, DC.

1917: On to Victory

Although Catt had planned to head the 1917 New York campaign, she was unable to fulfill that role because the following month she was drafted to take the place of Anna Howard Shaw as president of NAWSA. At the emergency convention she called in September 1916, Catt revealed that NAWSA would now take the federal suffrage amendment as its major goal (previously, the group had put most of its effort into state-by-state campaigns like New York's, while Alice Paul's Congressional Union had favored a federal strategy). Catt's "Winning Plan" proposed that NAWSA focus simultaneously on state campaigns where success was likely and on a federal campaign, using state victories to influence and propel the eventual passage of a federal amendment. In 1916, NAWSA also convinced both the Republican and Democratic Parties to include woman suffrage in their platforms.

With the advent of World War I in 1917, Catt set aside her lifelong pacifism and announced that NAWSA would work for a second goal: the war effort. Catt had learned a lesson from Stanton and Anthony, who had put their push for women's rights on hold during the Civil War and subsequently regretted that decision. As she later wrote, "the suffragists of 1917 had read history; they knew how prone men were to accept the help of suffragists in the hour of need and forget women's case for suffrage in the hour of calm. So while working loyally and energetically as special war organizations in support of the needs of the nation in its time of crisis, the New Yorkers did not lay aside their campaign" (Catt and Shuler 1923, 295).

1917: Effective Tactics

Though scholars may disagree about whom to credit for the ultimate suffrage victory, they all agree that new twentieth-century tactics making the struggle far more visible clearly made an important difference in the campaign. Flamboyant, popular events raised the profile of the movement and made it seem to be everywhere at once. With suffragists out in the streets of the cities and on the roadways of the state, they engaged in numerous spectacles in support of the vote. In 1913, for example, Long Island suffragist Edna Buckman Kearns used a wagon called "The Spirit of 1776" to attract attention and promote the cause, arguing against women's "taxation without representation."

The suffragists' use of urban space in general, and office buildings in particular, enhanced their prestige. As the historian Jonathan Soffer has written of NAWSA, "A board of wealthy women devoted themselves full time to the cause, creating a well-financed lobbying, advertising, and political organization. Headquartered on two floors of a Manhattan skyscraper, they deployed the latest technologies to persuade Americans of women's right to vote and maintained transnational and intercontinental connections. They transformed NAWSA into a modern, urban, cosmopolitan lobby for women's right to vote." ("Modern Women Persuading Modern Men," 2012). But how did this new visibility and publicity translate into an electoral victory? Ann F. Lewis argues that we need to examine the suffrage victory as a political campaign, not only as a social movement. The movement provided an underlying groundswell, but the campaign delivered the votes. Lewis asks,

"What did they *do* to win?" Based on campaign literature and memorabilia (Lewis has collected over twelve hundred items, which are viewable online), her analysis considers their message, methods of persuasion, and ability to turn out the vote. At the center of her argument (made in her speech "Messaging, Media, and Motherhood: Political Strategies of the New York Suffrage Campaign" in 2018) is the leadership of Carrie Chapman Catt and her longtime friend and companion Mary Garrett Hay.

In promoting the importance of Catt, Lewis focuses on such political moves as her 1914 address to the Federation of Women's Clubs, convincing this powerful group (long ambivalent about voting) that it was women's "duty" to fight for and use the ballot for good. Equally important was Hay's triumph in convincing Tammany Hall (the Democratic Party machine that controlled so many immigrant votes in New York City) to drop its opposition to the New York referendum. Her tactic was to appoint the wives of Tammany officers to positions of responsibility within the campaign.

Santangelo also recognizes the importance and innovation of Catt and NAWSA's contributions to the New York campaign by "mapping" the suffrage campaign's organization onto existing assembly districts. She argues that the suffragists came to see Manhattan as a "richly textured map" that could be understood as a collection of communities and neighborhoods. Goodier and Pastorello (2017) also give Catt appropriate credit, but their work sets her contributions in the context of a much larger movement as they strive to encompass decades of activism across the state.

1917: Why New York?

New York, the first state east of the Mississippi to support full suffrage for women, was targeted by suffrage leaders for two reasons: because the size of the New York delegation to Congress made it the most powerful addition to the suffrage cause and because it seemed most possible to pass a suffrage referendum in such a progressive state. That is, suffragists deliberately chose to focus on New York as the most important, and the most likely, state to win in 1917.

The political process by which women suffragists attempted to win the vote was a referendum to amend the New York State Constitution. In order to get the referendum on the ballot again, as they had in 1915, the measure had to be approved by two consecutive sessions of the state legislature. This meant that the referendum could be placed before the voters again quickly.

The presence of NAWSA's national headquarters in New York City and the position of Hay as chair of the Woman Suffrage Party in New York City also meant that significant political experience and focus were brought to bear on the city campaign. In addition, New York had a strong state organization prepared to deliver votes across the state. In fact, women in the other eastern states where suffrage lost in 1915—New Jersey, Massachusetts, and Pennsylvania—did not win the vote until the federal amendment passed in 1920.

Suffragists were well aware of the pivotal position New York state could play in the national campaign. As the most populous state in the union, New York had the largest congressional delegation, whose representatives and senators would be forced to support a federal suffrage amendment once women could vote in the state. A victory in New York would begin to tip the scales and create what would start to feel like inevitable momentum.

1917: THE RIGHT MOMENT

We know that the suffrage referendum failed in 1915 but passed in 1917, and that the difference in the vote came from New York City. According to Santangelo, who has studied the New York City campaign extensively, proposals from a constitutional convention held in 1915 disrupted the political landscape, leading suffragists to believe that men voted against their referendum when they went to vote against constitutional changes. In addition, she cites New York's polio epidemic of 1916 as an opportunity for Progressive women to prove their value as "municipal housekeepers." As volunteers passing out literature and assisting in inspections, women reformers demonstrated their skills and their willingness to cooperate with (for example, canceling their open-air meetings), assist, and support the government.

Along with Goodier, Pastorello, and other scholars, I would also cite the immediate decision of Catt, Hay, and other suffrage leaders not to give up or even take time out after the 1915 defeat. Instead, they built on their previous efforts—essentially creating a four-year campaign that lasted from 1913 to 1917. To win in 1917, the movement also raised significantly more money. The state campaign of 1913 to 1915 started with a fund of less than $90,000; for the 1917 campaign, Whitehouse raised hundreds of thousands of dollars from wealthy men, and there was the extra infusion of cash from the Miriam Leslie bequest.

Suffragists continued to stress the importance of canvassing (soliciting votes or opinions one-on-one) in 1917. In order to prove that women *did* want the vote and counter the anti-suffragists' argument that most women did not, they undertook a house-to-house canvas. As described by Robert P. J. Cooney Jr. (2005, 370), "to answer anti-suffragist charges that most women did not want to vote, suffragists spent more than a year going door-to-door in nearly every city and town in the state, collecting the signatures of over one million women who said that they wanted to vote. Organizers climbed thousands of tenement stairs, walked country lanes, and visited the homes of the rich and poor. The result was the largest individually-signed petition ever assembled, eventually totaling 1,030,000 names, a majority of the women in the state."

To gain the vote in New York City (where the campaign had lost by more than eighty thousand votes in 1915), NAWSA organized an "effort focused on a combination of sophisticated advertising and block-by-block organizing, both particularly geared to the city's unrivalled population density and political culture" (Soffer 2012). Immigrant working-class heroines, like the socialist labor organizer Rose Schneiderman, lobbied tirelessly to convince immigrant, working-class men to support suffrage for their mothers, wives, and daughters.

Finally, most scholars agree that the entry of the United States into World War I and NAWSA's active support of the war effort were important in turning the tide. Suffrage organizations also used the war to publicize their cause. For example, when distributing government pamphlets about conserving food or canning, suffragists were not shy about pasting on labels that promoted the suffrage referendum. In addition, suffragists lobbied soldiers and sailors at home and abroad, stressing women's support for the troops and courting their votes. Anti-suffragists, in contrast, supported the war wholeheartedly to the exclusion of their former campaigns.

On the eve of Election Day in 1917, Catt was quoted in *The New York Times* as appealing to the voters on the basis of the petition and American ideals: "Remember that our country is fighting for democracy, for the right of those who submit to authority to have a voice in their own government. Vote for woman suffrage, because it is part of the struggle toward democracy." In the end, suffrage won in every borough, and the large majority in the city overcame a slight loss upstate, so that the measure carried by more than a hundred thousand votes statewide. Suffrage won in Auburn, Binghamton, Buffalo, Newburgh, Ossining, Oswego, Schenectady, Syracuse, and Westchester but lost in Albany, Kingston, and Rochester. Hugely disappointed two years earlier, suffrage supporters were now jubilant.

On to 1920

In November 1917, as a result of multiple efforts and an army of volunteers, New York state passed the referendum supporting the vote for women in all elections. This put the power of the largest state in the union, with its congressional representatives, behind the Nineteenth Amendment. And, as the war continued, women's efforts—on the home front and overseas as drivers, nurses, telephone operators, and translators—increased, and were valued and praised. To do their part, women across the United States (not only suffragists) knit and nursed but also worked in factories and on farms, filled in as office workers and streetcar conductors, drove ambulances, and even joined the navy as clerical workers. Women, whether active suffragists or not, proved their patriotism and citizenship. Meanwhile, NAWSA kept up its pressure on Congress and the president, as did Paul's National Woman's Party.

Women's leadership, organizational skills, and contributions of time, money, and energy led to the ultimate suffrage victory in 1920, when the Nineteenth Amendment to the US Constitution was finally ratified by the state of Tennessee, the thirty-sixth state to approve—thus meeting the required threshold for state support. The amendment passed by a single, unexpected vote, cast by a young representative from East Tennessee, Harry Burn. It seems that Burn's decision to vote in favor of the amendment was largely based on a letter he had received from his mother, Febb Ensminger Burn, who wrote that he should "be a good boy and help Mrs. Thomas [*sic*] Catt." Here is yet more evidence of the importance of Catt as the national leader of the suffrage campaign.

The suffrage victory called for celebration, and New York City was the site of a series of tributes to Catt. Her train was greeted at Penn Station by New York Governor Al Smith (and a band), where Catt was almost overwhelmed by a huge bouquet. An informal parade of suffrage workers then surrounded her car and marched to a reception at the Waldorf Astoria. Catt's arrival was met with thunderous applause.

Why Not Catt?

The lack of recognition of Catt as part of both the 1917 and 1920 centennials was shocking. Although women's historians may argue that she has been given too much credit, most Americans have never heard of her. While Susan B. Anthony's Rochester grave has become a site of pilgrimage, covered with "I Voted" stickers, the Woodlawn Cemetery monument for

Catt and Hay receives little attention from the press or public—except from the LGBTQ community, who have on occasion placed Pride flags next to the stone. A recent children's book by Senator Kirsten Gillibrand, *Bold and Brave: Ten Heroes Who Won Women the Right to Vote*, does not even include Catt as one of the ten leaders, though it features other women who were not very active in the suffrage movement. Almost unbelievably, "Votes for Women" (2019), a five-hundred-piece puzzle and matching set of informational flash cards portraying forty-one US suffragists, also ignores Catt (in favor, it appears, of mixing iconic figures such as Stanton, Anthony, Truth, Lucretia Mott, Paul, and Frederick Douglass with a wide range of relative unknowns who provide both geographic and racial diversity).

During Catt's lifetime, everyone knew her name, and the press gave her credit for the suffrage victory. In 1912, her picture appeared on a full-page spread in the Sunday *New York Times* featuring her international suffrage campaign; in 1926, Catt appeared on the cover of *Time* magazine. When she died in 1947, Catt's obituary in *The New York Times* stated categorically that "when the Nineteenth Amendment was ratified, she was the national heroine of a great victory. More than anyone else, she had turned Woman Suffrage from a dream into a fact. . . . Her attack was logical, organized, and unanswerable."

Why has Catt been written out of the popular suffrage story? Her racism and anti-immigrant attitudes could be blamed, but here she was certainly no different from—no worse than—Anthony, Stanton, or Paul. We can assume that, like most Americans, white, middle-class suffrage leaders were all racists to some extent, as that term is understood today. Certainly, the evidence shows that both Catt and Alice Paul were willing to accommodate racism in order to pass the federal suffrage amendment. Famously, Paul told African American women to march in a segregated unit, at the back of the line, in her great Washington, DC, suffrage parade of 1913. Although African American leader Mary Church Terrell claimed that Catt (whom she considered a friend) showed no signs of personal racism, Catt made no effort to advocate for racial equality or even allow issues of racial justice to be discussed at NAWSA conventions. However, Catt clearly argued for "Votes for All" in a 1917 article published in *The Crisis*, the magazine of the NAACP, in which she insisted, "Everybody counts in applying democracy. And there will never be a true democracy until every responsible and law-abiding adult in it, without regard to race, sex, color or creed has his or her own inalienable and unpurchasable voice in the government." Ann Lewis suggests that Catt's lack of recognition could be because neither she nor her tactics make a good picture. Suffragists may have gone from "frumpy to fashionable," as Neuman argues, but Catt and Hay remained distinctly frumpy. Alice Paul and Lucy Burns (both included in Gillibrand's children's book) were young and photogenic, but by the time of the suffrage victory, Catt was in her late fifties and early sixties, with dark circles ringing her eyes, and dressed in shapeless cloaks and gowns. While the demonstrators of the National Women's Party could be pictured picketing the White House, being arrested, or even sitting in jail, the lobbying and strategizing sessions led by Catt just did not make for good visuals.

There are geographic issues as well. Seneca Falls and Rochester, in the western part of New York state, have actively promoted their suffrage sites to encourage tourism. New York City, where Catt and Hay organized their campaigns, and Westchester, where they lived, have numerous attractions, but little has been done to make a suffrage trail through these areas.

Perhaps most important is the fact that Catt was moderate and accommodationist, an organizer and a politician. Her "Winning Plan" of 1916 won the vote in only four years. But it seems that many feminists don't want her to have been responsible. Today's activists prefer someone more confrontational, more radical—someone more like Susan B. Anthony, who was tried for voting illegally, or Alice Paul, who insulted President Wilson in the midst of World War I. However, our presentism should not blind us to the complex realities of the past. Flawed as she was, Catt must be recognized as a successful leader. She was a consummate political organizer; she accepted that getting the win required compromises and mixed tactics as well as different approaches for different populations of voters. Neither "great men" nor "great women" should have to be perfect to be remembered.

Where Are We Now?

In conclusion, disagreements among suffrage scholars, as discussed above, are a very positive sign of the vitality of recent research into the 1917 and 1920 suffrage victories. Like all other important historical events in US history, the long struggle to end voting discrimination on the basis of sex deserves a robust historiography, including passionate debates. Historians are ready to move beyond Susan B. Anthony and other nineteenth-century heroines and to analyze the successful suffrage campaigns of the early twentieth century.

Research into this important topic is ongoing, while public appreciation of the complexity of issues surrounding the suffrage victory is only beginning. As Ann F. Lewis points out, the passage of the Nineteenth

Amendment represented the greatest expansion of suffrage in this nation's history. Surely it is time that the multiple stories surrounding the final campaign—especially the leadership of Carrie Chapman Catt—become well known to the public and students across the United States. Finally, it is vital that feminists analyze the successful tactics and strategies of the past to see if they can prove useful in addressing the limits of suffrage today.

☙

The inspiration for this essay developed out of the 2017 Women in Politics conference organized by the Benjamin Center at SUNY New Paltz and the FDR Presidential Library in Hyde Park, New York. I would particularly like to acknowledge the Eleanor Roosevelt scholar Allida Black and the political strategist Ann F. Lewis as well as the historians Susan Goodier, Karen Pastorello, and Lauren Santangelo, all of whom participated and shared their ideas. My interpretation was also informed by teaching courses on the suffrage movement, especially the research and analysis of my students in those classes.

11

Prohibition in New York City, 1920

Ellen NicKenzie Lawson

Adapted from Ellen NicKenzie Lawson, "Smugglers, Bootleggers, and Scofflaws: Prohibition and New York City" (SUNY Press, 2013).

Revolutions take many forms, including, sometimes, resistance to and eventual defeat of unpopular laws.

The Eighteenth Amendment to the Constitution, passed in 1920, prohibited the production, sale, and transportation of alcohol for consumption. But the law implementing it was widely violated. New York City became a hotbed of violation as its citizens found many ways to skirt the law or just to break it outright.

Violation and resistance to the law in New York City had a Gotham flair—pre-Prohibition organizations and gangs, seeing a new opportunity, transitioned to a new business, supplying booze to thirsty New Yorkers who wanted it. A variety of gangs controlled the trade on the Lower East Side, Irish Americans were prominent on the West Side and in the Hell's Kitchen area, and another gang catered to Broadway. Italian Americans had their own approach. Black New Yorkers in Harlem organized groups to meet the needs there. Speakeasies, where drinks were easy to get if you knew where to look and the right code word, sprang up all over the city.

Public opposition elsewhere in the nation grew, in part because of news coverage of violations of the law by "organized crime" and "the Mob" in New York City (and a few other cities, especially Chicago). The result was national *repeat under President (and former New York governor) Franklin D. Roosevelt soon after he took office in 1933.*

༄

When the Eighteenth Amendment became law in January 1920, Americans were obliged to abstain from alcohol for purposes of personal enjoyment. Production of alcohol for religious, medicinal, military, or industrial use remained legal. Poisonous or nauseating agents called denaturants were added to industrial alcohol to discourage diversion. "Near beer," made by producing real beer and then weakening its alcoholic content, remained legal. The production, transportation, and sale of liquor for personal use was forbidden.

The US Senate spent thirteen hours debating the merits of the Prohibition Amendment before approving it. The House of Representatives considered and approved it in eight hours. The Wartime Prohibition Act, in effect at the end of World War I, enabled many Americans to view Prohibition as merely an extension of a wartime measure. The Progressive movement, which successfully called for an end to child labor; the regulation of food, meat, and drugs; and the extension of the suffrage to women, was also behind passage of the Eighteenth Amendment as a solution to the perceived abuse of liquor and alcoholism. Industrialists also supported the dry amendment to ensure a sober workforce come Monday morning.

New York was one of the last states to ratify the amendment, doing so only after enough states had already approved it. The New York State Assembly voted 81 to 66 in favor, and the New York State Senate voted 27 to 24. Voters outside New York City held disproportionate power in the state legislature because the US Supreme Court did not rule that legislative apportionment must follow a "one man, one vote" principle until the 1960s. Even within the city, "dry" forces proved effective lobbyists, convincing some voters it was progressive to be for a cause that would weaken the Tammany political machine, whose organizational strength was in the city's saloons.

Prohibition began at midnight on January 16, 1920. Guests and waiters wore black at New York's Park Avenue Hotel, where liquor was served in black glasses. At midnight the ballroom was darkened, and a spotlight focused on two couples ceremoniously taking a black bottle from an open coffin in the center of the room, pouring out the last drops, and holding black handkerchiefs to their faces to wipe away tears. At Reisenweber's, a popular Manhattan dance hall, the ballroom orchestra played Chopin's *Funeral March*. One hundred cases of legal champagne were given away at midnight at the Hotel Vanderbilt while an orchestra played "Goodbye Forever."

Wealthy New Yorkers stocked their wine cellars with last-minute purchases, and private clubs rented storage space in bonded warehouses. Those who made their living from the production, transportation, and sale of liquor—captains, sailors, longshoremen, owners of saloons and bars, waiters, bartenders, and liquor store owners—wondered how they would make a living in the new era. On the other hand, urban gang leaders and their associates contemplated how to exploit what promised to be a new, highly profitable black market in liquor.

The Rise of the Mob in New York City

Most Americans are taught that Prohibition spurred the development of the US underworld, but few know exactly how this happened. New York City's large liquor-smuggling syndicates emerged from well-known neighborhood gangs in Manhattan on the Lower East Side, the West Side, and Little Italy. These new syndicates diverted legally produced domestic liquor intended for industrial, military, medicinal, and religious uses. They marketed this diverted liquor, along with smuggled liquor, to thousands of bootleggers supplying nightclubs, speakeasies, drugstores, and individuals.

Lower East Side

The Lower East Side, bounded by the East River, the infamous Bowery, and Fourteenth Street, was once home to the legendary McGurk's Suicide Hall, a saloon famous for knife fights, flying glasses of ale, and a high mortality rate for those brave enough to enter and order a drink. The neighborhood housed immigrants from southern and eastern Europe crammed into six-story tenements on twenty-five foot by one hundred foot lots with little natural light, twenty-four families to a building. Reformers claimed Prohibition would clean up the Bowery, but it remained wide open for drinking: secretive passwords and cards, used at nightclubs and speakeasies elsewhere in the city, were not needed on the Bowery.

There were five hundred synagogues in Lower East Side neighborhoods to accommodate the flood of immigrants. Jewish religious wine stores remained open. The Volstead Act permitted a Jewish family to have from two to ten gallons a year for home services. (Catholic and Protestant churches also had continued access to wine for communion services.) Circumventing of Prohibition began with these wine stores dispensing far more than needed for religious purposes. The Prohibition Bureau hired Isadore "Izzy" Einstein, an immigrant Austrian Jewish postal worker from the neighborhood who understood German, Hungarian, Yiddish, Polish, French, Italian, Russian, and a little Chinese, to investigate legal shipments to religious wine stores. He discovered that two hundred people were bootlegging, including rabbis knowingly reselling wine permits, a fake rabbi serving seventy congregations, a genuine rabbi claiming a congregation ten times its actual size, and rabbis with very Irish names like Sullivan and Moriarty. Einstein also discovered "synagogues" located in apartments, butcher shops, pool parlors, and one pork store. Wine stores were then closed and wine distributed only within legitimate synagogues.

Monk Eastman, commanding fifteen hundred men in the Lower East Side's largest pre-Prohibition gang, might have been expected to dominate smuggling and bootlegging in his neighborhood, but he was murdered in 1920. He was shot in front of a café in Union Square in an altercation with a drunken "friend," an employee, ironically, of the new Prohibition agency. Instead, Arnold Rothstein, thirty-eight, black sheep of a wealthy German Jewish family from the Upper West Side and a longtime associate of Eastman, became the kingpin of smuggling and bootlegging in Manhattan. As a teenager, Rothstein worked as a translator for immigrants dealing with Tammany bosses before he ventured into gambling. A successful underworld figure by 1920, he was able to provide loans to fellow gangsters. He had a reputation for gambling on a sure thing, and smuggling liquor seemed to fit that requirement. He had advance knowledge of the rigged 1919 World Series, known as the Black Sox Scandal, and may have used winnings from that for start-up funds for smugglers and bootleggers.

Rothstein's first foray into liquor smuggling was with "Waxey" Gordon (also known as Irving Wexler), former pickpocket and labor "thug" on the Lower East Side. They met on a bench in Central Park to discuss a partnership and began smuggling to eastern Long Island by bribing a local Coast Guard commander. They had a fleet of trucks to move the liquor to warehouses in Queens. When the commander was replaced, their next shipment had to be diverted at the last minute to the West Indies and sold at cost. This was too close a call for Rothstein, who retreated into the background, leaving the field to Gordon while remaining a major financial backer. Gordon's operation flourished for the next few years.

A lumber barge, used to smuggle liquor for Gordon, was seized near New York in 1925. Captain Hans Fuhrman agreed to testify against his boss. Supposedly, Mrs. Fuhrman had asked Gordon not to employ her husband as he was an alcoholic and returned home from sea drunk and penniless. Her request was refused, and she may have tipped authorities about her husband's last voyage. Federal authorities also raided Gordon's headquarters in the midtown Knickerbocker Building, obtaining incriminating documents including maps and names of contacts. Fuhrman, kept in a guarded Manhattan hotel room, died before any trial could take place. Police ruled his death a suicide, but his wife insisted he was murdered. The US district attorney for southern New York incredulously told a congressional committee investigating Prohibition enforcement, "There was the most important witness in our first direct challenge to a big, wealthy, powerful and hitherto unmolested gang of bootleggers, and our most important witness committed suicide within three weeks." Four witnesses against Gordon were murdered before his next encounter with the law, suggesting that Mrs. Fuhrman was right.

After this close call, Gordon followed in Rothstein's steps and quit smuggling, realizing he could be convicted on the word of any one of the many captains working for him. He took his millions and invested in illegal breweries in Elizabeth, Union City, Patterson, and Newark, New Jersey; illegal distilleries in Pennsylvania and New York; and Manhattan nightclubs. His wealth increased: He traveled abroad with his family and bought a "castle" with a moat on the Jersey Shore.

Maier Suchowljansky, eighteen, and Benjamin "Bugsy" Siegel, fifteen, had the "Bugs and Meyer" gang on the Lower East Side before Prohibition. When he was nine, Suchowljansky's family emigrated from Poland to the Lower East Side. Siegel grew up "over the Bridge" in Brooklyn. At the start of Prohibition, the two teenagers worked as enforcers for other bootleggers, hijacking liquor convoys or, conversely, riding shotgun to protect the convoys. Siegel, in particular, gained a reputation as a killer for hire, supposedly going "Bugsy" in the process of murdering someone.

Arthur Flegenheimer, another Jewish teenager in 1920, began as a lone gangster, not on the Lower East Side but in the Bronx. He rose to the top in a bootleg street gang and emerged on the public scene in the late 1920s as the infamous Dutch Schultz, engaged in a bootleg war for control of the city's beer supply. He also took over the Harlem numbers racket, founded by independent Black businessmen.

Hell's Kitchen on the West Side

Hell's Kitchen, stretching from Twenty-Third Street to the Fifties in the area west of Ninth Avenue to the Hudson River, encompassed slaughterhouses, docks, freight yards, and tenements inhabited by a large number of Irish immigrants. The railroad yards were frequently targets for robbery by two large pre-Prohibition neighborhood gangs, the Hudson Dusters and the Gophers. A smuggling syndicate, rivaling Gordon's on the Lower East Side, emerged in Hell's Kitchen under William "Big Bill" Dwyer. Born and raised in the neighborhood, the Irish American Dwyer had ushered in vaudeville houses in his youth. At the start of Prohibition, he worked as a stevedore in the Longshoreman's Union. With his union contacts, including truckers, garages, docks, and warehouses, Dwyer quickly developed his smuggling syndicate. Like Gordon on the East Side, he initially relied on Arnold Rothstein for funding.

Dwyer's syndicate was expert at bribing politicians, police, and federal agents. Top associates were "Broadway Bill" Duffy, John McCambridge, Walter Weider, and Max Bernstein. The syndicate maintained a fleet of contact boats near the East River's Hell Gate Bridge and operational headquarters in Times Square. Verbal deals, in the hundreds of thousands of dollars, were witnessed by lawyers each week. When "Legs" Diamond began hijacking Dwyer's truck convoys, Dwyer cut ties with Rothstein, believing the latter was backing Diamond. This was probably when Dwyer turned to piracy on Rum Row to obtain liquor, looting at least one ship and removing $800,000 worth of liquor.

Authorities developed leads about Dwyer's smuggling syndicate about the same time they were closing in on Waxey Gordon. An armed speedboat, used to decoy the Coast Guard on Rum Row, was captured, and a William Duffy, who had a tavern on Broadway, a "wide-open barroom," proved to own the speedboat. Duffy also owned the Sea Grille on West Forty-Fifth and managed the Silver Slipper nightclub. Authorities suspected that the gang met on the second floor of Dinty Moore's Restaurant at 216 West Forty-Sixth, "late at night drinking bottled Canadian ale." The Coast Guard learned, from an aggrieved family member of a sailor on a Dwyer boat lost at sea, that John McCambridge had an office on pier 38 on the Hudson River. There "negro crews" of longshoremen bossed by "Big Riley" unloaded liquor cases into furniture vans for distribution.

The big break against the Dwyer syndicate came from a Canadian engineer on another coal ship, befriended by a supercargo named George Ferguson. The supercargo bragged that he had been hired by Dwyer at a Montreal racetrack, that Dwyer smuggled more liquor into New York City than anyone else, and that this trip would be one of Dwyer's biggest hauls. The engineer also said that a Coast Guard patrol boat met the ship at sea and escorted it into the harbor at night, with its searchlight on, all the way into the dock at East Fourth, where the liquor was unloaded onto a large truck painted with signs for a newspaper company. Before daybreak, empty of liquor but still smelling of it, the coal boat moved to the Grand Street wharf. In the morning, it was boarded by an officer from the corrupt patrol boat as if he planned to search it. He went directly into the wheelhouse for a private meeting with the captain and mate because he knew there was no liquor aboard. In the same way that Captain Fuhrman was a weak link in the Gordon syndicate, so was Supercargo Ferguson the weak link in Dwyer's.

US District Attorney Emory Buckner charged the Dwyer syndicate with conspiracy, naming more than fifty New Yorkers as defendants to be tried in two separate trials beginning the summer of 1926 in the federal courthouse in Manhattan. Evidence offered in the first trial included the Dwyer syndicate's use of corrupted Coast Guard patrol boats and bribing of federal agents with Broadway dinners, theater tickets, prostitutes, and hotel suites. Coast Guard authorities already had some idea that the agency had been corrupted. The agency believed guardsmen on patrol boats operating close to shore were susceptible to corruption because they were not as well-trained or as well-paid as career men serving on destroyers and cruisers at sea. The fact that the Dwyer syndicate deliberately painted one of its boats to look like a patrol boat, escorting ships into the harbor, might have also distorted reports of corruption.

Dwyer and his payoff agent were convicted, but everyone else in the first trial was judged not guilty. After a year in prison, Dwyer quit smuggling to become a silent partner in the Phoenix Cereal Company, the former Clausen and Flanigan Brewery at West Twenty-Sixth and Tenth. The Phoenix was to become the largest illegal brewery in Manhattan. Federal agents unsuccessfully sought four times to obtain a warrant to raid the West Side brewery. They were successful in the final year of Prohibition when they found a judge willing to say that smelling beer from the nearby street was sufficient for a warrant.

Dwyer's public partner in the brewery was Owney Madden, released from Sing Sing in 1923 after serving time for murder. Dwyer took him aboard after Madden began hijacking his liquor trucks. The top-selling beer of the brewery became "Madden's No. 1." Dwyer, Madden, and Frenchy de Magne, a third partner, bought political protection for the brewery from the West Side politician James J. Hines, who conveniently owned a trucking company probably used to distribute the beer. Then, the beer was sold to Tammany politicians, who marked it up 50 percent for resale to speakeasies and clubs in their wards and precincts. Madden soon had money to invest in nightclubs, including the Cotton Club, Silver Slipper, and Park Avenue Club, while also having interests in boxing and laundry rackets.

The city's most powerful Irish American bootleg gangster was not the least bit Irish: He was 100 percent Italian. Frank Costello, born Francesco Castiglia on the Italian mainland, immigrated as a young child with his family to East Harlem's Little Italy. He changed his name to Costello, the Irish-sounding equivalent of Castiglia, before Prohibition when he realized that the Irish controlled the police and dominated the corrupt Tammany political machine. He moved so much within Irish and Jewish social circles (his wife was German Jewish) that authorities never suspected he was Italian or had connections with Italian gangsters.

Costello took over the Dwyer operation when the latter was imprisoned. Costello's headquarters were near or in the new Chrysler Building. His syndicate owned European freighters such as the *Napoli*, *Sicilia*, *Bel Vino*, *Nonte*, and *Pollino* with foreigners fronting as owners, warehouses in St. Pierre and Miquelon in the North Atlantic, and a domestic fleet of small boats on the East River. While he was known to the public as a flourishing bootlegger, few knew he was a major figure in the underworld. Supposedly, John J. Raskob, manager of Governor Smith's presidential campaign, invited Costello to bring a fellow bootlegger to meet the candidate. Smith advised the two "bootleggers" to prepare for an end to Prohibition because he expected to win as a "Wet."

Little Italy

A major Italian American syndicate emerged in Manhattan's Little Italy. Before Prohibition, the Unione Sicilione was confined to Italian neighborhoods in Manhattan and Brooklyn. The Unione concentrated on traditional crimes such as gambling, prostitution, and protection rackets. Its headquarters were in an Italian restaurant and Marinelli's Garage, both at the intersection of Kenmare and Mulberry. Albert Marinelli, owner of a trucking business, was also a Tammany politician with two hundred thugs on call for use on election days. Here Sicilian-born Chief Joe Masseria met with top "soldiers," including Salvatore Lucania and Joseph Doto. Lucania, twenty-three, who was born in Palermo, arrived in New York City at the age of nine and grew up on the Lower East Side. He was in the pre-Prohibition Five Points Gang and, in 1922, killed Rocco Valenti, a rival to Masseria, on orders from his boss. Doto, eighteen, was born in Montemarano.

The Unione Sicilione might have become rich bootlegging and smuggling if Masseria had chosen to operate beyond Italian neighborhoods. But he was an old-time boss, known as a "moustache Pete," and did not recognize or act on the opportunity. If Al Capone and Johnny Torrio had not moved from New York to Chicago prior to Prohibition, New York City's Prohibition history might have been very different, probably more violent. On a visit to Manhattan early in Prohibition, Capone dined with friends in Little Italy, including Lucania and Doto, and challenged them to seize the day as he and Torrio were doing in Chicago. Lucania and Doto listened and began their own smuggling ring, with Masseria's blessing as long as they remained loyal. This ring included Albert Anastasia, Vito Genovese, and Thomas Lucchese as enforcers. Costello was invited and brought his smuggling experience with Dwyer's West Side gang. Suchowljansky was included because he and Lucania were friends; Siegel came into the gang with Suchowljansky. Masseria, a traditional Sicilian and also antisemitic, warned Lucania and Doto against Costello, a non-Sicilian inexplicably cozy with the police, and against the two Jews.

The first deal for the new Lucania–Doto gang was an offer from Waxey Gordon, at a Philadelphia boxing match, to sell them ten thousand dollars' worth of quality whiskey for resale. Gordon probably also directed them to Rothstein as their banker. Rothstein advised them not to dilute the liquor but market it at a high price to rich New Yorkers. Rothstein also mentored them on the proper suits for businessmen, the importance of good manners so they could relate to wealthy clients, and how to make decisions based on profitability. Costello had Americanized his name earlier, and now Lucania, Doto, and Suchowljansky Americanized their names—to Charlie "Lucky" Luciano, Joe Adonis, and Meyer Lansky.

This syndicate soon began smuggling its own liquor, first from the Bahamas—with Adonis hiring Bill McCoy, telling him there would be millions in it for him—and then from Europe. One of their earliest hauls was in an Azorean ship, which hovered off the *Lightship Ambrose* while gang members personally went out in speedboats to unload the liquor, making repeated trips to shore.

Two years later, a man unknown to the public was killed in the streets by hired gunmen in a car with Illinois license plates—New York City's first major gangland assassination. Few knew the dead man was Brooklyn's top bootleg gangster or that he also handled smuggled liquor for Capone in Chicago. New York reporters assigned to the story were surprised to see ten thousand mourners follow the man's hearse, as well as 250 cars, including thirty-eight carrying floral arrangements. The scene at Holy Cross Cemetery when a hundred men, each holding a single rose, simultaneously tossed these onto the coffin as it was lowered into the ground also amazed reporters except for those familiar with mobster funerals in Chicago. They thought this one in New York compared favorably. The corpse was Frankie Yale.

The Broadway Mob

By the mid-1920s, Lower Manhattan's three liquor syndicates, headed by Jewish Americans, Irish Americans, and Italian Americans, had relocated to Midtown near Broadway and Times Square. The Knickerbocker Building, once a fancy hotel, was now an office building known as a "warren" of bootleggers. The Prohibition Bureau, realizing the significance of Midtown to bootlegging, opened a sting operation called the Bridge and Whist Club at 14 East Forty-Fourth. This proved short-lived due to negative publicity in Congress about using government funds to run a speakeasy.

The big Midtown draw for bootleggers and smugglers was not only that it was the commercial hub for the entire metropolis but that it provided access to the banker Arnold Rothstein, "AR," "The Big Fellow," "The Man Uptown," who rarely left Midtown except for occasional jaunts to the racetracks at Saratoga. Rothstein's Midtown business operations included twenty-six holding companies, among these a bail bond business, insurance, and real estate. Most nights, he could be found at his regular table at the Midtown Lindy's Restaurant, popular with newsmen, politicians, gamblers, theater people, and con artists. At Lindy's, he made loans from $50,000 to $100,000 in cash. If a single payment were missed, he would hound the borrower or send the Diamond brothers to "enforce" quick repayment. Borrowers, both legitimate and underworld figures, were uniformly pressured to patronize his other businesses for bail funds and insurance needs and to rent rooms and apartments in his buildings and hotels at rates above the market.

A slim man of moderate height, Rothstein dressed like a conservative, successful Manhattan businessman. He pressured borrowers to patronize his Broadway tailor, who gave him kickbacks. New York City during Rothstein's "reign" undoubtedly boasted the best-dressed gangsters in America: Several owned at least one $250 suit, very expensive for that era. When gangsters gunned down a victim in an Italian American grocery store in Greenwich Village in the 1920s, onlookers described the killers to police and reporters as well-dressed men wearing pinstriped suits with fedoras pulled down low over their foreheads.

The Broadway Mob took in an estimated twelve million dollars a year. The group paid $200 a week to one hundred employees in an era when the average store clerk took home twenty-five dollars a week. In addition, $100,000 a week was paid in graft to police, federal agents, and city magistrates and other court officials. Ten percent of that, or $10,000, was dedicated to top police officers and politicians and carried to city hall in a paper bag, as if it were lunch, by an Irish American workman. The remaining millions were divided among bootleg gangsters.

Speakeasies

New York City had thousands of speakeasies, hundreds of nightclubs, and hundreds of thousands of customers drinking at home or in private parties. The *New York Telegram* published a list of places where residents and visitors could buy liquor, including dancing academies, drugstores, delicatessens, cigar stores, soda fountains, shoeshine parlors, barber shops, paint stores, fruit stands, vegetable markets, grocery stores, athletic clubs, boarding houses, Republican and Democratic clubs, and laundries. Bootleggers also had business cards, since they could not advertise in newspapers, for home and office deliveries.

Hotels in Manhattan were not usually raided or padlocked, even if liquor was consumed on the premises. They were too important to the city's tourist economy. Hotel managers disclaimed any responsibility for "private parties." When the mayor and police commissioner attended the banquet of the Police Lieutenants' Benevolent Association at the Hotel Commodore, no one was arrested although plenty of alcohol was consumed by attendees. They brought it in suitcases, handbags, and paper bags. Ten years into Prohibition, a debutante party of the Woolworth heiress Barbara Hutton was held at the Ritz-Carlton. Prior to the party, the Coast Guard began monitoring a yacht in the Upper Bay leased to Norman B. Woolworth, probably suspecting liquor was to be smuggled for the event; however, the yacht was never stopped or searched. Later, guests consumed two thousand bottles of champagne at the Hutton party, two per guest.

The first speakeasies and nightclubs opened in Lower Manhattan because immigrants in those neighborhoods opposed the Eighteenth Amendment from the outset. They also had access to liquor because the earliest smuggling syndicates were located there.

McSorley's, one of the city's oldest saloons and located in a brick tenement at 15 East Seventh, remained open throughout Prohibition. The saloon replicated the Irish saloon where the original Mr. McSorley worked before emigrating to New York in the mid-nineteenth century. Here homesick Irish immigrants could imagine that they had never left their country. During Prohibition, Barney Kelly made ale in its basement, diluting it so it could be called "near beer" yet customers could get drunk on it. The saloon was never raided because police and politicians, mostly Irish, were steady customers. Patrons of Gypsy Night Club, on Second Avenue on the Lower East Side, were from central Europe. The primary languages spoken in the club were German and Hungarian. The orchestra played ethnic music, and the walls were decorated with murals of European mountains and Romani people (often called "gypsies" in those days).

Greenwich Village, with Italian American tenements, second-generation Irish Americans, and bohemian rebels from everywhere, was connected to Midtown by subway a few years prior to Prohibition. Residents elsewhere in the city, as well as tourists and businessmen visiting Midtown, could easily travel by subway to the Village to seek out speakeasies and clubs. John and Jean's, at 139 West Tenth Street, required visitors to walk through a Franco-Italian restaurant, climb stairs to the next floor, and then descend in the back. Julius, at No. 159 on the same street, primarily served Villagers and was named after its popular bartender; here, people stood six deep at the bar despite the fact that the beer was heavily needled. Three Steps Down, a cellar club on West Eighth, was managed by Ira Gershwin's in-laws, and his brother George sometimes stopped in to play the piano.

The Fronton, at 88 Washington Place, was an elegant Village speakeasy popular with the poet Edna St. Vincent Millay, State Senator Walker, and the reporter Herbert Bayard Swope, of the *New York World*. The owners bought directly from Italian bootleggers who obtained liquor smuggled to the docks on the nearby Hudson River. When local gangs tried to shake down the two cousins who owned and operated it, a childhood friend, now a federal agent, brought five other agents to talk with the bullies and discouraged further harassment. This was the second of four speakeasies owned and managed by Jack Kriendler and Charlie Berns. Their first, begun when they were still college students, was the Red Head, also in the Village. Kriendler's widowed mother stored their first liquor supplies in her home, and his teenage brother pulled the bottles in a red wagon, camouflaged with groceries, across town from the Lower East Side to the Village. Kriendler said the Prohibition agents Izzy Einstein and Moe Smith, from their same East Side neighborhood, never raided the Red Head and sometimes stopped in for a free drink.

Chumleys, at 86 Bedford Street, attracted Village radicals and writers, including Willa Cather, F. Scott Fitzgerald, and Ernest Hemingway. The place had several entrances and exits including an underground tunnel a block away as well as a secret door behind a bookcase leading to a side alley. It was popular with radicals because owner Lee Chumley published pamphlets and circulars for the International Workers of the World, the "Wobblies." The police seemed more interested in his political activities than in the speakeasy: Chumley was never accused of violating the Volstead Act, but he was once arrested for possessing a penknife.

Don Dickerman's Pirate's Den was on Minetta Lane and later, still in the Village, on Sheridan Square. Dickerman, in his youth the "man-mangling Human Gorilla" at Maine county fairs, recreated a carnival atmosphere in his club: Waiters dressed as pirates, there was a talking parrot, and background effects of stormy winds and ships' bells were provided along with murals of pirate scenes. Using cutlasses and pirate slang, the waiters occasionally acted out scenes from *Treasure Island*.

Jo's, located in the basement of a Village tenement, was furnished with chairs, old sofas, and tables. Its patrons were young people and middle-aged single men, all interested in the topic of sex. Weekly discussions included the "social position of a gigolo" and the meaning of "sex appeal," about the time Hollywood films were introducing Clara Bow as the "It Girl." There were theatrical presentations with gay patrons giving imitations of "pansies." Lesbians and women experimenting with the lesbian lifestyle danced together in the narrow space between tables.

By the mid-1920s, speakeasies and clubs in Midtown began to surpass those in the Village in popularity because more middle-class New Yorkers, not just immigrants and ethnic groups, were beginning to scoff at the Eighteenth Amendment.

The Forty-Fourth Street Club, at 405 West Forty-Fourth Street on the third floor, was popular with musicians, music publishers, booking agents, and mail-order people and was unlike most dark and dim speakeasies because it had windows on two sides filling it with sunlight. According to one expert, "booze fights" were welcome at this place, and the beer was not needled. Some called Forty-Fifth Street itself, near Broadway, the wettest in the entire country. The first two floors at Dinty Moore's on Forty-Sixth were popular with theater people as a place to rendezvous. James "Dinty" Moore lived on the third floor and stored liquor on the fourth. At the Pansy Club on Broadway and Forty-Eighth, female impersonators and a "pansy" chorus entertained a straight crowd.

The Mansion, a speakeasy in a former banker's mansion at 27 West Fifty-First with chandeliers, drapes, and a grand staircase, admitted those with selectively given out "wooden" cards. Less elitist was the speakeasy over a garage on Fiftieth, west of Sixth, called the Old-Fashioned Club, a hard-drinking establishment popular with horse players, gamblers, the unemployed, and the Broadway fringe. When the beer was terrible, the bartender would dismiss complaints saying it came from a "bad barrel," adding that he had to serve what "they" gave him, meaning underworld bootleggers. Every third drink was on the house. The Ship Ahoy, at 52 West Fifty-First, was decorated like a tropical island, and visitors walked up a gangplank from the sidewalk to the dining room. To get into the bar, they had to say, "The captain sent me." Neighborhood residents, chorus girls, people with a walk-on part on Broadway, and gay people—called the "middle sex regiment"—patronized this club.

On one block of West Fifty-Second Street, there were thirty-nine clubs and speakeasies. Mac Kriendler and Robert Benchley, a theater critic, visited every club in one night intending to take notes, but gave up documenting after they got hopelessly drunk. The first speakeasy to open on Fifty-Second—Jean Billiams—was in a converted millionaire's mansion. Club 21, the most famous and lasting of Kriendler and Berns's speakeasies, was at 21 West Fifty-Second and known informally as "Jack and Charlie's." The Onyx, famed for appealing to musicians, was at No. 35. Here patrons descended stone steps to a basement door, walked down a short hall, climbed a dark staircase, and walked down a dark hallway to a silver door. A man behind a peephole then asked for the password, rumored to be the name of a famous jazz musician but actually the number of the New York Musicians Local. The Dizzy Club, at 64 West Fifty-Second, had a sign behind the bar with the letters "WYBMADIITY." If a patron asked what it meant, they were asked, "Will you buy me a drink if I tell you?" The club's motto was "A rolling tomato gathers no mayonnaise." Little Maison Doree, at 72 West Fifty-Second, was popular and issued cards of admission but did not demand these. In fact, the staff was suspicious of anyone who insisted on showing one. The Park Grill at No. 106 had a nonalcoholic bar at street level; those in the know went upstairs to a barred door and used a password or a special knock to be admitted to the real bar. Photos of Governor Al Smith and Mayor Jimmy Walker were posted on the walls along with a copy of an 1840s liquor license issued to Abraham Lincoln and his Illinois partners. The place was popular with Broadway people, musicians, and songwriters.

The Silver Mattress, on Park Avenue near Fifty-Third Street, offered its patrons silver mattresses placed on the floor as its seating, surrounded by silver walls and curtains. Debutantes, musicians, Broadway chorus girls, and rich Park Avenue residents loved the club. Husbands walking dogs late at night could drop in, with the dogs accommodated in a separate room, until their wives read about this in Walter Winchell's gossip columns and put a stop to it. The club was run by Belle Livingstone, who also owned and managed the short-lived Philanthropy Club and the highly successful Country Club, later called the Park Avenue Club, in the same general neighborhood. A tall, long-legged woman who had danced on Broadway in the Gay Nineties, Livingstone was a confident, heavyset individual in her fifties and reputedly acted as her own bouncer, once personally tossing out an entire squad of federal agents. Her club was raided soon after that. Captured in red satin pajamas while fleeing across the club's rooftop, she was sentenced to thirty days in the women's prison in Harlem. A young actor named Cary Grant waited outside the prison on the day of her release to escort her home in an armored car, loaned by another nightclub hostess.

Helen Morgan had several Midtown nightclubs during Prohibition. A mere twenty years old when she arrived in Manhattan at the start of the era, Morgan sang in many clubs and eventually had two named after her, Chez Morgan and Helen Morgan's Summer Home, both on Fifty-Second Street. She achieved wider fame when she sang two showstopping songs in *Showboat* when it opened on Broadway. She once spent a night in jail after a raid at one club where agents did $75,000 worth of damage. When she appeared on Broadway the following night, the sympathetic audience spontaneously gave her a round of applause, some shouting out what a shame it was that she had been arrested. When her next club was raided, she was charged in court as its owner. Government attorneys told the jury a star like Morgan had a particular "duty" to American youth to model good values and not influence them to visit nightclubs. She was found not guilty because she never owned any of her clubs; she died a decade later from liver complications.

Harlem

Harlem's population in the 1920s made it the nation's largest "Black city" within a city. Scofflaws, who began patronizing clubs and speakeasies in

Lower Manhattan and then moved to Midtown, discovered the northern part of Manhattan at the end of the 1920s during the Harlem Renaissance in the arts, music, and literature. Clubs and speakeasies were also part of the renaissance. Most white scofflaws who journeyed to Harlem were exposed to Black culture for the first time. Some Harlem clubs preferred white customers, others favored Black patrons, and a few welcomed integrated audiences.

The Cotton Club, at 644 Lexington Avenue and 142nd, formerly the site of the boxing champion Jack Johnson's Club Deluxe, was the most famous Harlem club. Owned by gangsters like Madden, the club was primarily for white patrons, admitting a few Black couples but refusing admittance to most Black people; racially mixed couples were not allowed. With Duke Ellington, Cab Calloway, and Ethel Waters performing, the club's fame spread far beyond New York City with live radio broadcasts of the music. On Sunday nights, major Broadway actors and actresses showed up at the club to take bows and, sometimes, to perform.

Connie's Inn, at 132nd Street and Seventh Avenue, was another stop for white clubbers. The entertainer Jimmy Durante called it the swankiest place in Harlem, with its classy red canopy outside, high prices inside, and waiters cautioning customers to keep bottles in their pockets and not on the floor. Brothers Connie and George Immerman, who owned the place and squeezed 125 couples inside, refused admittance to "mixed parties" but admitted a few Black couples. According to the *Daily News*, the club lacked a Harlem atmosphere and was merely a Black version of Midtown white clubs. There was a gunfight outside Connie's one night. Two bystanders were injured, and a Harlem society woman was killed. Baron Wilkins' Exclusive Club was popular with white people, including Southerners reputedly "nostalgic" for Black society. The club was also popular with African American sporting men and leaders. White and Black couples shared tables, but working-class African Americans were unwelcome. The Nest, at 169 West 133rd, was popular with white women who supposedly ogled Dickie Wells, its handsome proprietor. This club was the first in Harlem to be padlocked, although clubs had been padlocked downtown and in Midtown years earlier. This delay was probably less due to racism, not caring about Harlem clubs or thinking they were worth padlocking, than to the fact that few prominent clubs existed in Harlem until the late 1920s.

Small's Paradise, on 135th in Harlem, was owned and operated by African American Ed Small. It had one of the best floor shows and bands in the city and was "the hottest spot in Harlem" for jazz, with fifteen hundred patrons flocking there to listen or dance. Waiters sometimes danced the Charleston while carrying trays to and from the kitchen. Black and white patrons, looking for genuine Black music and entertainment, were always welcome. Langston Hughes, who lived nearby at East 127th, wrote a short story, "Who's Passing for Who?," about a Midwestern white couple and their Black escort at Small's. When the escort told them light-skinned Black people sometimes passed for white, they "confessed" to being Black, fooled him, and succeeded in having him show them the real Harlem, a richer experience than most white people had.

Harlem millionaire Casper Holstein financed the Lenox Club and hired Jeff Blount as manager. Everyone was welcome—Black, white, and mixed parties—and people danced together on the crowded floor. The club was known for its early-Monday-morning breakfast dances, which began at four o'clock when Black entertainers from downtown shows and other clubs arrived to relax and perform in return for free liquor and food. These jamming sessions ended at eight o'clock when customers rushed from the club to start work.

White people wanting an "authentic" Black experience visited the Sugar Cane near 135th, primarily a Black club, with a low ceiling, worn plank floor, kitchen chairs, and "rickety" tables. One tourist said white visitors to the club might find themselves dancing with their maids or elevator operators. Technically speaking, the Savoy Ballroom at 596 Lenox Avenue was neither a nightclub nor a speakeasy as its bar provided soft drinks and setups, and patrons brought their own liquor. (Later on, liquor was probably served.) African American Charles Buchanon managed it. When it opened in the middle of Prohibition, it was one of the first integrated public places for dancing. Every night, for six months, the Black writer George Schuyler courted his white fiancée at the Savoy; he thought interracial couples were good for New York and for the United States. (After Prohibition, the Lindy Hop, Stomp, and Jitterbug originated here.)

Pyle's Club at 138 Fifth Avenue, managed by Harry Pyle, served middle-class Black patrons. Mike's, in the 140s on Seventh Avenue, which had a Black manager and a white bartender, had a policy of tolerating but not encouraging white patrons. The message was emphasized by differing drink prices based on race: white patrons paid a quarter for a drink, and Black patrons paid a dime for the same purchase. After the 3:00 a.m. city curfew, patrons moved to a cellar annex two doors down, where the bar was made from packing cases pushed together, glasses were unwashed, and patrons could hit their heads on pipes hanging from the ceiling; they tolerated the inconvenience because the place had hot piano playing, good singers, and risqué songs. Ethel Waters said the nearby Banks' Club, on 133rd Street between Lenox and Fifth, was another "low-down" nightclub. Harlem's "fast set" hung out at Casper Holstein's Turf Club on 111 West 126th, where Holstein ran a numbers racket.

Danger at the Clubs

Many clubs had violent confrontations between gangsters; some were extreme, and a few involved well-known people or mobsters. At the Blossom Health Club on Fifty-Seventh, Vinnie Higgins pressured the owner to order beer from his gang and was knifed instead. Casablanca owner Larry Fay was murdered by a disgruntled doorman whose pay had been reduced due to the Depression. Joey Noe, partner of Dutch Schultz, was assassinated at the Chateau Madrid. A man was shot and stabbed at the Club Abbey on Fifty-Fourth. The Club Chantee, run by the Whittemore mob, was deliberately destroyed by fire. Frank Wallace was murdered on the doorstep of La Vie, and it was then closed. A gangster club on Fifty-Third was bombed. Three people, including the bartender, were murdered at Porky Murray's Club on West Fifty-Second. The Plantation Club in Harlem was destroyed within a week of its opening for stealing Cab Calloway away from the Cotton Club. Baron Wilkins was murdered in front of his club in Harlem by a liquor supplier named "Yellow Charleston." Then there was the infamous Mingo's at 167 East Fourth, where police and gangsters would meet to fix cases and to arrange police escorts for liquor convoys.

The Hotsy-Totsy Club, at 1721 Broadway between Fifty-Fourth and Fifty-Fifth, owned by Hymie Cohen fronting for Legs Diamond, was an infamous Manhattan club. Two patrons were shot in a drunken brawl here one night while the bandleader ordered the orchestra to play "Alexander's Ragtime Band" loudly to drown out the gunfire. Twenty-five people witnessed the shooting, but no one would admit to seeing anything. Diamond disappeared from the city for eight months and only returned once two witnesses were silenced by death, two others assumed dead, and one permanently missing. The case was never solved.

Nightclubs in Midtown hired the detective Johnny Broderick for protection. A retired boxer, he refused on principle to carry a gun and stationed himself on the sidewalk outside Lindy's, awaiting calls for help. When Legs Diamond began trashing a nearby club whose owner refused to buy "protection," Broderick arrived, beat up Diamond, and warned him to leave the city. Diamond swore revenge and did not leave Manhattan. When Broderick was informed that Diamond was still in the city watching a movie in a certain Broadway theater, Broderick invited Mayor Walker and the police commissioner to stand across the street and watch. Then he went inside the theater and emerged holding the tuxedoed Diamond high off the ground, walked over to the nearest alley garbage can, and dumped him in it. When Broderick rejoined his audience of two, they asked why he hadn't arrested Diamond, and the detective replied that clever lawyers would get the gangster released, whereas this incident might shame him into leaving the city.

Besides hiring private detectives, some speakeasies and clubs hired perceptive doormen. Sherman Billingsley, a member of a Western bootlegging gang before he arrived in New York City to run a pharmacy dispensing illegal "medicinal" liquor, started the Stork Club on West Fifty-Eighth Street. It foundered until Frank Costello stopped by to leave $100,000 for "safekeeping" while he went abroad. Billingsley soon learned this "loan" came with a price: his legitimate business partner was fronting for Madden, Dwyer, and Frenchy de Magne from the Phoenix Cereal Company, who then pressured him to buy liquor from them. During the Beer Wars, Billingsley was kidnapped and held for ransom in Harlem before being released. After that, he offered to buy Madden and the others out. They told him they did not own stock that he could repurchase, that they actually owned him for the rest of his life. Nevertheless, his second Stork Club at East Fifty-First was free of gangster influence because he hired a doorman whose major claim was that he knew every gangster by sight. Billingsley told him to keep out everyone he knew.

New Yorkers, tourists, and visiting businessmen out for a night on the town during Prohibition could successfully avoid the dangers of gangster speakeasies and bad liquor by patronizing the Salvation Army's Temperance Saloon in the Hotel Argonne on West Forty-Seventh. But it would be a tame affair. There would be no raids, no arrests, no gangsters, and no bootleggers. The choices for liquid refreshment would all be legal—coffee, tea, ginger ale, or buttermilk.

12

Radical Roots

The Rise of the United Federation of Teachers
and the First Teachers' Strike in New York City, 1960

Dennis Gaffney

Adapted from Dennis Gaffney, "Teachers United: The Rise of the New York State United Teachers" (SUNY Press, 2007).

For more than a century, New York has been a leader in supporting organized labor and encouraging labor unions. But it took a determined group of New York teachers and a strike to secure teachers' right to organize and bargain collectively.

In the period after World War II, New York City teachers were burdened by low pay, heavy teaching workloads, and hovering school bureaucrats. Their response was revolutionary: an effective, determined teachers' union, the United Federation of Teachers (UFT), founded in 1960. The new union carried out a strike that year in the face of a state law that prohibited strikes by public employees. Teachers' strikes at that time were practically unheard of. The strike was short but resulted in the city school board acknowledging the teachers' right to collective bargaining and recognizing the UFT as the collective bargaining agent for all the city's teachers.

With that success, New York teachers opened a new chapter in the history of the organized labor movement in New York, and the nation, extending the right to unionize to public employees. A few years later, a New York law granted public employees the right to collective bargaining, established impasse procedures for the resolution of collective bargaining disputes, and created a Public Employment Relations Board to oversee the law.

Once again, New York had led the way in improving wages, rights, and respect for working people.

☙

On most mornings in the fall of 1960, Fred Nauman, a thirty-year-old New York City science teacher, would rise before dawn to commute from his home in Brooklyn's Kensington neighborhood to Junior High School 73, in Bedford-Stuyvesant. He usually arrived well before the 8:40 a.m. bell to ready science experiments for his students, and he had hoped that the morning of November 7, 1960, a Monday, would unfold like all these others.

But as the day approached, it became clear that it wouldn't.

Over the weekend, he and his fellow teachers had phoned one another, and in each call Nauman expressed his disbelief: How had this happened? Why hadn't the conflict between teachers and the New York City Board of Education, over salaries and the recognition of their new teachers' union, been resolved? Would he and other teachers really have to *strike*?

On that Monday morning, Nauman gobbled down his bagel, gulped his coffee, and was out before his wife, Judie, had awakened. She had not been pleased the year before, when Fred had left his $6,000-a-year job repairing office machines at IBM to become a $4,800-a-year public school teacher. Family finances had become even tighter three months before, when the couple moved to a larger, more expensive apartment and Judie had stopped working as an executive secretary at the Associated Press to stay home with Steven, the couple's first child. On November 7, Steven was just over a month old.

Judie worried that if Fred walked the picket line that day, he'd be fired. It wasn't an idle worry. In the weeks prior, New York City Superintendent Dr. John J. Theobald had repeatedly stated that he would enforce the Condon-Wadlin Act, the State of New York anti-labor legislation that made it illegal for public employees, including public school teachers, to strike. If Theobald enforced the law, any striking teachers would be fired. If rehired, Nauman would have to wait three years before receiving a pay raise. Still, Nauman was set on walking a picket line. Teachers needed to raise their pitiable salaries, and a strike just might deliver that.

His gray Dodge sedan pulled up to JHS 73 by 6:00 a.m. He and the other strikers around the city established their picket lines hours before schools opened. That way, teachers who refused to strike couldn't slip into the school without having to cross the line. Nauman counted only ten other teachers, all men and most of them younger than thirty, walking the picket line with him, a small percentage of the sixty teachers in JHS 73. As he walked that cold morning, he was anxious to know what was happening across the city and how it would all turn out. How many of the other fifty thousand teachers at the city's public schools were walking picket lines? Would teachers, divided for so long in New York City, act in unity on this one day? Or would today be the day he lost his job?

Nauman and the city's other public school teachers would not have had to choose whether to strike that November day in 1960 if it weren't for the meeting of a few young men seven years earlier. Two were teachers who had met on the first day of school in 1953. They weren't introduced by other teachers, or by teacher unionists—unless you place their mothers, both working-class seamstresses, into those two categories.

Mamie Shanker and Pauline Altomare worked together at a sewing factory called J. & J. Clothing, at the corner of Prince Street and University Place in Lower Manhattan. The factory employed two hundred people, mostly women, who cut and sewed men's coats and jackets. Pauline Altomare was full of spunk, a natural leader who was chosen by her peers at J. & J. Clothing as shop chairperson for the Amalgamated Clothing Workers Union. Pauline was a neighbor of Mamie Shanker's in Astoria, Queens. Mamie was a Jewish immigrant from czarist Russia who had come to America before World War I. At first, she worked in sweatshops, putting in upwards of seventy hours a week at her sewing machine for meager wages and no benefits. During her years in the trade, Mamie discovered that unions were willing to defend workers from unsafe conditions as well as fight to whittle down exhausting weekly hours and increase paltry wages. She joined both the Amalgamated Clothing Workers Union and the International Ladies Garment Workers Union, and in Mamie's home unions were revered just below God.

One day in the spring of 1953, Mrs. Altomare and her son George picked up Mrs. Shanker from work in their twenty-year-old Chevy. George, then a graduate student at City College in Harlem, mentioned to Mrs. Shanker that he was planning to teach in the fall. "You know, my boy is going to be teaching, too, my boy Albert," Mrs. Shanker replied in her thick Russian accent. "Vere are you going to be teaching?" "Astoria Junior High

Radical Roots | 197

School," George said. "That's vere mine boy Albert's going to be teaching," Mrs. Shanker replied. "Vy don't you get together?"

On Monday, the day classes started that fall, George, just twenty-two years old, sought out Al, as he was known, at the faculty meeting in the auditorium at Astoria Junior High School. Shanker, then twenty-five, was tall, lanky, and academically inclined. He fell into teaching because he was having trouble completing his doctorate in philosophy at Columbia University, and he had begun to feel guilty that he hadn't earned a dime since he married three years earlier. Altomare and Shanker began eating their brown bag lunches together with a few other teachers who would later become union activists, including Delores Tedesco, Dick Thaler, and John Stam. Another was Dan Sanders, a social studies teacher, who would become a close confidante of Shanker's and a statewide teacher leader.

The lunchtime colleagues shared their experiences in the classroom. None of them were paid well—that was no surprise. Shanker and Altomare started at about fifty dollars a week, about a quarter of what their mothers were making at the clothing factory. Many junior high school teachers in the system were full-time substitutes and were paid even less than regular teachers and received no benefits. Sanders, who was a full-time substitute, was once out for a month with the mumps—and he received no salary during his illness.

Two years after these teachers came together, *The New York Times* would print an editorial titled "Teach or Wash Cars." It asked why anyone would bother to teach in the New York City schools for an average salary of $66 a week when they could make more—$72.35 a week—washing cars.

Work conditions matched the pay. A junior high school teacher might teach two hundred or more students in five periods, an average of forty students in each class. Teachers had no prep periods and were often assigned to oversee students during lunch. The newcomers at Astoria Junior High complained about these conditions during their lunchtime gatherings, but perhaps their most colorful complaints were about Abe Greenberg, the school's assistant principal. Greenberg used to look out through his office window with binoculars to spy on teachers during the day. Were you sitting down? Greenberg believed teachers should be standing up. Were the students standing up? Greenberg believed they should be sitting down.

The school bureaucrat's behavior might have been merely an unpleasant footnote in all their lives, had he not been the catalyst that roused Sanders, Shanker, and Altomare to leave their school in Astoria one day and travel to a small, two-room union office in Lower Manhattan. It was a trip that would bring the men to teacher unionism in New York City and, over time, launch a teachers' revolution.

☙

The office that the men visited was rented by the Teachers Guild, the New York City union that was affiliated with the American Federation of Teachers (AFT). The office, located at Broadway and Fifth Avenue, was a fourth-floor walk-up above a cut-rate barbershop and had but two rooms with loft ceilings. The office was grimy and untidy, and in the early morning or late at night, little visitors could be heard scurrying along the wood floors. They were rats.

When the teachers from Astoria Junior High School entered the guild's office, they were stepping into a thirty-seven-year-old stream of teacher labor unionism in New York City. The guild was descended from the Teachers Union (TU), the small band of New York City teachers who formed the city's first teachers' union in 1916. That same year, teachers in the TU joined with those from other urban areas, including Chicago, Gary, Oklahoma City, Scranton, and Washington, DC, to form the AFT, a small national teachers union that was founded with fewer than three thousand members. The AFT was affiliated with the American Federation of Labor.

By forming a union, teachers made a dramatic break from their usual habit of joining associations, such as the National Education Association (NEA), which had dominated the New York state and national education landscape for many decades. Teachers in the NEA considered themselves professionals, like doctors and lawyers, and they yearned to share the same social status. By joining a union, New York City teachers were admitting they were like other workers who had to negotiate and sometimes tussle with their bosses to win better wages, rights, and respect.

Teachers devoted themselves to the TU, but those who did so were a small minority of New York City teachers. At the onset of the Depression, just twelve hundred of the thirty thousand teachers in the city belonged to the union. In the Depression, teachers, along with other workers, became more radical, and the TU became dominated by Communist Party members. Seeing this, many of the TU founders broke off to form a new union in 1935, which became the Teachers Guild. In 1940, the AFT revoked the TU's charter and granted a new charter to the guild. By 1953, many of the guild's original members were in their fifties and sixties and had been fighting for teachers' rights for decades. Many, including Charlie Cogen, guild president at the time, and Rebecca Simonson, Cogen's predecessor, had been among those who had broken off from the TU.

Cogen and the other guild leaders—who all volunteered their time—were the cream of the teaching profession. Sanders was shocked by the quality of the people he met; almost everyone in the guild had a doctorate in something. Shanker compared the guild to a debating society. "You'd go to a guild meeting and listen to some very brilliant people expound on the state of the world," Shanker said. "After three hours you'd leave edified with nothing done."

But during their first visit to the guild's office, Shanker, Sanders, and Altomare didn't meet these well-educated guild leaders. Instead, they met another man, who was neither Jewish nor from New York City. He was a blond Midwesterner who liked to wear bow ties, and he would serve as mentor to the spirited young men from Astoria. He had arrived in New York City only a few months earlier to work as an organizer for the union—its only employee other than the secretary. His name was David Selden.

Selden was a Socialist. He had come to New York City to do a job that most labor organizers of the day considered a Sisyphean task: organizing teachers. Previously, he had been based in Poughkeepsie, New York, as the AFT's "Eastern organizer," directing all organizing drives east of Lincoln, Nebraska. His turf was later narrowed to New York, Pennsylvania, and New Jersey, and his job put him on the road almost constantly, organizing new AFT chapters and bolstering established ones. Often it seemed that as soon as he had set up one chapter, another would dissolve.

After Selden took a job as the guild's sole paid organizer in the spring of 1953, he learned fast that organizing New York City teachers wouldn't be any easier. Each morning, some eight hundred thousand New York City students—the equivalent of the entire population of Cincinnati—made their way to school. More than forty thousand teachers taught those students in six hundred elementary schools, one hundred junior high schools, and ninety high schools. When Selden arrived in New York City, the vast majority of those teachers didn't belong to any teachers' group, much less to the guild.

The Midwesterner must have been relieved when Shanker, Sanders, and Altomare walked into his office. When he was done listening to them, Selden "grabbed hold of us," Altomare remembered later, and got them to work. Sanders, who had written for the campus newspaper at City College and had been a stringer for *The New York Times*, was recruited to write for the *Guild Bulletin*, the union's newspaper. All three were put to work organizing their school, Astoria JHS.

The men used many tactics to encourage other teachers to join the guild. Sanders and his wife, Elaine, used to invite "the Guildies" from PS 126 to their apartment for weekend get-togethers. Each Friday, Shanker would mix whiskey sours for after-school parties at his apartment on Twenty-Ninth Street in Astoria, located about a mile from the junior high. The rules were unwritten but understood: If you hadn't joined the union, you wouldn't get an invitation to the parties. Teachers would ask, Can I come? Sure, they'd be told, but you have to give nine dollars—half a year's membership—to join the guild. The method might not have been ideologically pure, but it was effective.

In less than two school years, the majority of teachers at Astoria Junior High had joined the guild, a success rate that dwarfed that in any other school in the city. Shanker, with a smile, would later compare the concentration of guild activity in the Queens junior high school to the concentration of "dissidents who met under the czar in Siberia" before the Russian Revolution.

After two years at the guild, though, Selden had made little headway. New York City was a hotbed of American radicalism, yet its teachers, like those elsewhere, were averse to joining a union. The staunchest anti-unionists were the school system's older generation of teachers, who were largely Irish American women. These were the teachers who declined invitations to join the guild with the phrase, "We are professionals." Shanker would sometimes discuss this attitude with his mother. "Teachers are so smart, they're stupid," Mamie Shanker would tell her son. "They don't realize that they have to have a union."

But Selden was also surprised to bump into opposition among many younger Jewish teachers, the most recent wave of educators to roll into the city's public school system. These were the sons and daughters of eastern European and Russian Jews who had immigrated to New York City in the late nineteenth and early twentieth centuries. Many of these families had settled in the Lower East Side and worked in the clothing industry. They were unabashedly liberal, even radical, and almost always pro-union. The rub, though, was that they expected their sons and daughters to climb the social ladder and become professionals, who didn't need unions. Selden found Jewish teachers almost always sympathetic to unions; they just wouldn't join one. My parents, one said, would drop dead if I ever joined a union.

Other times, teachers rebuffed Selden by explaining that they already belonged to a teachers' group. And they did. In the 1950s and earlier, teachers paid from fifty cents to a few dollars to join one of the city's roughly one hundred teachers' groups. Teachers in Manhattan met on one side of the East River; teachers from Brooklyn met on the other. Queens teachers didn't take subways to the Bronx, and Manhattan teachers weren't inclined to make a ferry crossing, which left the Staten Island educators with their own teachers' group. High school teachers, who believed they should be better paid than elementary and junior high teachers, had formed their own organization. English teachers met separately from math teachers, who met separately from science teachers.

How else could teachers divide themselves? Religiously, of course. Catholic teachers had their group; Jewish teachers had theirs. As if to prove their point, Orthodox Jewish teachers broke from non-Orthodox ones. It wasn't long before Shanker, making fun of all the splinter teachers' groups in the city, was referring to the "Female Health Education Teachers of Bensonhurst." It was a joke, but barely.

It was as if teachers had used that old political tactic—divide and conquer—against themselves. New York City's Board of Education took full advantage of the divisions. Each year, the board would invite dozens of the teachers' groups to appear before them to make their case. All were aware that they were competitors. If science teachers convinced the board to purchase more beakers, English teachers might be allotted fewer Shakespeare texts. If high school teachers convinced the board they deserved a raise, elementary teachers might have to forgo one. Each year, the board listened politely—and then did what it pleased. What the board meted out was more often crumbs from the tin than pieces from the pie.

Selden dreamed of building the guild membership until it was the dominant teachers' group in the city. A few times a week, he would visit schools and discuss pressing educational issues with teachers over brown-bag lunches, and at the end of the hour, a few teachers might sign membership cards for the guild. But the pace of guild growth was glacial. In two years on the job, the guild's membership had risen from about eighteen hundred members to about two thousand. Selden calculated that at this rate it would take about twenty-five years to herd the majority of New York City teachers into the guild. His worst-case estimate was a century—or never. For a missionary, even a patient one, this was a dismal prognosis. Selden applied for a teaching job in Westchester County, the suburban district just north of New York City, and considered quitting his New York City job.

Instead, he decided to stay and make recruitment more lighthearted. He began scheduling guild meetings at night rather than just after school, which allowed for more leisurely get-togethers, including a monthly beer-and-peanuts party. At gatherings, Selden entertained new members by playing labor songs on his cheap banjo while Altomare played his guitar, strumming songs such as "Teacher's Blues." Guild get-togethers were becoming fun.

The organizer also believed that the guild needed to do a better job at setting itself apart from other teachers' groups. In the in-house paper "Big Guild, Little Guild," Selden suggested that the union should sell itself like a candidate for public office in order to become the city's dominant teachers' group. The first thing it needed to do was to stop taking positions that repelled members, such as opposing prayer in the public schools. Instead, the paper called for the guild to focus on bread-and-butter issues such as salaries, benefits, and working conditions.

Selden also saw another key issue that the guild could promote to separate itself from competitors: collective bargaining. Establishing the right to bargain collectively would mean that a single united union would represent them at the bargaining table, where administrators would be required to bargain with them "in good faith."

Private employees had gained the legal right to bargain collectively in 1935 under the National Labor Relations Act, also known as the Wagner Act because Senator Robert Wagner of New York, who had attended the city's public schools as a boy, had championed it. The law was often referred to as the "Magna Carta of Labor." It gave workers more power in their relationship with their employers, and it also brought order to the relations between management and employees during a time of strikes and violence and near-revolt by the masses. Under the act, unionism in the private sector flourished.

But the act specifically excluded public employees from the rights of collective bargaining—and in the 1950s nearly all public employees, including teachers, still didn't have these rights. In the spring of 1956, Selden and the more militant guild members were able to convince the organization's delegate assembly to make collective bargaining the group's first priority.

Selden's plan also included another crucial idea: that bold actions by the guild would bring in members. The older Guild leaders maintained that membership had to grow more before the group could take more decisive action, a traditional organizing approach. But Selden and his young recruits believed that bold actions would bring in members. Evolution was proving too slow. They wanted a revolution.

Buoyed by his successes organizing at Astoria Junior High School, and eager to add members to the guild, Altomare took an appointment in 1956 to teach history at Franklin K. Lane High School in Woodhaven in Queens. In doing so, he became a "union colonizer," intending to recruit a new group of workers: high school teachers.

But in his first year at Lane he recruited only eight new guild members. The problem was that most high school teachers who joined a teachers' group joined the High School Teachers Association (HSTA), which, along with the guild and the TU, was one of three major teachers' groups in the city. HSTA had one issue: It demanded that high school teachers receive more pay since their job required more education than elementary and junior high school teachers. High school teachers avoided the guild because the union had long supported the single salary schedule for all teachers; "equal salary for equal work" was the guild's slogan.

Altomare soon realized that he wasn't going to convince many high school teachers to join the guild. But he and the other young guild recruits had another idea: Why not merge the guild, which consisted of maybe two thousand teachers, with the HSTA, which had maybe three or four thousand members? In 1957, Altomare broached the idea with HSTA leaders. They told him they would only merge if the guild supported the policy of paying high school teachers more, something that Altomare knew wouldn't fly with guild leaders.

While Altomare was thinking merger, HSTA upstarts took a bold action that would change teacher politics in the city forever. In January 1959, eight hundred teachers who taught at evening high schools resigned to protest their pitiful wages. In labor parlance, it was a wildcat strike because it was initiated not by union leaders but by the rank-and-file. The young guild activists were amazed. Teachers rarely talked strike, much less launched one. High school teachers were taking the kind of bold action that insurgents at the guild had only dreamed of.

Hoping to find a bridge to these militant high school teachers, Shanker, Altomare, and Selden came to the nightly picket lines at Jamaica High School in Queens, offering donuts and coffee to the shivering strikers. The three returned from those picket lines and suggested a radical move to the guild leadership: support the evening high school teachers and their strike. The older guild leaders hesitated. To support it would increase the likelihood of its success and thereby give the HSTA the upper hand in the ongoing organizing battles. But Selden pushed another argument: Teachers needed to support all their fellow teachers, because as one teachers' group gained muscle, all teachers would gain strength. Selden put it succinctly: What if they won the strike without your support? Guild leadership reluctantly endorsed the action.

The HSTA strike, the first one by teachers in New York City history, was an unequivocal success. After a few weeks, the Board of Education raised the daily wages for evening high school workers, who taught the equivalent of four courses each night, from twelve dollars to twenty-one dollars, beyond what even the strike organizers had hoped. The strike was a lesson of what a daring act could win teachers—and the potential of teacher unity. On the picket line, Altomare and John Bailey of the HSTA made a pact: We will meet with each other until a merger is forged. Shortly thereafter, the young guild leaders met with three HSTA activists at Altomare's apartment in Astoria. The young teachers swore to keep the meetings secret from their leaders, because they might kill the delicate negotiations if they knew of them, something the young organizers didn't want to risk.

Inspired by the high school strike, Selden wanted the guild to organize its own one-day strike to win a salary increase for all teachers. It was the kind of bold action he believed would attract new members. But the guild's senior membership feared that if it failed, the move could destroy their group. Rebecca Simonson, the guild's well-respected former president, challenged the young activists to bring out five thousand teachers for a mass meeting to show that there was support for the action. Selden knew that five thousand teachers had not come together anywhere, anytime, for any purpose. So he counterbargained: two thousand teachers. They compromised: bring out three thousand teachers, and the guild's leaders would endorse the strike.

Attracting three thousand teachers to one meeting was a Herculean task. To make matters worse, HSTA's senior leaders refused to support the guild's action. Guild organizers scheduled a rally at the St. Nicholas Arena on West Sixty-Sixth Street, which was often used for sporting events. On the night of the rally, the arena was nearly filled with teachers.

In a voice vote, the crowd approved the guild's one-day action for April 15, 1959. It marked the first time that a teachers' organization in New York City had openly called for a strike. The evening before the stoppage, the guild president, Cogen, went on TV to exhort teachers to "stick to their guns." While the guild president was being interviewed, an aide passed him a note saying that Superintendent Theobald wanted to meet with union leaders for last-minute negotiations. Cogen came on the eleven o'clock news later that night and called off the strike; teachers had been promised considerable

Radical Roots | 205

raises. The next day, the guild printed bulletins hailing the victory. A flood of new members—upwards of eight hundred teachers—joined the guild.

The young guild members continued to push for a merger with HSTA, convinced that unity would bring teachers even better results. They suggested a compromise on the salary issue. Allow a salary differential, they proposed, but apply it to anyone, even elementary school teachers, who completed a master's degree. The HSTA's Samuel Hochberg, Roger Parente, and John Bailey were intrigued by the offer, but the more conservative leadership rejected it.

The guild negotiators' next move was to suggest that Parente, Hochberg, and Bailey abandon the HSTA and form a new group of high school teachers that supported teacher unity. In the fall of 1959, Bailey and Altomare scraped some of their own money together to put an ad in the *New York World Telegram and The Sun*'s education page, which was read by thousands of teachers daily. It announced the formation of the Committee for Action Through Unity, or CATU (pronounced *kay-too*), a group of high school teachers who supported teacher unity and better pay for all teachers with supplemental education. The response to the ad was phenomenal. Within days, CATU had twelve hundred new members, almost half the size of the guild.

The effort to create a willing partner to merge with would have been an unambiguous success if not for a few powerful teachers who were outraged by the plan: the guild's old guard. Guild leaders immediately attacked the young rebels for secretly negotiating a potential merger with the high school teachers without the approval of the guild's leadership or members. After some back and forth, the younger leaders successfully argued the merits of their plan, and the guild's board initiated formal merger talks with CATU.

Through the fall of 1959 and into early 1960, CATU and the guild leadership hammered out an agreement. But what to call the new group? "Teachers Union" was taken. They avoided the word *association*; it smacked of the NEA. The name United Federation of Teachers (UFT) was suggested, and the name stuck. On March 16, 1960, at the old Astor Hotel, five hundred guild delegates overwhelmingly voted for the merger, and with the fifteen hundred sign-ups from CATU, the UFT boasted a membership of roughly five thousand. New York City teachers had finally come together. Now it was time to act.

Almost cocky, UFT leaders presented the Board of Education with a list of demands. These included an across-the-board raise, including a

$1,000 bonus for all teachers who had received additional education; duty-free lunch periods; ten days a year paid sick leave for full-time substitutes; and an automatic deduction of union dues from paychecks. The Board of Education and Superintendent Theobald balked at these requests, especially the UFT's key demand: that the union represent all of New York City's teachers in collective bargaining.

"I do not bargain with members of my own family," was Dr. Theobald's response to the demands. The UFT called a strike for May 17, 1960, Teachers' Recognition Day, when parents would traditionally walk through the city's schools pinning flowers onto the blouses and jackets of teachers. At the last minute, Theobald agreed to the bulk of the demands, and the action was put off.

But in June, representatives from all city teachers' groups except the UFT were invited to the board offices at 110 Livingston Street. These teachers' groups, which had opposed collective bargaining, came from the meeting advocating "divisional bargaining," or separate bargaining for elementary, junior high, and high school teachers. UFT leaders assumed the board was up to an old trick: dividing teachers in order to conquer them. All summer, Theobald ignored pleas from UFT leaders that the superintendent follow through on his promises. The UFT's collective bargaining committee voted to launch a strike on November 7, the day before the Kennedy–Nixon election, figuring that NYC Democratic leaders wouldn't dare shut down the strike lest it alienate Democratic voters.

The UFT's executive board and delegate assembly approved the strike on October 4 and 5, but no other teachers' group in the city endorsed the measure, seeing it for what it was: a power play by the UFT to become the dominant teachers' group in the city. Superintendent Theobald, as well as the Board of Education and James E. Allen Jr., the state education commissioner, also warned that any teacher who went on strike would jeopardize "that teacher's state certificate and his rights to teach in any school district in New York State." Many old-timers were told they would lose their teacher's pension if they walked that day. Nervous school officials forbade teachers to meet on school grounds to discuss a strike. Instead, guild teacher leaders met at churches, synagogues—even at a funeral parlor.

In the days prior to the strike date, Shanker remembers a guild meeting where some of the old-time leaders, aware of Theobald's threats and the skepticism about the strike from the city's labor unionists, spoke of calling off the strike. "Look," Shanker told them, "we have no choice but to go out. There's no argument that anybody can come up with to call this strike off that allows us to continue to have a union or any chance of building one. I admit this is risky. But the other way is a certain death warrant."

The last editorial before the scheduled strike in the UFT's paper, *The United Teacher*, said, "This is a strike for our dignity, our self-respect. We will smash once and for all the concept that teachers are educated fools."

As the Monday strike day approached, the tiny UFT headquarters was jammed with volunteers who staffed phones, turned out mimeographed flyers, and painted signs. "It was all thunder and lightning, do or die," recalled Jeannette DiLorenzo, a teacher at JHS 142 in Red Hook, Brooklyn. "Even the old were young again."

UFT organizers moved their headquarters to Selden's and Shanker's apartments during the weekend. Each apartment had two phone lines. In one call after another, the men told the teacher troops not to believe what would be reported on the radio the next morning since the Board of Education would likely underestimate the number of teachers out. Altomare also suggested a technique to keep administrators from knowing who stayed out: drop paper clips into the school's time clocks.

At about three o'clock on Sunday morning, Selden and Altomare, their preparations over, walked over to Shanker's to get some more wine, which they had been sipping while they worked. The three men knew that not all—or even most—of New York's teachers would walk out. What they hoped was that enough teachers would strike to cause havoc in the schools. Striking with such meager forces was like putting your head in a lion's mouth and hoping it didn't bite. The men hoped the lion—the liberal Mayor Robert F. Wagner Jr., son of Senator Wagner—was sympathetic to their dreams. On the walk over to Shanker's house, Altomare asked Selden a question he hadn't dared consider: "What happens if teachers cave in?"

Win or lose this strike, Selden told him, we'll have created a teachers' union movement that won't fail.

On the morning of November 7, all over the city, teachers strung placards over their shoulders and joined picket lines. "Better Salaries, Better Schools," said one sign; "United We Stand," said another. One parent on the line wore a sign: "Parents Want Justice for Teachers." A news clip about the strike was titled "Reading, Writing—and Pickets." The newscaster said, "When problems hit the nation's biggest city, they're usually big—such as the first strike of schoolteachers in New York City's history."

At JHS 73 in Brooklyn, Fred Nauman and his fellow teachers got out early to walk their picket line; it was cold enough to see their breath. The picketers passed a transistor radio around, spinning back and forth between local news channels. Would the strike be a success? It was a question on the mind of nearly every public school teacher in the city.

At Public School 165 on the Upper West Side, a teacher named Ray Frankel walked the picket line with just four of her colleagues. Some of the other teachers appeared in the school's windows to watch the picketers, and a few started crying. "Stop crying and come out," she yelled at them. As each hour passed, the radio reported higher and higher estimates of strikers. One thousand teachers . . . two thousand teachers . . . with each announcement, the dread that Nauman had felt slowly began to lift. Three thousand teachers . . . four thousand teachers . . .

At Public School 100 in Queens, Nat Levine, bowing to the vote not to strike by his UFT colleagues at the school, showed up for work. But by lunchtime he could no longer stomach the choice he had made. He grabbed a piece of chalk and wrote a message on the board for himself, but also for his students who would enter the classroom in the afternoon: "To thine own self be true."

Outside JHS 142 in Red Hook in Brooklyn, Jeanette and John DiLorenzo and about eighty other teachers picketed, joined by longshoremen and merchant seamen from the nearby piers. Later that morning, Jeanette drove around to check out other public schools in south Brooklyn, and at many of the elementary schools, not a single teacher was walking. By the time they circled back to JHS 142, half of the striking teachers had deserted their picket line, and by day's end Jeanette was hoping "to find a way to get back in that building with some kind of dignity."

DiLorenzo's observations were accurate: the turnout from elementary school teachers had been dismal. Most of the strikers came from the more militant staff at the junior highs. By the end of the day, the board had conceded that 4,600 teachers had gone out. Later newspaper accounts would report that 5,600 teachers had walked picket lines and that another 2,000 teachers called in sick. Whatever the exact numbers were, Nauman was exhilarated come the end of the day: thousands of other teachers had risked their jobs as well.

That night, the teachers once again returned to the St. Nicholas Arena, and from the cheers that rose up from within, a passerby might have thought that a raucous crowd had gathered for a professional wrestling match. As the meeting was breaking up, Selden was told that he had a phone call. "Okay, listen," the caller said. "Vill you take mediation?"

"Who is this?" Selden asked.

"Dubinsky. I vant to meet with you." It was David Dubinsky, the legendary president of the International Ladies Garment Workers Union, the union that Mamie Shanker and Pauline Altomare belonged to. Dubinsky was well connected to the Democratic Party, and he didn't want the strike to embarrass the mayor or disrupt the election. That night, Cogen, Hochberg, Jules Kolodny, and Selden met in Dubinsky's Manhattan apartment, and by the end of the evening, a compromise had been worked out. The mayor would appoint a special labor committee consisting of three labor unionists, all of whom were sympathetic to the cause and to collective bargaining, to investigate the teachers' demands. The UFT leaders called off the strike.

Superintendent Theobald announced that the Board of Education would not enforce the Condon-Wadlin Act and reversed his command to fire strikers. The labor committee that was established recommended that the board make concessions on pay and working conditions to teachers and that a collective bargaining election be held before the end of the school year. In June 1960, the Board of Education polled New York City teachers as to whether they wanted collective bargaining. Despite the opposition to collective bargaining by the NEA, 27,367 teachers voted "yes," and 9,003 voted "no." In October 1961 the Board of Education directed the city labor department to hold a collective bargaining election to decide which group would represent teachers.

The most serious rival to the UFT in the election was the NEA, which came into New York City with organizers and established the Teachers Bargaining Organization (TBO), an alliance of many of the scattered teachers' groups in the city. Money flowed from NEA headquarters, and the association's organizers sent teachers anti-union leaflets headed, "Do You Want Hoffa and Bossism?"

Meanwhile, organized labor, including the United Auto Workers, mobilized behind the UFT, providing $250,000 to the union over a half-year period before the vote. In *The New York Times*, an ad supporting the UFT was endorsed by political giants such as Eleanor Roosevelt and Herbert Lehman, the former New York governor. On each of the ten days that teachers had to return their ballots, a hundred UFT volunteers phoned teachers to urge them to "vote for the organization that won the right to vote."

On December 16, 1961, the votes of 33,000 teachers, 77 percent of the city's teachers, were counted. The UFT won overwhelmingly, receiving 61 percent of the vote: 20,045 votes cast for UFT, 9,770 cast for the TBO, and 2,575 for the TU. The UFT would now speak for all of New York City's teachers.

But negotiations between the UFT and the Board of Education broke down almost immediately when the board dragged its feet over money, offering little. "What other means are there besides a strike?" asked an exasperated Cogen. "We've tried everything else—like gentle persuasion. This is time to stop talking and get a little action." Teachers, though, were still reluctant to strike and voted to support one on April 11, 1962, by a margin of only 313 votes: 2,544 to 2,231. Once the day arrived, though, teachers heeded the call—about twenty-two thousand of them walked picket lines in this second teachers' strike, seven thousand of whom weren't even members of the UFT. Teachers held signs that read that they were tired of being treated as "low-paid babysitters."

The board was stunned by the teacher response; in that 1962 strike, a full one-half of the city's teachers didn't report to their classrooms, crippling the city's nine hundred public schools. The president of the Board of Education called the stoppage "reckless, irresponsible . . . immoral, and illegal," and the board convinced a state supreme court justice to invoke the Condon-Wadlin Act and issue an antipicketing order. The afternoon of the strike, seven thousand teachers surrounded city hall, packing Murray Street and overflowing onto Broadway.

Charlie Cogen, the UFT's five-foot-tall leader, scrambled onto a sedan to address the crowd. "This is the greatest day in the history of education in the city of New York," he said. The crowd of teachers broke into a chant of "Stay out, stay out" and cheered their gray-haired leader, a veteran of the Teachers Guild who had taught in the 1930s for $4.50 a day.

The court injunction ended the strike, but the Board of Education made concessions. In the negotiations that followed, teachers secured a $1,000 across-the-board annual raise—the largest pay raise in New York City school history—and established new salary differentials for teachers who had different levels of experience. The contract also guaranteed teachers a free lunch period. For many teachers who had worked during their lunch hour their entire careers, it was like manna from heaven. The most important gain, though, was not more money, or even better work conditions, but more power.

UFT leaders had won the right to bargain collectively, which meant that the Board of Education would have to negotiate with the UFT, which represented all teachers in the city. Now, every contract negotiation, said Al Shanker, who would become the most prominent leader of the UFT, "opens up afresh opportunities for direct teacher participation in the revitalization of our schools."

With this success, New York City's teachers had ushered in a new era in the history of the American labor movement. The 1880s saw the consolidation of the craft unions and the founding of the American Federation of Labor. The 1930s saw the creation of the great industrial unions and the Congress of Industrial Organizations. The 1960s, with teachers at the forefront, would see the unionization of government employees. In January 1961, President John F. Kennedy would sign Order 10988, giving legitimacy to union organizing among public employees. New York City teachers had led the way, becoming the first teachers in any major city to win the right to bargain collectively.

Teachers all over the country watched this three-year transformation of their New York City colleagues. They saw the city's teachers, once dismissed as disorganized and impotent, become a powerful, unified force. The word of their success spread from New York City like a fire, igniting rebellion and organizing efforts in elementary schools, high schools, and universities all over the state. Teachers no longer pleaded for respect, decent wages, and fair working conditions; they saw they could demand them—and win.

For New York teachers, the 1960s had arrived.

13

The Empire State Plaza and the Remaking of Downtown Albany, 1963

C. R. ROSEBERRY

Adapted from the third edition of C. R. Roseberry, "Capitol Story," with revisions by the New York State Office of General Services and Diana S. Waite (SUNY Press, 2015).

Governor Nelson A. Rockefeller (1959 to 1973) was the architect of the modern New York state government. He built low-income housing, established a robust medical care program for the needy, enacted a state minimum wage, increased the state highway program, and created several other new programs.

Rockefeller's vision of a robust state government led him to the realization that the New York State Capitol (completed in 1912), the other state office buildings in Albany, and rented space around town were too cramped to accommodate burgeoning state offices. Modern state government, in the governor's view, required something much more magnificent. He conceived of a vast new government office complex, stretching south from the capitol nearly to the New York State Executive Mansion on Eagle Street. Building the complex required razing many older buildings.

Built between 1965 and 1978, it was originally called the South Mall and is now called the Nelson A. Rockefeller Empire State Plaza. The plaza included space for agencies, a building for legislative offices, a performing arts center, a convention center, and a Cultural Education Center housing the New York State Library, Museum, and Archives.

The Plaza remains the most innovative and striking state building complex in the country, a tribute to Rockefeller's vision and determination and a testimony to New York's historical record of leadership in the nation.

☙☀

A reporter at a press briefing once asked Governor Nelson A. Rockefeller if it was correct to refer to him as a frustrated architect. The governor gestured toward the great south windows of the Red Room and replied, "Not anymore." In a speech on another occasion, he noted that he might indeed have an "edifice complex." It is a fact that Rockefeller, while a student at Dartmouth, seriously contemplated architecture as a career.

The governor's allusions were to the complex of marbled buildings known as the South Mall during much of its creation but rechristened by Rockefeller himself as the Empire State Plaza. Not long before his death, that name was expanded by Governor Hugh L. Carey to the Governor Nelson A. Rockefeller Empire State Plaza. It rears resplendently as the tangible symbol of his governorship. No other chief executive of the state of New York left so prodigious an imprint on the face of the capital city.

The principal architect, Wallace K. Harrison, of Harrison and Abramovitz, declared that the plaza was an extension of the New York State Capitol. This was how Rockefeller regarded it, although the style of architecture was drastically different. Far from downgrading the capitol, the extravagant new complex of governmental structures complements and enshrines it. The massive, century-old building has been brought into true focus as it never was before, particularly when viewed from the south end of the Plaza along the line of reflecting pools and framed by tall marble buildings.

One of the early things Rockefeller did as governor was to ask for a complete tour of the capitol. He was fascinated by the building and often roamed its corridors to study architectural details—the legislative chambers, the superb stairways, the profuse carvings. He mentioned to his secretary, Dr. William J. Ronan, that a book should be written on the history and the intriguing architecture of the capitol and set his staff photographer to taking pictures around the building. Such was the genesis of this book's first edition. Rockefeller felt that the much-maligned capitol ought to be rehabilitated and take its rightful place in any future state plans. By his order, the grounds were improved with floriculture, a fountain, and the removal of dying trees. The east facade was floodlit at night.

Nelson Aldrich Rockefeller was not only the wealthiest of all New York's governors. With the single exception of George Clinton, the first governor, Rockefeller established a record for tenure in the office—fifteen years and election to four terms. During most of those years, he was directly involved with erecting the South Mall. He was able to watch its progress day by day from his office windows, and he frequently donned a hard hat to inspect the working areas. It was his obsession. He stated his philosophy on the project in this fashion: "Mean structures breed small vision. But great architecture reflects mankind at its true worth. [The Mall] should fulfill us aesthetically as well as serve us practically."

Rockefeller had come to Albany with no preconceived notion of making over the capital city, with which he was scarcely familiar. But fresh in his memory were visits to Brazil's spectacular new capital, Brasilia, by which he was much impressed. Upon moving into the New York State Executive Mansion on Eagle Street in January 1959, he was taken aback at the unkempt, down-at-heels aspect of the nearby streets verging on the South End slums. The realization that his family had become residents of a badly deteriorated inner city went against his aesthetic grain. Soon the new governor became aware of a related problem—namely, a severe shortage of space for the needs of state government. Rentals were being paid for state offices scattered in at least ten commercial buildings around the city.

Talking with his budget director, T. Norman Hurd, Rockefeller learned that there was additional office space available at the state campus, a spread of twelve office buildings three miles west of downtown Albany, a plan for which had been formulated under Governor Thomas E. Dewey as a hoped-for solution to the space dilemma. (That development, pushed through by Governor Averell Harriman in the 1950s, had no connection with the campus of the State University of New York at Albany later constructed a little farther west.) Harriman voiced doubt as to the wisdom of moving so many state units to the outskirts. Those doubts were echoed by the downtown merchants.

An episode that had an incidental bearing on Rockefeller's reaction to Albany during his first year in office was a visit by Princess Beatrix of the Netherlands. The state was holding a Hudson–Champlain Celebration in 1959, marking the 350th anniversary of the exploratory voyages of Henry Hudson and Samuel de Champlain. Holland sent the country's twenty-one-year-old princess as the official delegate of the former Dutch colony. A motor tour of historic places up the Hudson Valley climaxed at the city of Hudson, where Beatrix boarded Laurance Rockefeller's yacht *Dauntless* to enter Albany by water as Henry Hudson's *Half-Moon* had done. The princess was landed at the foot of Madison Avenue, where she was met by Mrs. Nelson Rockefeller and their daughter Mary and whisked to the executive mansion on Eagle Street in the governor's limousine. Nelson himself was in New York City that day, meeting with the Soviet premier, Nikita Khrushchev, but returned to play the gracious host to Princess Beatrix at the mansion. The governor afterward admitted to embarrassment at having a royal guest see some decrepit samples of the capital city, and the press made a considerable point of this, but it was by no means crucial in triggering the South Mall.

Rockefeller learned that Albany's Democratic mayor, Erastus Corning 2nd, was allied with a group of business leaders in urging a joint state-city effort to salvage the ailing downtown. The governor, by executive order, called a halt to further construction at the state campus. At his behest, in March 1961 the legislature created a Temporary State Commission on the Capital City, headed by Lieutenant Governor Malcolm Wilson. Rockefeller had already decided that the ideal solution would be to combine the twin objectives of more space and the resuscitation of the Albany center. The Wilson commission produced a report in January 1962, recommending that the state concentrate all future building in the heart of the city. Of several potential locations, it favored a "South Mall" along a north–south axis extending from the capitol nearly to the executive mansion, between State Street and Madison Avenue. Not only would this site be handy to the existing state complex on Capitol Hill, but its elevation would make a dramatic skyline.

The commission submitted a map showing boundaries of the tract to be taken by the state under right of eminent domain. The tract embraced forty city blocks, plus a right-of-way for arterial highway approaches and ramps down to the river, and a narrow strip along the riverfront to accommodate pump houses for the use of Hudson River water in the huge air-conditioning system. The total area came to 98.5 acres. The forty-block tract contained 3,300 dwelling units, 350 business establishments, and a population of 6,800. It was predominantly residential, with three-story brownstone and brick row houses dating as far back as the early nineteenth century. The neighborhood was in decline, but not (as often asserted) a part of the vice-ridden Albany "Gut," notorious for its bordellos and winos.

The South Mall proposal was kept under wraps as long as feasible, to guard against land speculators moving in and buying properties cheaply.

The governor asked for twenty million dollars in his deficiency budget to cover acquisition of the parcels to be condemned. By the end of January 1962, the legislature had given the go-ahead signal by approving the deficiency budget including this sum. No statute specifically authorizing the construction of the South Mall was legislated. Instead, the legislature—in a mood to give Rockefeller anything he asked—sanctioned the project by voting appropriations for it as budgetary items.

At this juncture, Mayor Corning was invited over to the capitol, informed of the plan, and shown the map. The mayor went back to city hall and dictated a letter of protest to the commission, saying its proposal would violate "human rights" and deprive the city of about $500,000 in realty taxes per year. Ignoring this remonstrance, the machinery of eminent domain ground steadily forward. By the governor's order, on March 27, 1962, the State Department of Public Works filed with the Department of State and the Albany County Clerk maps of the tract the state was appropriating. With that, Mayor Corning fired off a yet-stronger letter to Rockefeller, charging "ruthless misuse of power by the Executive" and "what might be expected of a dictatorship." As the final touch, he wrote, "Do not build this magnificent monument on a foundation of human misery."

The aristocratic Albany mayor backed up his words with legal action. The city filed for an injunction to prevent seizure of the properties and on April 4 was granted a temporary stay by a judge of the state supreme court. The state appealed, and the appellate division reversed the lower court's ruling on June 29. Corning, having made his point, carried the appeal no farther. On the contrary, after Rockefeller's reelection sweep, the mayor swung over into a cooperative role, recognizing that the South Mall would be beneficial to the city. Corning afterward explained that he had begun the action because he was concerned about the state taking the streets as well as the blocks. The plan was changed to leave the streets to the city for maintenance of water, sewer, lighting, and cleaning.

Having cleared the way for South Mall construction, in July 1962 Rockefeller mounted the operator's seat of a giant crane and aimed a steel clam shovel against one of the doomed buildings. By this act, he symbolically touched off one of the largest, most complicated, and most costly single construction projects in history. All down the line, he repeatedly proclaimed that the South Mall would make Albany one of the most beautiful and spectacular capitals in the world.

Now Rockefeller found his opportunity to be allied for the final and climactic time with Wallace Harrison, an eminent New York architect and personal friend of long standing. When he became assistant secretary of state for Latin American affairs during World War II, Rockefeller had called Harrison to Washington and made him coordinator, with special reference to cultural relations. Their close association dated from the 1930s, when Harrison designed Rockefeller Center and the Radio City Music Hall for John D. Rockefeller Jr., who appointed his son Nelson as president of the center. Harrison had since been the principal architect on such noted structures as the United Nations building and the Metropolitan Opera House in Lincoln Center and had built a private mansion for Nelson on the family estate at Pocantico Hills.

On a flight together from Washington, DC, to New York, Rockefeller told Harrison about the planned Albany Mall and, on the back of an envelope, sketched his rough notion of what it should be. Harrison tossed in ideas of his own. Not surprisingly, when the time came, the firm of Harrison and Abramovitz received the contract as chief architects for the South Mall. Before the job was done, six architectural firms were involved. Most notably, James and Meadows and Howard, of Buffalo, designed the Legislative Office Building; Sargent, Webster, Crenshaw, and Folley, of Syracuse, was selected for the Justice Building; and Carson, Lundin, and Shaw, of New York City, was responsible for the motor vehicle building. The total architectural and engineering fees were $37.8 million, of which the Harrison firm's share was $10.1 million.

As yet, however, no financial prescription for the South Mall had been worked out. Rockefeller was not so politically naive as to imagine that the voters would approve a bond issue of the necessary dimensions in a referendum. The first published estimate of the cost was four hundred million dollars—about as realistic as the initial four-million-dollar limit for the capitol had been. It is uncanny how, on a hugely magnified scale, the capitol's history was repeated in the building of the South Mall—in the ballooning cost, the constantly lengthening time schedule, and the barrage of criticism. While the demolition was going on, Mayor Corning performed so complete an about-face that he came to the aid of the South Mall and earned the title of its "financial architect." He called on Governor Rockefeller to propose a lease-purchase formula by which the city of Albany would employ its credit in floating municipal bonds to defray the construction costs; the city, as technical owner, would then lease the buildings to the state. The state's annual rental payments would be applied to the principal while also meeting the carrying costs of the bonds. With the final payment in the year 2004, if not before, the mall would become the property of the state. Rockefeller "went for the plan like a trout for a fly," to quote Corning, an ardent fisherman. The mayor afterward said, "It was a tremendously tricky arrangement, and lots of lawyers worked on it." Some referred to it as "backdoor financing." In January 1964, at Corning's suggestion, the method was amended so that Albany County, instead of the city, issued the bonds.

The Wilson commission had also recommended that the capitol be given an external cleaning for the first time since it was erected. The big scrub-down was done in 1966 with a combination of steam and chemicals. The public had come to accept the unsightly coating of grime as the capitol's normal hue. People were agreeably surprised as the pristine off-white beauty of the Maine granite was revealed. The cosmetic treatment spruced up the capitol for its coming marriage with the South Mall.

With announcement of the financing formula, a scale model of the architectural dream was unveiled in the east lobby of the capitol. A feature of the model was an Arch of Freedom thrusting skyward at the south extreme of the mall, facing the capitol. But the governor sensed that the arch would be a weak southern terminus for the giant plaza, as if it were dwindling away into nowhere. It was replaced by the Cultural Education Center, a far more effective counterweight to the capitol.

As the old buildings were being obliterated, powdered plaster drifted across the capitol like a smokescreen. Excavation followed, and streets and sidewalks were alternately muddy and dusty. The mall ran into the same initial problem as the capitol had—the deep deposit of glutinous blue clay streaked with sand that had to be removed. In all, 3,124,000 cubic yards of earth were excavated. This basic task in itself served notice that the South Mall job was not going to be accomplished thriftily. The foundations took twice as long and cost twice as much as the original estimate.

Digging was followed by pile driving, a procedure that shattered the calm of the capitol for more than five years. The decibels of this assault upon the eardrums of state workers and nearby residents were a reminder of the engineering strides that had been taken since the capitol was built. As many as twenty-six thousand H-shaped steel pilings were driven as foundation supports to an average depth of seventy feet to get into glacial gravel underlying the clay. In addition, around the rectangular perimeter of the mall area were driven twenty thousand tons of interlocked steel sheet pilings for cofferdams—to preserve the normal water table in the ground outside the foundations.

Long before the South Mall had been envisioned, Rockefeller had established the Office of General Services in 1960, appointing as its first commissioner General Cortlandt Van Rensselaer Schuyler. Schuyler had been chief US military representative on the Allied Control Commission for Romania at the end of World War II, and the Pentagon had later assigned him to Rockefeller's staff in Washington, DC. Construction of the South Mall was at first under jurisdiction of the Department of Public Works, while the Office of General Services had charge of overall planning and design. Before long, Rockefeller transferred supervision of the whole job to General Schuyler and the Office of General Services. Schuyler needed a coordinator, and Dr. Ronan recommended Brigadier General William W. Wanamaker, at that time with the State University of New York Construction Authority. In this way Wanamaker became the initial director of mall construction. But in the last analysis no one could dispute that the real boss was Nelson Rockefeller.

Now that the die was cast, the first critical decision to be made was what kind of stone to use. The choice fell upon marble as being the most economical as well as attractive and abundant. The bulk of the marble for the mall was to come from Vermont and Georgia, some from Alabama, and in one instance from Greece. The Grecian *verde tinos* serpentine was used on the floor and columns of the tall, spacious central lobby of the Legislative Office Building. For several years the Albany Mall was to devour nearly the entire output of Vermont marble; indeed, one Rutland quarry was depleted. Other varieties of stone were used, here and there, including granites for some paving and stairways. In the latter category, a considerable amount of the relatively rare dark-gray igneous rock meta-anorthosite was obtained from an Adirondack quarry at Upper Jay. Because Harrison wanted touches of darker stone for contrast with the glaring whiteness of all the marble, a quantity of brownish sandstone called llenroc (*Cornell* spelled backward) came from a quarry near Ithaca. Its use is noteworthy in the eastern wall and parapet of the plaza and in the lower part of the Cultural Education Center.

The architectural plan crystallized down to twelve buildings. The pivotal "topmast" of the complex is the Tower Building, 589 feet high, the tallest skyscraper in the state north of Manhattan. The others, ranged about the quarter-mile-long plaza, are the four agency (office) buildings, the Legislative Office Building, the Justice Building, the Cultural Education Center, the Performing Arts Center (commonly known as "The Egg"), the Swan Street Building (Motor Vehicles Department), a low restaurant building beside the Tower, and the Platform Building. The last named is the largest—in fact, one of the biggest in the world—but the casual visitor would hardly sense its existence because it is mainly underground. Most of the other major buildings rest upon it.

The bubbling enthusiasm of Rockefeller could not wait for the actual "laying" of a cornerstone. Instead, he unveiled one. On June 21, 1965—barely two months after disclosing the financial plan—he staged the unveiling ceremony on a plank platform near the northwest corner of the Swan Street Building, for which only a fragment of the foundation was yet complete. The carefully chosen stone, to be mortared in place at a later date, was a 7,500-pound block of white granite quarried at Concord, New Hampshire—an obvious symbol of the capitol connection.

Beaming broadly as he dropped the covering, Rockefeller hailed the event as beginning "Albany's transformation into one of the most brilliant, beautiful, efficient, and electrifying capitals in all the world." He then filled a document box that was to be sealed into a slot behind the cornerstone. As a copy of the financial agreement was handed to him for deposit, he quipped, with a grin at Mayor Corning, "Handle that with care. It took us a year and a half to draw it up."

The same day, a release from the governor's office deferred the mall's estimated completion date from 1970 to 1972 and hinted that the four hundred million cost might creep upward by as much as one hundred million.

The Swan Street Building was the first to be occupied, in 1971. It is five blocks (1,200 feet) long, with two porticos for breaks between segments. This stretched-out structure was purposely designed with a low profile, making it a transitional step between the mall towers and the ranks of brick townhouses across the street. The massive granite cornerstone today faces Swan Street with large, deep-carved letters: SOUTH MALL.

The South Mall project was plagued with problems from its inception. Among the first to rear its head was an acute shortage of labor in the capital area, especially of carpenters and pile drivers. Many workers were brought in from New York City and Montreal, and this bred discontent among local unions. Wage scales escalated. When a bearded young Canadian worker called "Frenchy" quit to return to Montreal, his compatriots gave him a farewell party with the toast, "Here's to the project that never ends!" The workforce at its maximum numbered over three thousand. Wildcat strikes, slowdowns, and featherbedding multiplied. In one year, 1970, the labor disputes totaled 217.

Of greater import was the hurried, almost impetuous way in which primary contracts were let. At the outset, while he had a compliant legislature,

Rockefeller got funds committed, so if political winds shifted work would go on. The capitol was an object lesson in this respect. Another factor spurring him on was the certainty of inflating costs as time passed. Behind it all, however, was the impatient driving force of the governor. The state signed six major contracts almost simultaneously, stipulating the approximate starting date for all, when each depended, in some degree, upon the completion of one preceding. A consequence was that at times workmen were fairly tripping over one another. In retrospect, General Schuyler frankly avowed, the mall would have been erected in a more orderly manner had it not been pushed so fast in the beginning. The difficulties began, according to Schuyler, when the contractor on the foundation fell behind schedule, thereby delaying the others. At the peak of construction, 359 contractors and subcontractors were onsite at one time. By 1970 the South Mall was running three years behind schedule, and Schuyler publicly admitted that the state was largely responsible for the delays. "There was more complexity to the project then we realized," he said. To keep contractors from suing in the Court of Claims for losses due to improper planning, a number of "equitable adjustments" costing millions were made.

The original contract figure for the five-level Platform Building was $97,777,000, and the job was so gigantic that it was shared by two New York City contractors. It proved the classic instance of cost overruns. Before it was finished, the Walsh-Corbetta company, alleging that the state had not properly coordinated and scheduled the work, was awarded without contest an additional $49,725,971, bringing the total contract value to $149,750,000. The enormity of the Platform Building may be appreciated by reflecting that it contains the Grand Concourse extending the length of the mall beneath the plaza; the convention center, whose main room, unobstructed by pillars, will accommodate twenty-seven hundred people, and which has six meeting rooms besides; four levels of the New York State Health Department's laboratories; a bus terminal; and underground parking spaces for three thousand cars, along with the various utilities installations.

Cost estimates for the mall were revised upward year by year. The Democratic state comptroller, Arthur Levitt, predicted that the figure would escalate to at least a billion. In 1968, Levitt sent a letter to both houses of the legislature asking for an investigation into the soaring costs, referring to the mall as "an insatiable project." Rockefeller revealed how stung he was by Levitt's attacks by going before the legislature with a special message in reply. He acknowledged that the price tag had recently been increased from $480 million to $610 million but reminded the legislators that extending the construction period over still more years could only result in far higher costs. The governor wound up his eloquent defense by heaping praise on the legislature for its "continued support" and its "great vision."

By 1971 the cost estimate was up to $850 million. By 1975 the total of mall bonds authorized by Albany County was $985 million. In 1976, Levitt proclaimed that the lease and interest payments would boost the total past $2 billion. Actually, the more accurate final figure, including rental and carrying costs, turned out to be around $1.7 billion.

History was repeated in the torrent of ridicule that fell upon the architecture long before the project was completed. The more strident of its critics called it such things as "a naïve hodgepodge of barely digested design ideas," "a compendium of clichés of modern architecture," and "Buck Rogers creating a seat of government." Others wrote that "stylistically, the Albany Mall leaves one not knowing whether to laugh or cry," or "its characteristics are pomposity and banality," or "reality is in short supply in this complex."

The mall had its defenders as well—generally less vocal, as had been the case with the capitol. They maintained that "its roots were aesthetic" and hailed it as "an artistic triumph." The chief architect, Wallace Harrison, took the brickbats in stride. With him it was an old story. Time would bring acceptance and approval. Shortly before his death (in 1981), he commented that there was no better governmental complex anywhere else in the world. Under sharp questioning in the Senate hearings for his appointment as US vice president, Rockefeller gamely defended the mall project, observing that similar statements were made about Rockefeller Center.

While the Tower was rising to its forty-four stories in height, the cranes operating on its summit were a long-term spectacle on Albany's skyline. Twice during its construction, fires flared through its upper levels. One workman was killed in a fall down an elevator shaft. The lofty structure is faced with more marble than the United Nations building, and its windows contain a million dollars worth of glass. The observation deck comprising its forty-second floor affords a stunning panorama. The Tower looks down upon the row of four identical nineteen-story agency buildings on the opposite side of the reflecting pools. In Harrison's view, this plaza, which was the crown of his long artistic career, "is the only place I know of where skyscrapers are used with space around them so everybody can enjoy the light and air."

At the time the plaza was being designed, the State Department of Health, then quartered on Holland Avenue, was petitioning for a new laboratory building in the vicinity of the Albany Medical Center. Rockefeller seized the opportunity to entice a major state operating department into the mall. He offered the health commissioner, Dr. Hollis Ingraham, the option of waiting years for the money to build a new laboratory or moving downtown into the Tower Building. The result was a drastic change in design planning for the Tower.

The four subsurface levels in the Platform Building beneath the Tower were set apart for the laboratories, while the departmental offices were assigned the first fourteen floors of the Tower. The move gave the health department the enviable good fortune of acquiring the most advanced laboratory equipment while developing, in collaboration with the architect, fail-safe controls over all laboratory processes. Consequently, the laboratory became a building within a building. Harrison worked long hours with the lab staff, planning the ambience down to the finest details, even to the colors of paint on the walls.

A latecomer to the South Mall plan, the Cultural Education Center was the happiest thought of the entire complex.

First called the Museum-Library Building, it eventuated as the shared domicile of the New York State Museum, Library, and Archives. The contract for its construction was let in 1969. Architecturally, it is regarded as the jewel of the plaza, and Harrison himself considered it his best contribution. Characterized by distinctly separated layers with vertical window slots, it flares outward toward the top with a faint resemblance to a pagoda. The strongest reason for so substantial a building at the south end of the mall, instead of a frivolous arch, was the severely overstrained condition of the New York State Library after a half century in the pillared Education Building following the disastrous capitol fire of 1911. Everyone mourned the evacuation of the magnificent reading room and rotunda created by Henry Hornbostel, but books were being piled in stack corridors and overflow resources stored in an outlying warehouse. The new reading room is purely utilitarian, with no vaulted ceiling and no tall, ornate windows, but the well-ventilated stacks beneath occupy entire floors and allow for future expansion of contents by millions of volumes. The library has seventy-seven miles of shelving.

The New York State Museum, occupying the lower floors of the Cultural Education Center, took the opportunity to create an entirely new museum environment, employing the latest museum techniques. The exhibits were developed around the theme of "Man and His Environment."

Governor Rockefeller had never felt comfortable with the South Mall name. It reminded him too much of a shopping center. On November

21, 1973, he presided over a dedication ceremony with which he formally rechristened it the Empire State Plaza. Crane booms were still swinging, air compressors chugging, and a bitter wind blew. A knot of spectators gathered around a massive block of polished Brazilian granite on which were graven the words, EMPIRE STATE PLAZA—DEDICATED TO THE PEOPLE OF NEW YORK. This monument stands at the north end of the plaza, nearest the capitol. Speculation as to the reason for this unseasonable event was confirmed on December 11 when Rockefeller announced he would resign the governorship to pursue "a new national role," saying he felt he had accomplished all he could as governor. Malcolm Wilson moved up to governor, and in February 1974 he appointed his former superior as chairman of a Citizens Advisory Committee on the Empire State Plaza, with duties of "guidance and suggestions."

The most controversial structure in the plaza is the oddly shaped Performing Arts Center, commonly referred to as "The Egg." It has been variously compared to half a grapefruit, to a watermelon cut on a bias, or a radar disc with a lid. Instead of marble, its material is concrete. There is not a straight line in the whole structure; even two of the elevators are round. The shape is somewhat elliptical—more precisely, an oblate spheroid. To John C. Byron, it was "the biggest headache of all." Byron was director of construction from 1971 until the Empire State Plaza was finished. The reason for the extraordinary difficulties was that the Egg was a totally new construction form, with no engineering precedent. An exact model was first built for study and experiment. A computer was used to calculate curvatures and stresses. Concrete pouring was a ticklish problem because of the curving wooden forms and differing thicknesses of the walls. Because concrete generates heat as it hardens, ice cubes were mixed with some pourings to ensure uniform curing.

The nickname "The Egg" was hatched as a jocular term among engineers and hardhats working on its construction. A public relations agency promoting its formal opening in May 1978 picked up the catchword and made it endure. The label was distasteful to many, including Rockefeller and his architect, but, once embedded in the vernacular, impossible to eradicate. Harrison took the Shakespearean attitude that "a rose by any other name would smell as sweet." The sobriquet, at all events, did not hinder the building's flowering into an entertainment center.

Much as the Egg has been deprecated by critics, it provides a striking counterpoint to the austere vertical lines of the Tower and the agency buildings. Perched atop a slim concrete pedestal, it leaves open vistas of the

Hudson River and the hills beyond that a conventional structure would have blocked off.

A meeting hall, spacious enough to accommodate fifteen hundred guests at dinner, was quietly added to the plaza's design in 1965 beneath the future site of the Egg. This eliminated the need for a convention hall in Albany as had been recommended by the Commission on the Capital City.

The Grand Concourse (the adjective has since been dropped) is walled with travertine from Italy. It evolved into far more than a passageway between buildings. Lined with a variety of stores, branch banks, restaurants, and cafeterias, it functions as a subsidiary shopping center for state workers. Its midline spaces are frequently utilized for special exhibits and trade shows. The Concourse also serves as a remarkable art gallery.

Ornamental aspects of the open-air plaza itself were well provided for in advance. For example, as early as 1967 a nursery was contracted to begin growing 576 trees for the final cosmetic touch when the plaza was completed. Little saplings were planted and grew "faster than the Mall." By 1975, the maples were twenty feet high, and fears were heard that they might grow too big to be moved. The worry proved groundless. Transplanted in neat rows along either side of the reflecting pools and fountains, the trees and shrubs were trimmed in cubic forms to harmonize with the buildings. In winter, the reflecting pool adjacent to the capitol is converted into a skating rink.

Another stamp that Nelson Rockefeller left indelibly upon the Empire State Plaza was his personal taste in art. The dream nursed by some early planners of the capitol to make it a repository of fine art finally came true in the plaza, though in a radically different idiom. Rockefeller thought of it partly as a gallery of contemporary art. At the outset, a sum of $2,653,000 was earmarked for works of art, both paintings and sculptures, to adorn the plaza and its buildings. The governor, famed for his private art collections, appointed a commission of experts to select the works. As chairman of this commission, he named Wallace Harrison, who saw eye to eye with him on modern abstract art. Rockefeller personally approved every piece before its purchase. The main criterion was that they be contemporary works by New York state artists, although there were exceptions. The choices were made during the 1960s. A total of ninety-two pieces were acquired at a cost of $1,887,610. Viewed simply as investments, apart from their aesthetic worth, they have appreciated greatly in value since their purchase. A New York art critic wrote of the collection, "Its quality is such that any museum in the western world specializing in contemporary art would be proud to have it."

Forty of the paintings adorn the walls of the Concourse.

The Concourse also presents, at intervals, a number of arresting metal sculptures. Even visitors who decry the bold abstractions must admit that representational works of art would have seemed out of place, and too small for these expanses of wall. Nor would pictorial canvases blend with the architecture. One does not find here the pompous portrait, the English hunting print, the soothing harbor scene, or a Grandma Moses primitive. In four instances, the paintings are of unusual length, and these were commissioned for the spaces they occupy. The longest, an untitled entry by Sven Lukin, stretches to 118 feet, 7 inches.

Three sculptures on the plaza win particular notice. The most conspicuous, due to its location in the south reflecting pool silhouetted against the facade of the Cultural Education Center, is Alexander Calder's stabile *Triangles and Arches*. A jagged cluster of black sheet metal uprights, aiming sharpened spikes at the sky, makes a powerful impression from any angle. Fascinating to all visitors is George Rickey's *Two Lines Oblique*, a kinetic creation, whose elegantly tapered arms of stainless steel mounted on a forked post wave about in varied geometric attitudes, powered by the slightest breeze. The largest and costliest sculpture of the entire collection is an intricate wooden composition, which spreads itself in the southeast corner of the plaza. Entitled *Labyrinth*, this was done on commission by a French sculptor, Francis Stahly. It is fashioned from iroko blocks and covers an area measuring 180 by 70 feet.

The Legislative Office Building was hastened to early completion to mollify grumbling legislators impatient to escape their crowded capitol nooks. They began moving into their spacious office suites in January 1972. This building, too, was favored with its modest share of art, but with a difference. A minor revolt against the Rockefeller taste occurred among some lawmakers who disliked modern art. Accordingly, the legislature set up its own committee to select pieces, which were to be "strictly representational."

The Empire State Plaza was destined for more ceremonies of a dedicatory nature. A much-publicized celebration, tied in with the US Bicentennial, took place on July 1, 1976. This observance marked the opening of the Cultural Education Center along with the new New York State Museum, but it signalized the public debut of the plaza as a whole. Governor Hugh L. Carey led a retinue of state officials to the platform and pronounced the plaza "a monument to the people." A band played and toy balloons ascended. As a climax, the Chancellor of the Board of Regents, Theodore M. Black, officially opened the Cultural Education Center by snipping a ribbon crossing the doors at the terrace level. Crowds trooped through the Adirondack Hall, the first completed wing of the state museum.

On Memorial Day, 1978, another ribbon-cutting ceremony was held for the Egg—the Performing Arts Center—which signified not only the completion of that structure but of the mall project in its entirety. With that occasion, John C. Byron retired, amid plaudits, from his crowning career as director of construction. Within a few days, Nelson A. Rockefeller observed his seventieth birthday.

In May 1978 the AFL-CIO of New York state launched a movement asking the legislature to rename the mall as the Governor Nelson A. Rockefeller Empire State Plaza. The Senate quickly and overwhelmingly passed a resolution endorsing that request, and a bill was introduced to that effect. The bill died a quiet death in the Democrat-controlled assembly. Ignoring the legislative inaction, Governor Carey issued an executive order declaring that the plaza "shall henceforth be known as The Governor Nelson A. Rockefeller Empire State Plaza."

By now "out of politics" and a private citizen, Nelson Rockefeller made his farewell appearance at his beloved plaza on October 6, 1978, to accept that honor. He was accompanied by his wife, Happy, and several other members of the Rockefeller family. A considerable audience assembled around the granite monument he had previously placed there for dedication of the Empire State Plaza. They heard Governor Carey intone, "Today we are gathered at the most beautiful state capital in America, to honor one of America's most civic-minded citizens. What was constructed was more than buildings. This complex is a unique concentration of great architecture, great art, and of New York's place in history. . . . A deteriorated capital city could not, and cannot, be accepted as part of New York state's legacy."

On January 26, 1979, Nelson A. Rockefeller died of a heart attack in New York City. The great plaza bearing his name became an enduring symbol of Rockefeller's governorship. It bloomed into a civic, convention, entertainment, and cultural center as well as a magnetic tourist and visitor attraction. Long before its completion, its impact on the surrounding community became obvious. Neighborhood improvement groups sprang up around its periphery: the Center Square Neighborhood Association expanded its prior efforts; others were organized—Hudson Park, the Washington Avenue Association, Robinson Square, and the Mansion Neighborhood Association. In response to the demolition of countless structures, Historic Albany Foundation was organized in 1974 to protect and preserve the city's historic buildings.

14

The Stonewall Uprising and the Fight for Gay Rights, 1969

Ashley Hopkins-Benton

Throughout New York's history, people whose sexual practices and beliefs ran counter to prevailing customs, norms, and behaviors have faced discrimination and persecution. Sometimes, that took the form of social pressure and condemnation. Other times, it took the form of laws enforced by police. A major turning point came on June 28, 1969, when police raided the Stonewall Inn, a bar in New York City that catered to gay patrons. The raid led to several days of protests, and, in turn, that led to a redoubling of efforts to secure equal rights for gay people. That effort slowly gained adherents and momentum and continues to the present time.

The "Stonewall uprising" is an example of how a single dramatic event can energize and galvanize a reform or protest moment that was already beginning to grow. It also shows the need for protesters to get organized, to make appeals in the media, to advance their cause in local and state legislation, and to fight for their goals in court. It shows the need for determined, persistent leadership.

The long struggle for gay rights in New York is a reminder of how long it can take to effect revolutionary-scale change.

⁂

Early in the morning of Saturday, June 28, 1969, police raided the Stonewall Inn in New York City's Greenwich Village. Rather than returning to their homes as they were released, the patrons stayed and fought back; their numbers soon swelled by both passersby and others who heard about the action and came to join. This raid was not the first on a bar or restaurant catering to the LGBTQ+ community in New York City or across the country. It was also not the first time the community fought back against actions by law enforcement. The LGBTQ+ community had faced years of laws and harassment that targeted them and had started to organize for change. Prior to Stonewall, the homophile movement already existed; groups like the Mattachine Society and the Daughters of Bilitis had been raising awareness and organizing protests to support gay rights. For a generation steeped in the actions of the civil rights movement and anti-war protests, something shifted during the nights of the Stonewall uprising—it was a call to action.

The Stonewall uprising—or rebellion, or riot—is a challenging historical event to study. It is vitally important to the development of the LGBTQ+ rights movement but also not its start. Over time, as it has been told and retold, the details have gotten muddied. Players that might not have been as central on the actual nights of the uprising have been raised up and their stories amplified, while others who were key have been forgotten altogether. The very language we use, whether Stonewall is called an uprising, a rebellion, or a riot, speaks to the distinct meanings the event holds for different groups and the ways it has been used to project a message in the intervening years. Academic historians have been slow to understand the importance of LGBTQ+ history, and museum curators have been slow to collect it; both are a detriment to its preservation. The story and the significance of Stonewall have been protected by groups like the National Stonewall Rebellion Veterans Association and co-opted by many others. The spirit of Stonewall has been used as a rallying cry for protests and is also preserved in a National Monument.

In 1969, there were no protections for New Yorkers against discrimination on account of sexual orientation or gender presentation. A person could be fired from their job for being gay, evicted from their housing for being a lesbian, or denied services for being transgender. In fact, until the 1980 *People v. Ronald Onofre* decision in the New York Court of Appeals repealed New York's penal law on sodomy, homosexuality itself was illegal.

Until 1967, drinking while gay was also illegal. Laws that allowed for bars and restaurants to be closed for being "disorderly" were frequently used to punish homosexual activity, including same-sex dancing, kissing, or flirting. The New York State Liquor Authority outlawed the service of alcohol to gay people. These laws were tested by the New York chapter of the Mattachine Society, beginning with a "sip-in" on April 21, 1966, by Dick Leitsch, Craig Rodwell, John Timmons, and Randy Rickert. Inspired by the sit-ins employed in the South during the civil rights movement, the group ordered at several Greenwich Village establishments, stating that they were homosexuals, and members of the press were invited along. The first couple of bars that the group tried, one of which displayed a sign in the window that read "If You Are Gay, Please Go Away," were tipped off ahead of time and either decided to close or to serve the men without protest to avoid problems. At Julius' Bar, they began with a prepared script: "We are homosexuals. We are orderly, we intend to remain orderly, and we are asking for service." The bartender, having been told that the Mattachine would provide support for any legal troubles the bar faced, put his hand over the glass and refused to serve them. Having been denied service, Mattachine had a potential court case. Following the action, which was covered in *The New York Times*, *The Los Angeles Times*, and *The Village Voice*, the chairman of the State Liquor Authority, Donald Hostetter, stated that the agency had never discriminated against homosexuals, and that regulations "leave service to the discretion of the management." From there, the matter was passed to the New York City Commission on Human Rights, but since it did not concern hiring, the Human Rights Commission could not investigate. Despite an anticlimactic end in New York City, the action began the process of chipping away at discrimination faced by gay people in New York City bars and led to action and court cases in New Jersey.

Despite the outcome of the sip-in at Julius' Bar, obtaining a liquor license as an operator of an openly gay bar was still challenging in New York. The result was many Mafia-run establishments, the Stonewall Inn included, catering to the LGBTQ+ population. The Mafia felt no kindness toward the LGBTQ+ population and operated the bars with a balance of negligence and disdain. The bars were often dirty and rundown, had discriminatory door policies targeting people of color and those who were cross-dressing, and were frequently raided. Watered-down liquor, likely often stolen, was served, ensuring a high profit margin. There was a type of gentleman's agreement between the police and the Mafia, wherein bars were often raided early in the evenings, the police were paid off, and the bars reopened shortly afterward. The Stonewall Inn had no running water, and glasses were "washed" after each patron in a tub of standing water, then reused. As Morty Manford recalled to Eric Marcus in 1989, "The Stonewall was a dive. It was shabby, and the glasses they served the watered-down drinks in weren't particularly clean."

Arrests and harassment for cross-dressing were also a common occurrence for queer people on the streets of New York City. These arrests were likely based on old masquerade laws still on the books. In New York state, these laws were established in 1845 to prevent tenant farmers from dressing as "Calico Indians" while evading sheriffs and rent collectors during the anti-rent wars. Technically, this law made it a crime to wear a costume or mask in order to go undetected while committing a crime. New York did not actually pass what became known as the "walking while trans" ban (section 240.37 of the New York Penal Code) until after Stonewall, in 1976. This law, meant to prevent loitering "for the purpose of engaging in prostitution," was not repealed until 2021. The law was used to target transgender people as well as those in drag. It was also used to make arrests during protests, including during the 2011 Occupy Wall Street movement, when protestors demonstrating against economic inequality and corporate greed set up an encampment in New York City's Zuccotti Park as well as in locations around the state and the world.

While it would serve as a spark that would lead to further organizing and actions, the Stonewall uprising does not mark the beginning of the gay rights movement. A number of homophile organizations had already formed in New York City and across the country. At the time, most organizations used the term *homophile* as a more neutral term, as *homosexual* was still included in the American Psychiatric Association's original *Diagnostic and Statistical Manual of Mental Disorders* (*DSM-I*) as a "sociopathic personality disturbance," from 1952 to 1973. The Mattachine Society was founded in 1951 in Los Angeles, and a New York Area Council was created in 1955. The group fought for the rights of gays and lesbians to simply exist as themselves, without risk of persecution or arrest. The Daughters of Bilitis (DOB) was formed in San Francisco in 1955 as the first lesbian organization in the homophile movement. It was originally focused on providing a secret social outlet for lesbians to meet others and avoid persecution, but soon after began discussions of rights issues. The New York chapter of the DOB was formed in 1958 by Barbara Gittings and Marion Glass, and the group frequently collaborated with the Mattachine Society of New York. Through the 1960s, most members who attended Mattachine and DOB meetings did so under pseudonyms, as the risks of being out were so great. Both organizations emphasized assimilation into heterosexual culture. Members were encouraged to present as model citizens and look respectable, wearing suits and ties for men and dresses for women, when appearing at public-facing actions. At the time they were founded, the ideas and actions of the Mattachine and DOB were considered radical, but by the time of the Stonewall uprising, there were some in the community who were frustrated with this conservative and staid approach and who had begun to push for a more open and assertive course of action. These conversations and growing schisms within groups were already percolating by the mid-1960s.

On September 19, 1964, Randy Wicker, of the Homosexual League of New York (HLNY), organized the first public demonstration for gay rights in the country, a picket in front of the US Army Building in Lower Manhattan to protest the army's treatment of gay people. Wicker had first volunteered for the Mattachine Society when he arrived in New York City but frequently pushed back against the organization, advocating for better publicity for its events and more visibility in working for gay rights, and ultimately forming the HLNY. While those picketing made themselves visible in joining the action, they still wore suits and ties or dresses.

Police harassment and brutality targeting the LGBTQ+ community were common throughout the twentieth century, and Stonewall was not the first time those targeted fought back. Across the country, pickets were organized to protest unjust laws and harassment, ramping up in the late 1950s. In July and August of 1966, protesters in San Francisco first picketed, and then rioted, protesting harassment by police and private agents at Compton's Cafeteria, a popular hangout for trans women of color (an event almost lost to history, save for the work of the historian Susan Stryker).

It is important to note why the raid on the Stonewall Inn, as well as the broader pattern of raids at gay and lesbian establishments (including Cooper Do-nuts and Compton's Cafeteria), was so hurtful to members of the queer community. In an era before the internet, before LGBTQ+ community centers, and without legal protections (keeping most people in the closet at their workplace and in other parts of their lives), gay and lesbian bars and clubs were one of the few places to go to meet other LGBTQ+ people. To meet friends or potential romantic partners or to cruise, or even just to feel less alone as a queer person in a straight world, bars were essential. The Stonewall veteran and artist Thomas Lanigan-Schmidt described the role of the Stonewall Inn in the queer community in his 1989 essay "1969 Mother Stonewall and the Golden Rats":

> WE [queer "street rats"] ALL ENDED UP TOGETHER AT A PLACE CALLED THE STONEWALL. Safe and sound. All you had to do was find an empty beer can, so the waiter would think you bought a drink, and the night was yours. . . . We

were happy. This place was the "ART" that gave form to the feelings of our heartbeats. Here the consciousness of knowing you "belonged" nestled into the warm feeling of finally being HOME. And home engenders love and loyalty quite naturally. So, we loved the Stonewall.

The perceived welcoming nature of bars like the Stonewall varied greatly depending on who you asked. Mafia-run bars operated with bouncers (often to promote the idea that they were clubs rather than illegal bars), and many discriminated based on race, sex, or gender presentation. Sylvia Rivera explained to Eric Marcus in 1989, "If you were a drag queen, you could get into the Stonewall if they knew you. And only a certain number of drag queens were allowed into the Stonewall at that time." The Stonewall Inn was not a common hangout for lesbian women, although some did go. In a 1989 "testimony" with Michael Scherker at the Lesbian and Gay Services Center, a lesbian who did frequent the Stonewall (who chose to remain unidentified) noted, "There didn't seem to be hostility, but there didn't seem to be camaraderie."

The raid on the Stonewall Inn, located at 53 Christopher Street in Greenwich Village, began early in the morning of June 28, 1969. It was the third targeting Greenwich Village bars that week. Police actions took place under the direction of Deputy Inspector Seymour Pine. Similar raids had often occurred just as the night was getting started, at nine or ten o'clock, but the actions at Stonewall started much later, as celebrations were in full swing. Also unusual was the fact that two pairs of undercover officers were first sent in, prior to the bar actually being shut down. When the police did enter around 1:20 a.m. and announced the raid, they closed the front door and checked IDs, dismissing patrons one by one. Whereas the police probably hoped that each dismissed patron would head home, glad to no longer be in police custody, those dismissed lingered on Christopher Street and in Sheridan Park, waiting for friends to be released and to see what would happen. Passersby also stopped to see what was going on, and the crowd swelled. Some patrons struck campy poses as they were let out the front door of the bar and were met with applause from the onlookers. A police wagon was parked right in front of the Stonewall Inn, and the bar staff, as well as some patrons who were cross-dressing, were arrested and put inside. The wagon was never locked, however, and some of the arrested parties simply left. Some note that a drag queen was treated roughly during her arrest, and that raised the temperature of the crowd. There are also several accounts of a butch lesbian, dressed in men's clothes, who was either harassed by the police or acted against them as she was arrested—some cite this as the moment the crowd began to shift.

Soon after, the gathered crowd started throwing coins at the police, an action recounted as a reference both to "dirty coppers" and to the idea that the police had gotten their payoff and could leave. From there, things escalated—larger objects were thrown, the original police contingent barricaded themselves inside the Stonewall Inn, a parking meter was used by the crowd as a battering ram, and there were attempts to set the building on fire.

The police called in backup, including the Tactical Police Force (TPF). The geography of Greenwich Village, with its narrow streets, small blocks, and streets meeting at acute angles, meant that as a row of TPF officers approached the crowd, members of the crowd could break off, run around the block, and confront the officers from behind. At times, the crowd threw in bits of camp—high kicks and chants referring to the officers as "Billy Blue," a firm declaration of the fact that their pride remained intact.

The action did not only take place at street level. Just down the street from the Stonewall Inn was the Women's House of Detention, a looming, eleven-story edifice. The historian Hugh Ryan notes that the prison held some women for actual crimes and many others for behaviors viewed as transgressive, radical, or "obscene," including wearing pants, staying out late, being alone on the street, and lesbianism. Many incarcerated in the House of Detention were women of color, and many were likely queer women. During the Stonewall uprising, observers noted objects being lit on fire and thrown from the prison windows and chants of "gay rights, gay rights, gay rights!" from those incarcerated.

The action in the streets of Greenwich Village continued to flare up for six days. Leaders of the Mattachine Society called for an end to violent actions in favor of peaceful protest. By Monday and Tuesday, things were significantly quieter in the Village. On Wednesday, July 3, however, the weekly publication *The Village Voice* landed on newsstands, and the Mattachine Society claimed the paper was responsible for reigniting the violence. In recent years, *The Village Voice* has been seen as an open-minded publication, championing the arts and culture, the country's first alternative weekly. From its founding in 1955 through the 1960s, however, the paper was not kind to gay people; Dick Leitsch declared in the Mattachine's August 1969 newsletter, "That paper's editorial policy has long infuriated most homosexuals, as the paper pretends to be 'liberal' and avant-garde, but is actually conservative and uptight about homosexuality." In its first issue following the raid on the Stonewall Inn, the front page featured photographs by Fred W. McDarrah and articles by Lucian Truscott IV, who witnessed the events from outside with the protesters, and Howard Smith, who became trapped inside the bar with the police. It was far more coverage than the events had gotten in the mainstream press, and from a more local publication. (*The Village Voice*'s offices were just down the street from the Stonewall Inn.) Unlike the articles in the mainstream press, *Village Voice* reporters used both police and civilian accounts and framed the actions as just liberation rather than unprovoked rebellion. However, the reporting was biased, and both reporters used insensitive language, including Smith's reference to the crowd as "dancing faggots" and Truscott's note about "the forces of faggotry." While both reporters noted the root cause for the uprising was anger over harassment and lack of rights, the very language that they used called back to treatment the LGBTQ+ community had suffered under for so long.

The effects of the Stonewall riot rippled across New York state, the country, and ultimately the world. Organizers in the gay community made sure that there was press coverage, and news traveled through social contacts in various cities. The story of the way the community fought back against the same type of oppression that was felt in many other cities, including Albany, Syracuse, Rochester, and Buffalo, spurred on the foundation of activist groups, community centers, protests, and publications.

Before the dust even had time to settle in Greenwich Village, a new organization, the Gay Liberation Front (GLF), was founded. Energized by the events of Stonewall, young activists were interested in pursuing a more direct form of activism than the tactics used by earlier groups, including the Mattachine Society. Michael Brown formed the Mattachine Action Committee to capture and organize this energy, and the group soon spun off as its own organization. The GLF took a broad approach and worked to align itself with other activist organizations, including the Black Panthers and anti–Vietnam War protesters. Groups inspired by the GLF were founded in cities and on college campuses across the country. In the fall of 1969, the tensions that were already present between the LGBTQ+ community and *The Village Voice* were reignited and led to an early organized action and public protest by the GLF when a paid advertisement placed by the GLF was edited to remove the word "gay." On September 12, 1969, the GLF set up a picket line in front of the *Village Voice* headquarters. After hours of negotiations, the paper's management agreed not to alter paid advertisements and to allow the words "homosexual" and "gay" to appear in the publication. In celebration, the GLF ran a new advertisement reading, "The GLF sends love to all Gay men and women in the homosexual community."

In November 1969, several members of the GLF, including Jim Owles, Marty Robinson, Arthur Evans, and Arthur Bell, left to form an organization focused solely on gay and lesbian issues, the Gay Activists Alliance (GAA). The GAA formally adopted their name and preamble at a meeting on December 21, 1969, with a "structured, single-issue approach" toward an initial goal of "law reform, to give the homosexual citizen the rights and freedoms granted to every citizen." Taking a more direct approach to protesting than its predecessor homophile organizations, the GAA popularized the "zap," a form of direct political action that was used by a number of LGBTQ+, feminist, and AIDS activists from the 1970s through the 1990s. Zaps were intended to begin suddenly, were disruptive, and focused on gaining media attention. Protesters might abruptly appear at a political event, interrupting a speech, or yell at a politician as they entered an event. Bell referred to zaps as "political theater for educating the gay masses."

On Sunday, June 28, 1970, the first anniversary of the Stonewall uprising, the Christopher Street Liberation Day March was held in New York City—the first Pride parade. A group of GLF members, including Craig Rodwell, Fred Sargeant, Ellen Broidy, Linda Rhodes, and Foster Gunnison Jr., began meeting in July of 1969 to discuss a way to replace the Reminder Days (gay rights demonstrations held annually in Philadelphia, in which participants were expected to adhere to strict rules of dress and decorum, common for events held by the early homophile organizations). A proposal for such an event was put together by Rodwell and Broidy and presented to thirteen homophile organizations at the Eastern Regional Conference of Homophile Organizations meeting in November 1969, stating, "We propose that a demonstration be held annually on the last Saturday in June in New York City to commemorate the 1969 spontaneous demonstrations on Christopher Street and this demonstration be called Christopher Street Liberation Day." The march began on Washington Place in Greenwich Village, moved up Sixth Avenue, and ended in Central Park with a "gay-in" in Sheep Meadow. Thousands of marchers joined.

In Albany, Gary Pavlic, one of the founders and later board president of what would eventually become the Pride Center of the Capital Region, recalled in a June 4, 2020, interview with the author (recording collection of the New York State Museum, H-2021.77):

> We had a visitor, someone who was involved with the uprising, the Stonewall uprising in New York City. We had a drag queen; that's what she called herself, not a trans person, but a drag queen. . . . She told us about what had happened. We were

having some of the same issues in this area with bars, being treated unfairly, and, obviously, there were no laws to protect us. We had the same issues; we had crazy bars to go to, and the police would beat us up on a regular basis walking home from the bars. There were real issues here too as well. Then we decided to get organized, and eventually we formed . . . the Gay Community Center . . . I think we just had to stand up for our rights. And it was time, and I think people were just tired at that point. Tired of being abused and having no rights. So that's when we decided to organize.

It is possible that the speaker mentioned by Pavlic and others was Sylvia Rivera, who was also documented in Albany in 1971 for a gay rights march. Rivera recognized the significance of Stonewall and shared her experience regularly with various groups.

Learning about the Stonewall uprising in New York City spurred the gay community in Albany to organize. Shortly after the visit, they formed the Tri Cities Gay Liberation Front (inspired by the Gay Liberation Front in New York City), which first met on September 9, 1970. The organization subsequently changed its name several times to better represent its mission and the communities it serves: the Capital District Gay Community Council (CDGCC), the Capital District Gay and Lesbian Community Council (CDGLCC), and finally the Pride Center of the Capital Region (hereafter referred to as "the Pride Center" for clarity). From its first location at 250 Lark Street to its longtime home at 332 Hudson Street, the Pride Center has served as a hub for Albany's queer community, a space for social and activist gatherings, a visible presence and reminder of the LGBTQ+ community in the broader media, and an incubator for other special interest groups and organizations, providing meeting space and communications assistance as these groups got off the ground.

In March 1971, Albany held its first gay rights march, supported by both the Pride Center and the Gay Activists Alliance (a student group founded at the University at Albany earlier that year, now called the UAlbany Pride Alliance). Unable to get an official permit from the city, marchers walked single file down the sidewalks. Groups from across the state attended the march and a rally on the New York State Capitol steps, including a contingent from New York City with Sylvia Rivera, Mattachine Buffalo, and the Gay Alliance of the Genesee Valley (with their then new publication,

The Empty Closet, now one of the longest-running continuously published LGBTQ+ publications in the country).

Local activism in cities around New York state turned to work to pass local laws, and then state laws, that improved protections for the LGBTQ+ community. The infrastructure that was created in the months and years following Stonewall helped make this work possible, while the rise of the AIDS epidemic gave further urgency to the cause. Grassroots efforts led to the passage of city-level legislation in Ithaca (1984), New York City (1986), Syracuse (1990), and Albany (1992), barring discrimination in housing, employment, and services on the basis of sexual orientation. Similar protections were passed for city employees, but not the general public, in Troy (1979), Rochester (1982), and Syracuse (1990). These local laws helped build momentum for the successful passage of the State of New York's Sexual Orientation Non-Discrimination Act (SONDA) in 2002. Notably, none of these laws addressed discrimination against transgender New Yorkers, who would finally get protection at the state level in the Gender Expression Non-Discrimination Act (GENDA), passed in 2019. There is still no federal law barring discrimination based on sexual orientation or gender expression.

New York City's process to pass a law protecting the LGBTQ+ community began as Intro 475, the Clingan–Burden Bill, and provides insight into the discussions about inclusion or exclusion of transgender rights into such legislation. The result of pressure from the Gay Activists Alliance, it was announced by City Council Minority Leader Eldon R. Clingan on June 2, 1970. In its first version, the law was focused on barring discrimination based on sexual orientation in employment, but it was later expanded, under New York City's Human Rights Law, to cover discrimination in housing and public accommodation as well. Hearings and concurrent protests were fraught, and both featured activists who were tied to the Stonewall uprising. Testimony was presented to the committee from a number of individuals who today might consider themselves transgender (at the time, they referred to themselves as drag queens, transvestites, and transsexuals), including Sylvia Rivera, Marsha P. Johnson, and Bebe Scarpi. Scarpi advocated for protecting the rights of both sexual orientation and gender expression, noting, "We are constantly being used to put down the whole issue of gay liberation. We are part of that. Sure, we have our own rights. As this particular bill was worded, to my knowledge, it does not include us. As it is worded, it states about our sexual preference, which is not the issue. That we choose to dress as females is an entire different thing when we choose to do it."

Scarpi went on to recount the ways in which those who dressed outside of their sex at birth were targeted by the police and harassed.

Intro 475 was rejected by committees on January 27, 1972; July 19, 1972; and April 27, 1973. The April vote was looking positive until several committee members turned their votes. The resulting anger among the LGBTQ+ community led to numerous protests, including at the site of the Stonewall uprising. Days later, the GAA targeted New York City's Diamond Jubilee celebrations with a zap, and Sylvia Rivera was arrested for climbing the walls of city hall. A fourth failed committee vote in December of 1974 saw growing infighting in the GAA, with many pointing fingers at the transgender community for its failure. An amended version, renamed Intro 2, provided protection solely based on sexual orientation and was voted out of committee in April 1974. The plan did not work, however, when the Catholic Church and the Firemen's Association came out in force against it, and Intro 2 was voted down in the full city council on May 23, 1974. A new version, Intro 554, was introduced in September of 1975, still without "references to 'transvestitism,'" but the law did not pass until March 20, 1986.

The momentum built by work for passage of local laws banning discrimination on the basis of sexual orientation, and ultimately passage of SONDA in 2002, also fed into work toward the Marriage Equality Act, passed in 2011. Many of the same activists that had been lobbying for legal protection in city halls from New York City to Buffalo went on to work with organizations at the state level, including Empire State Pride Agenda. New York was not the first state to make same-sex marriage legal, but passage of the law in such a populous and influential state helped increase awareness and support nationally prior to the 2015 Supreme Court decision in *Obergefell v. Hodges*, which determined that same-sex couples have the same right to marry as different-sex couples.

In the years following the 1970 Christopher Street Liberation Day March, Pride celebrations have grown around the world. In New York City, Pride is held on the last weekend of June to coincide with the anniversary of the Stonewall uprising. Pride is many things to many people, shifting at times due to the urgent issues of the day. It can be a jubilant celebration of queer joy and the ability to be out, a reminder of the violent action that took place at Stonewall for the sake of winning the right to live peacefully and of the need to continue to fight for equal rights, a protest, a somber memorial to those lost to the AIDS epidemic, a time when products in stores are covered in rainbows for the sake of more sales, a place to belong in community, and more. Conflicting ideas about what Pride means and how to make use of it mean that events are not without conflict or opposing factions.

In 1994, Stonewall 25 events commemorated the Stonewall uprising, and the city hosted the Gay Games, welcoming athletes from around the world. The Stonewall 25 committee focused its march on the demand of adding LGBTQ+ people to the United Nations Declaration of Human Rights. At the same time, in the throes of the AIDS epidemic, the Spirit of Stonewall coalition, the AIDS Coalition to Unleash Power (ACT UP), and Councilman Thomas Duane called for a countermarch, and ACT UP distributed leaflets about the toll of AIDS on the city. When organizers of the Pride march announced that leathermen and drag queens were not allowed at official events, Gilbert Baker (creator of the rainbow Pride flag) and Brian Griffin (a.k.a. Harmonie Moore Must Die) created the New York City Drag March. The city also saw its second annual Dyke March, a protest organized by the New York Lesbian Avengers, created to celebrate "our beautiful and diverse Dyke lives, to highlight the presence of Dykes within our community, and in protest of the discrimination, harassment, and violence we face in schools, on the job, and in our communities." It takes place without permits or sponsors, calling back to the root of Stonewall's history, protest. Both the Dyke March and the Drag March have continued annually.

For the fiftieth anniversary of Stonewall in 2019, New York City hosted World Pride, the first time the celebration took place in the United States, and the largest LGBTQ+ event in history. The events, which began even before June, included museum exhibitions, lectures, community discussions, drag performances, and concerts. The Reclaim Pride Coalition was founded in 2019, with the goal of pushing back against the commercialism of Pride events. It held the Queer Liberation March, without corporate sponsors or police involvement.

In smaller cities and towns across New York state, Pride can take the form of a parade, a flag raising, a party, or a festival. In some places, the act of raising a Pride flag for the first time can be as controversial and rebellious today as it was for the participants of the Christopher Street Liberation Day March to appear defiantly and proudly in public in 1970.

The Stonewall uprising marks just one battle in the fight for LGBTQ+ rights, a revolution that is still very much ongoing. The actions of the

LGBTQ+ community across those six nights in Greenwich Village were a spark, bringing new energy and passion to the movement that had already begun, raising new leaders, organizations, and ideas to the forefront. Stonewall's reverberations can still be felt today when a Pride flag is raised, protesters take to the streets, and members of the queer community live unapologetically as themselves.

15

The 9/11 Attacks and New York's Resilience, 2001

Bruce W. Dearstyne

Adapted from Bruce W. Dearstyne, "The Spirit of New York: Defining Events in the Empire State's History" (SUNY Press, 2nd ed., 2022).

New York state and, particularly, New York City are always on the move. Throughout its history, the state has shown a remarkable capacity to bounce back from adversity and keep going. That is particularly true of New York City, which takes setbacks in stride and uses them to rally and build a better future. Most residents, proud of their unique city, assume without question that it is indestructible and will recover from whatever catastrophe may befall it. That can-do spirit was particularly evident as the city recovered from the terrorist attack on the Twin Towers on September 11, 2001. New Yorkers made plans not only to rebuild but to develop something even better for the future.

On September 11, 2001, terrorists hijacked four commercial airliners and flew two of them into the Twin Towers of the World Trade Center (WTC) in New York City. The resulting explosions and fires led to the collapse of both towers, and 2,752 victims were lost. The WTC included five other buildings, all destroyed or substantially damaged when the towers collapsed.

At its dedication in April 1973, Governor Nelson Rockefeller said the center would reaffirm New York's "accustomed place as the major capital of world commerce." By 2001, the Twin Towers, each 110 stories high, were home to 430 banking, finance, insurance, import/export, bond-trading, and transportation companies, as well as several trade and professional associations. On an average day, about 50,000 people worked there and 140,000 people rode the elevators to visit offices, dine in restaurants, or take in the breathtaking view from the observation deck at the top of the South Tower.

The Twin Towers were a symbol of New York City's proud and assertive leadership in American finance and commerce. Terrorists had detonated a truck bomb in a public parking area beneath the North Tower in February 1993. They killed six people and injured a thousand but failed in their goal of toppling the North Tower into the South Tower.

In 2001, they succeeded in their destruction. The devastated site came to be called Ground Zero.

The same day, terrorists flew another plane into the Pentagon, causing substantial damage. Another hijacked plane crashed in Pennsylvania.

It was a catastrophic loss for the nation and the state. New York City, which had given little thought to its security in recent times, was stunned. The nation responded by invading Afghanistan, and later Iraq, to extinguish the sources of terrorism. New York, the nation's largest—and arguably most resilient—city began to build back bigger and better than ever. The stories of the New York City Fire Department's recovery, a memorial and grand new building on the WTC site, and a citywide renaissance provide insights into this broader story of resilience.

Fire Department: Devastation and Resilience

The Fire Department of the City of New York (FDNY) lost 343 of its members in the attack, including many who went inside the towers to rescue people and died when the towers collapsed. FDNY, which traces its origins to the "fire watch" established by Dutch colonial authorities in New Amsterdam (as the city was then called) in 1648, was confident and used to victory over fires. During the 1990s, it had strengthened fire regulations, upgraded equipment, improved training, and created five new squads to fight major fires. Firefighters were known for their selfless dedication and esprit de corps. By 2001, the numbers of annual firefighter deaths and injuries were at a fifty-year low. Firefighters liked to say that their department always beat the fires.

Yet the 9/11 attack overwhelmed its capacities. "The firefighters arriving at the towers faced a situation that spun wildly and rapidly out of their control, in a way we had never anticipated," Fire Commissioner Thomas Von Essen recalled. "Firefighters are accustomed to bringing order and control. In this case, that was impossible."[1] Mayor Rudolph Giuliani came to the scene and established an overall command post a few blocks north of the towers. Von Essen, the chief of department, and other top officers arrived on the scene, established their own command post in the North Tower, quickly concluded that the fires could not be extinguished, and began dispatching firefighters to rescue civilians.

But they had to move the post up the street after the South Tower collapsed and the North Tower was weakened. Radio communication was deficient in the towers. The police developed their own command center, and communication between the fire and police departments was sporadic. Police and fire department radios were incompatible. Fire officers did not hear dispatches about the extent of damage from a police helicopter hovering above the towers. Chain of command was unclear after the chief of department and the deputy chief were killed when the North Tower collapsed.

The fires were extinguished soon after the towers collapsed. Firefighters worked on the sites of the fallen towers to rescue colleagues and, later, to be sure the bodies of their dead colleagues were retrieved. They joined city officials for one funeral after another. Many of the people who worked on the sites later suffered health-related problems from the toxic materials they encountered.

But, typical of New York's resilient spirit, the department went beyond mourning its losses to actively plan for a better future. A month after the attack, Von Essen initiated an oral history project to interview firefighters and emergency medical technicians who had been on the scene that day. The interviews revealed the department's disarray on 9/11: Radios were insufficient to communicate from the ground to the men in the towers, many firefighters were uncertain what to do, leadership was scattered, chains of command were disrupted, and the magnitude of the disaster was unprecedented. One firefighter recalled, "I have to tell you that I'm not sure what happened or where the command post was at this point. I didn't know—see, this situation was like war in that, you know, you've heard the expression the fog of war. Too much stuff happened sometimes too quickly for you to sort it all out and make logical decisions based on what's real." Hastily compiled

---

1. Thomas Von Essen, *Strong of Heart: Life and Death in the Fire Department of New York* (New York: Regan Books, 2002), 279.

books published in 2002 with interviews of firefighters and survivors of the collapse presented additional evidence of uncertainty and disorder.

Michael Bloomberg, a wealthy business magnate who had made a fortune as an entrepreneur assembling and selling business information, was elected mayor in November 2001. The mayor appointed a new fire commissioner and engaged McKinsey and Company, a highly regarded New York–based consulting firm, to study both the police and fire department.

McKinsey and Company's report on FDNY acknowledged that that the attack was "unparalleled in nature and magnitude. . . . Never before had such buildings been so severely damaged by explosion and fire that they collapsed to the ground."[2] It acknowledged the bravery and heroism of firefighters but did not spare the department from criticism for lack of a clear command structure in the emergency, failure of radios, and firefighters not having clear orders. But, in line with Bloomberg's direction, the report emphasized the future rather than the past—its official title was *Increasing FDNY's Preparedness*. The report recommended improved planning and management, stronger communications and technology capabilities, and enhancement of the department's system of member and family support services. It also recommended increased operational preparedness, including an incident command system to ensure fire and police coordination at major disasters.

FDNY moved quickly to implement the McKinsey recommendations. It began with a major reorganization, adding more chiefs at the middle-management level. It strengthened training. It began consulting with the US Military Academy at West Point and the Naval War College for advice on strengthening its chain of command and fighting terrorist attacks. It drew on the US Forest Service, which had longtime experience with coordinated responses to forest fires, for advice on how to develop an effective incident command. It established a task force headed by R. James Woolsey, former director of the CIA, to assess and strengthen technical readiness, including communications during unprecedented emergencies such as terrorist car bombs.

A major advance came with the establishment of a state-of-the-art operations center in 2006. The center enabled top-level commanders to monitor fire and emergency medical activity throughout the city, supervise daily responses, and manage large-scale disasters. Strategic planning and measurable benchmarks became standard operating procedure. It all

---

2. McKinsey and Company, *Increasing FDNY's Preparedness*, Fire Department of the City of New York, 2002, 3.

represented a sea change for an agency that had been accustomed to setting up ad hoc command sites, improvising at the site of disasters, and counting on the courage of its firefighters to overcome any obstacle.

Mayor Bloomberg in May 2004 announced adoption of a "Citywide Incident Management System" to integrate police and fire operations in emergencies.

The progress and changes in the department can be traced by following the career of Joseph W. Pfeifer. A battalion chief on 9/11, he was first on the scene at the North Tower, directed firefighters up the stairs to rescue people, then evacuated them just before the tower's collapse. He personified the department's—and the city's—spirit of resilience and moving forward after a disaster. Determined to make a difference, he volunteered to help implement the McKinsey report. Over the next few years, during which he was promoted several times, he led in many ways—convincing firefighters that the department had to change, bringing in new firefighter technologies, designing new fire boats with the capacity to reach the tops of higher buildings, and working out counterterrorism response plans.

Pfeifer's ideas, expressed in articles, book chapters, and lectures, exemplify the sorts of new approaches that came to permeate the department. He explained the need for real-time information being available to frontline responders, for command resiliency in case senior commanders were injured or killed, and for interagency cooperation in crises. He ran training seminars for FDNY officers and firefighters. He went on to publish some of his ideas in national journals.-

The fire department evolved and strengthened its capacities after 9/11, just as the city of New York did. Firefighters were trained for the new, more complex responsibilities that 9/11 and its aftermath had thrust on their department. Response times decreased. The year 2012 set an all-time record for the fewest fire fatalities in the city's history up to that year. The department cooperated with the police on several major incidents including a blackout in August 2003, an airplane emergency landing in the Hudson River in January 2009, a car bomb in Times Square in May 2010, and a major flood caused by Superstorm Sandy in 2012.

Place of Remembrance

New York leaders debated what to do with the WTC site after the bodies of the dead had been removed, the funerals were held, the mourning waned, and the debris was cleared away a year after the attacks. The Bloomberg administration sought public input through surveys and discussion forums. Two ideas emerged. One, dedicate and use the site only as a commemoration of the event and a memorial to the people who perished there. Two, rebuild the destroyed buildings or put something in their place that was equally grand and demonstrated New York's (and America's) defiance of the terrorists and also restored an important city center for commerce. In the end, New York got both.

The situation was complicated. The Port Authority of New York and New Jersey owned the WTC site. The Lower Manhattan Development Corporation (LMDC) was established in November 2001 as a subsidiary to the Empire State Development Corporation, a state public benefit corporation. Half of the LMDC's members were appointed by the governor of New York state; half by the mayor of New York City. Giuliani made his appointments just before leaving office, so Bloomberg could not make any right away. Later, the membership was expanded, but the governor's appointees still outnumbered the mayor's. Moreover, the legislation gave the governor the power to appoint the director, who had charge of operations. The LMDC was charged with developing plans for the sixteen-acre WTC site and Lower Manhattan generally and received $10 billion in federal funds appropriated for rebuilding Lower Manhattan. Mayor Bloomberg and Governor George Pataki often bickered over how to proceed and how to allocate available funds.

The LMDC invited proposals for what to do with the WTC site. In February 2003, it chose the architect Daniel Libeskind's master plan, which he called "Memory Foundations." It was designed to balance memory of the 9/11 attacks with the need to revitalize the neighborhood. The plan included a large memorial at the center of the site; a museum; five large office buildings arranged in a spiral with the tallest, to be called One World Trade Center (also called the "Freedom Tower," it was to be 1,776 feet high to evoke the nation's revolutionary past), at the top; a performing arts center; and other features.

Libeskind's plan was a start but was modified over time. The LMDC decided that part of the site would be devoted to a memorial. That part of Libeskind's plan was vague and needed fleshing out. Should the memorial mourn those who were lost or celebrate their lives? Should it reflect tragedy or the spirit of resilience? The LMDC established a Families Advisory Council, consisting of members of families of those killed at the site, to help develop parameters for the memorial. It carried out a "Public Perspectives" campaign through which people could express their aspirations for the winning design.

In April 2003, the LMDC launched what would become the largest design competition in history to that time to gather ideas for the memorial. Entry was open to anyone over eighteen, regardless of nationality. All entries would be evaluated by a memorial jury that consisted of a representative of the Families Advisory Council, world-renowned architects, prominent arts and cultural affairs professionals, a Lower Manhattan resident and a business owner, and others.

The competition brought in more than five thousand proposals from across the nation and around the world. The jury undertook a long review and discussion process. "People are responding from the heart," one juror remarked.[3]

In January 2004, they selected "Reflecting Absence," submitted by the architect Michael Arad. His would be an open-air memorial with the names of all the victims on display and a minimum of interpretation. The jury liked the concept but rejected some features, such as the location and shape of a proposed museum. The site looked stark, they felt. The jury urged Arad to collaborate with another architect, Peter Walker, to soften the landscape with trees and landscaping. The Arad–Walker plan was then accepted. The two architects described the memorial:

> This memorial [is] a space that resonates with the feelings of loss and absence that were generated by the taking of thousands of lives on September 11, 2001 and February 26, 1996. It is located in a field of trees that is interrupted by two large voids containing recessed pools. The pools and the ramps that surround them encompass the footprint of the Twin Towers. A cascade of water that describes the perimeter of each square feeds the pools with a continuous stream. . . . The surface of the memorial plaza is punctuated by the linear rhythms of rows of deciduous trees, forming informal clusters, clearings and groves. The surface consists of a composition of stone pavers, plantings, and low ground cover. Through its annual cycle of rebirth, the living park extends and deepens the experience of the memorial.[4]

---

3. Allison Bailey Blais and Lynn Rasic, *A Place of Remembrance: Official Book of the National September 11 Memorial* (updated ed., Washington, DC: National Geographic, 2015), 129.

4. Blais and Rasic, *Place*, 139.

The names of the fallen, including those killed in Pennsylvania on 9/11 and as a result of the attack on the towers back in 1996, are inscribed along the edges of the pools. The names are grouped in what Arad calls "meaningful adjacencies"—the names of victims who worked together in life or flew on the doomed planes are grouped together on ledges around the pools.

A separate, indoor museum was developed to tell the story of the attacks. There is a sign on the wall as you walk into the museum, a quotation from the *Aeneid* by the Roman poet Virgil: "No day shall erase you from the memory of time." Both the memorial and the museum were paid for mostly by private donations, including from individuals and several large foundations and corporations.

The memorial opened on September 11, 2011, the tenth anniversary of the attacks. The museum opened on May 21, 2014. They are both operated by the same nonprofit organization, called the National September 11 Memorial & Museum, which is dedicated to preserving the memory of the 9/11 attacks at the World Trade Center site.

"Great memorials cause you to think and to remember, to reflect, and to walk away determined to make sure that some tragedy like this doesn't happen again," said Mayor Bloomberg at the memorial's unveiling. The official book of the memorial, issued at the time of its unveiling, is titled *A Place of Remembrance*.

The memorial is visited by millions of people each year. Visitors report finding it an emotional and moving experience due to its design and the connection to the victims of the attack that it conveys.

Freedom Tower at One World Trade Center

In the meantime, the Port Authority moved ahead with plans for the construction of new buildings to replace the others, beyond the towers, destroyed in the attack. The centerpiece would be One World Trade Center, also known as the Freedom Tower, near the memorial. Rising to 1,776 feet, as architect Libeskind had envisioned, it would be the tallest structure in the Western Hemisphere and the seventh tallest in the world. It is more than four hundred feet taller than the towers of the original World Trade Center, symbolic of New York's spirit of daring and grandeur.

But getting there involved another New York–sized story. There were several years of negotiation and sometimes public bickering among the City of New York, the Port Authority, the governor, the Lower Manhattan Development Corporation, and the developer Larry Silverstein, who had leased space in the WTC just before the attacks. He recalled in his memoir *The Rising: The Twenty-Year Battle to Rebuild the World Trade Center* that "the reconstruction was a seemingly never-ending battle" against what seemed like "impossible odds."[5] But, in the end, a complicated deal was worked out. The Port Authority would construct the Freedom Tower, while Silverstein would rebuild the smaller towers that had been destroyed on 9/11. Insurance from the destroyed buildings, funding from the state and the Port Authority, and a special bond issue would support the work.

Construction plans moved ahead. Eventually, the site came to include One World Trade Center (the "Freedom Tower"), 2 World Trade Center, 3 World Trade Center, 4 World Trade Center, 7 World Trade Center, the National September 11 Memorial & Museum, and a transportation hub.

The Freedom Tower is the most prominent by far. It opened on November 3, 2014, and was soon filled with a variety of commercial tenants. But the contrast with the tenant makeup in the Twin Towers reflects the change in the city's business base. Those towers had held primarily financial institutions such as Bank of America and Cantor Fitzgerald, reflecting the city's status as a global financial hub. The Freedom Tower has more media companies, such as Condé Nast, prestigious publisher of *The New Yorker* and *Vanity Fair* magazines; Infosys, a global information-services company; and Progantics, a biotech company.

The Freedom Tower has an observation deck on floors 100 to 102, called the One World Observatory, the highest vantage point in the city. From there, people can get a 360-degree view of the city, and, on a clear day, up to forty-five miles can be seen in each direction. The tower is also visible for miles around, a symbol of New York City's grandeur. It is a monument to America's defiance of terrorists and New York City's determination to rise from the ashes of any disaster. It also attracted tourists to the area, aligning well with the Bloomberg administration's work to bring more jobs and people into southern Manhattan.

Reviving the City

The stories of the fire department, the memorial, and the Freedom Tower played out against a broader saga of renewal and transformation in the post-9/11 years under Mayor Bloomberg, who served from 2002 to 2014.

---

5. Larry Silverstein, *The Rising: The Twenty-Year Battle to Rebuild the World Trade Center* (New York: Knopf, 2024), 329.

New York was a place of contentions for power, such as the governor, mayor, city council, Port Authority, LMDC, and very vocal residents. Outgoing Mayor Giuliani took Daniel Doctoroff, Bloomberg's incoming deputy mayor for economic development and rebuilding, aside one day just before leaving office. Doctoroff recalled the conversation in his 2017 memoir, *Greater Than Ever: New York's Big Comeback*. "Dan, I want to give you some advice," Giuliani began.

> This is New York. On any issue, if there are four New Yorkers discussing it, there are going to be five opinions. No matter how good an idea you have . . . some people are going to hate it. You can go into Times Square and start handing out one hundred dollar bills. Somebody will criticize you for it being too much. Somebody will criticize you for it being too little. And somebody will criticize you for not distributing it fairly. No matter how much you are criticized, stay true to what you believe in.[6]

That proved to be good advice, though Giuliani might have added that sometimes you have to compromise, improvise, outmaneuver, and find a way around obstacles and obstructionists to make big things happen in New York.

When Bloomberg assumed office in January 2002, as Doctoroff recalled, "it was fair to question the very premise of New York" as a vibrant city with a great future.[7] The city had lost about 430,000 jobs and $2.8 billion in wages, and around $2 billion in tax revenues. About eighteen thousand small businesses had been destroyed or displaced as a result of the attacks. People left—in some neighborhoods around Ground Zero, the apartment vacancy rate shot up to over 40 percent.

Over the next few years, though, New York recovered, thanks in large measure to Bloomberg's and Doctoroff's policies. The Bloomberg administration pursued several policies:

TRUMPET NEW YORK'S RESILIENCE

Before leaving office, Mayor Giuliani worked with BBDO, one of the city's leading advertising agencies, to create six short TV spots to highlight New

---

6. Daniel Doctoroff, *Greater Than Ever: New York's Big Comeback* (New York: Public Affairs, 2017), 15–16.

7. Doctoroff, *Greater*, xii.

York's buoyancy and encourage shoppers and tourists to resume visits to the city. They were titled "The New York Miracle." The idea was that well-known New Yorkers excel at unexpected things, demonstrating the can-do spirit of their city. At the end of each segment, Mayor Giuliani appears, imploring viewers, "The New York miracle! Be part of it!"

Mayor Bloomberg's inaugural address explained that New York had problems in the past but never failed, always came back stronger than ever. It would do it again—rebuild better than before. City reports and media coverage reinforced that message: New York, undaunted, was on the move and could not be stopped.

Articulate a Bold Vision

In speeches just before and after entering office, Bloomberg talked about "the City of Tomorrow, with marvelous parks and buildings, finer hospitals, safter and more beautiful streets, better schools, and more swimming pools." He outlined a "Five-Borough Economic Development Plan" and a focused vision for Lower Manhattan. His administration spearheaded the effort, but he kept repeating that it was really up to the businesses, cultural institutions, and people of New York to propel their city into the future. The rhetoric was soaring, but it buoyed confidence and hope. That appealed to New Yorkers. In the end, much of what Bloomberg called for got done.

Make Use of Available Resources

Bloomberg raised property taxes to get much-needed resources. He made use of funds granted by the federal government for the city to respond to and rebuild after the attack. Where necessary, he floated municipal bonds to support investments.

Bloomberg supported a bid by the City of New York for the 2012 Summer Olympics. To attract the games, his administration undertook several massive public works projects. These included development of Long Island City's Hunters Point (site of the proposed Olympic village), Williamsburg and Greenpoint waterfronts (sites for swimming, diving, and beach volleyball), and a mega project at Hudson Yards on the west side of Manhattan (the planned site of a new Olympic stadium). New York was a runner-up (London got the bid). But the building had revitalized several areas of the city, and the planned and partially begun projects were transformed into housing, recreation, and park areas.

On the other hand, the mayor stopped spending on what he judged to be poor investments. He declined to pay companies to stay in New York, calling that policy "corporate welfare." He cancelled Giuliani's plans to build lavish new stadiums for the Yankees in the Bronx and the Mets in Queens (though later, when the city's budget outlooked brightened, he did agree to provide infrastructure upgrades and tax credits).

Support a Variety of Businesses

On 9/11, New York City's economy was overly dependent on the financial industry. Factories had closed; traditional manufacturing jobs had mostly evaporated. Bloomberg saw the need to diversify and encouraged new businesses to come to New York. But the city went after companies with a future, such as start-ups and innovative companies, particularly in the digital media sectors. Technology firms, advertising agencies, and media companies moved into New York as the number of financial institutions declined. He emphasized tourism, which grew steadily during his tenure, along with the number of hotel rooms and related service-industry jobs. The city's "Made in New York" initiative increased film and television production in the city through tax credits, free advertising on public transportation, and other incentives. The city grew by nearly 450,000 jobs from 2001 to 2013.

Make Affordable Housing a Keystone

New York was becoming too expensive a place to live. More space was needed for moderate-income housing. The mayor announced an affordable housing plan in 2002. Too much space was zoned only for manufacturing. His planning director, Amanda Burden, pushed through 140 rezoning laws, rezoning over 40 percent of the city to make room for housing. Bloomberg undertook an $8 billion investment in housing and launched what would become the largest city-driven affordable-housing program in US history.

Bloomberg also liked high-end development and welcomed the moneyed class to New York. He cheered the construction of high-rise towers, sometimes with conditions that the developers also build affordable housing and have plazas or parks open to the public. When he left office in 2013, more than twenty skyscrapers—nine of them taller than the Empire State Building—were in various stages of development.

Lift Southern Manhattan

Bloomberg did not have much control over the 9/11 site—that was mostly locked up by the Port Authority and Lower Manhattan Development Corporation, where he had limited influence. But he did comment on proposed memorial designs and publicly push for the construction to keep to deadlines (for instance, he insisted that the memorial must be open by the tenth anniversary of the 9/11 attacks). He opened up some streets that had been blocked by the World Trade Center to make the area more inviting. He pushed for the Freedom Tower to include a greater variety of companies than the WTC had.

Bloomberg also issued a plan for southern Manhattan, and his administration delivered on most of it: major investments in new parks and waterfront access, more affordable housing, new schools, playgrounds, riverfront esplanades, bike lanes, sports facilities, and better transportation. When he entered office, about 23,000 people lived in the area; a decade later, there were around 64,000. Five new schools opened in the area.

Projects to Boost Quality of Life

Several projects during the bounce back from 9/11 involved repurposing obsolete and sometimes abandoned structures. For instance, an abandoned New York Central Railroad elevated spur along the west side of Manhattan, originally authorized in the nineteenth century to carry freight trains with commodities such as coal, dairy, and beef products, was disused long before 9/11. It was transformed into an urban park lined with trees, artwork, and other features. It is owned by the city but operated by a not-for-profit group. It now attracts over eight million visitors annually and hosts educational and other events. It has boosted real estate values in the adjacent area.

New York's Resilience

The 9/11 attacks tested but did not break New York's spirit. The tragedy was an incentive for the city to reinvent itself. Most of the initiatives in those years had a positive impact—New York was a more robust, confident city a decade after the attacks than it had been on 9/11. And yet the city became an expensive place to live and do business. Critics acknowledged the affordable housing but said even more should have been built. Bill de Blasio, who succeeded Bloomberg as mayor in 2014, said that the previous decade had been "a tale of two cities"—one wealthy, one poor. But this ignored the fact that the majority of New Yorkers, the middle class, were in fact better off and more convinced that their city was the best in the nation than they had been right after the attacks. New Yorkers are never satisfied and keep trying to improve.

"The heart of crisis leadership is the ability to sustain hope by unifying efforts to solve complex problems in the face of a great tragedy," said FDNY leader Joseph Pfeifer in his 2021 memoir, *Ordinary Heroes*. "It takes courage to find resilience, to come back to lead with greater determination and purpose."[8] Pfeifer's comments capture New York City's importance and its key traits: strong, proud, defiant, and resilient. Building back from the 9/11 attacks reinforced those traits. When Superstorm Sandy flooded much of the city in 2012 and the COVID-19 pandemic hit in 2020, New Yorkers vowed, "We survived 9/11—we can survive anything!" and powered through. The city continued its upward trajectory—bigger, better, confident in the future.

---

8. Joseph Pfeifer, *Ordinary Heroes: A Memoir of 9/11* (New York: Portfolio, 2021), 237–38.

16

Inside the COVID-19 Era in New York

New York City Parks as Witnesses, 2020 to 2022

KEVIN C. FITZPATRICK

New York City has led the way through many crises in United States history. It has been the first to cope with health crises and to develop strategies for a large urban population to keep going even in the midst of serious public health challenges.

The New York City Department of Parks and Recreation is a good example. When the COVID-19 crisis hit in 2020, the department's leadership found ways to keep its employees safe, including having many work from home. Parks served the city by taking on some entirely new responsibilities, including serving as sites for food distribution, remote education to assist students who could not attend school in person, and vaccination against COVID-19.

The NYC Parks story is one of dedication and service, flexibility and improvisation, determination and perseverance. New Yorkers rise to the occasion during crises, and this agency's work during the COVID-19 crisis is an excellent example. This chapter relates the experience firsthand, as NYC Parks employees experienced and recalled it.

☙

The global COVID-19 pandemic that swept the world during 2020 through 2022 was a cataclysmic event in New York state history. The crisis brought life to a standstill and was devasting to the population. In less than a week in March 2020, regular life came to a halt that lasted for most of the year. As the death toll rose, businesses and schools closed, and governments on the local, state, and national levels struggled to manage the pandemic.

In this account, I will explore one slice of the New York story, as seen through the eyes of one agency in New York City. I sat down for one-on-one interviews with one hundred members of the New York City Department of Parks and Recreation during the waning days of the pandemic. The agency, one of fifty that report to the mayor, was caught in the middle of the crisis. NYC Parks maintains more than thirty thousand acres of land and five thousand properties in the five boroughs but was told to close all playgrounds and parks. Staff were instructed to put locks and chains on gates and remove basketball goals. In the summer, swimming pools were closed and beaches limited usage.

By interviewing these New Yorkers, from entry-level workers up to the commissioners who run the agency, I documented a story of perseverance, sadness, and relief. As the public was told to stay indoors and practice a new term called "social distancing," the "Parkies" had to continue working.

The Pandemic Begins

The roots of the pandemic first began in late 2019 in China, and by January 2020 the World Health Organization activated its Incident Management Support Team. The health crisis swept across Asia in January. By the end of the month, there were cases in the United States.

On March 1, 2020, news broke of the first confirmed COVID-19 case in New York, a woman in her thirties in Manhattan who had traveled to Iran. On March 7, Governor Andrew M. Cuomo declared a state of emergency for New York state. The first reported death attributed to COVID-19 in New York City was on March 14. Overnight, businesses and offices closed. Theaters and sports venues shut down. Airports halted international flights. City schools closed March 13 and sent all staff and more than one million students home.

For the next three years, the state coped with the deaths the disease brought, the damaged economy, and drastic changes in life, relationships, and values. In the United States, deaths in which COVID-19 was the underlying cause totaled 1,056,330 between 2020 and 2022; of those, New York accounted for 68,540, about 6.5 percent.

The most rapid period of change in the crisis in New York was a series of days in March 2020. On March 11, the World Health Organization declared the novel coronavirus (COVID-19) outbreak to be a pandemic. The next day, Mayor Bill de Blasio declared a state of emergency. That same day, theaters on Broadway closed, with thirty-one shows running and eight shows still in previews. New York schools closed, as noted above, bars and restaurants were ordered to be shuttered, and the St. Patrick's Day Parade was canceled. On March 13, President Trump declared a national state of emergency.

In the Parks

The seven thousand members of NYC Parks played a critical role in New York's response to the pandemic and had a unique view of the situation as the members of the staff continued to go to work.

The commissioner at the time was Mitchell Silver, who had been running the agency since 2014. He was in a city budget hearing when news broke that the city was going to close—and the governor had ordered immediate closures. Silver set up a war room in a boardroom of the third floor of the landmark Arsenal building in Central Park.

The agency's leadership faced uncertainty but also the need for critical decisions. The pace was hectic. "We were meeting in this room about twice a day," Silver recalled two years later. "We were getting guidance from City Hall on what to do, but we started planning ahead. What do we need to do? How do we prepare for what's about to come? We met in this room until we realized we could not be in the same space, and then we pivoted to Zoom like everyone else, very quickly, and started meeting in the morning and the evening. There were different teams, including a leadership team and the operations team, to be prepared for what was next."

Silver and his deputies had to quickly decide who could come to work. The agency did not at the time have anyone working remotely; the staff did not have the network, laptops, tablets, or cameras to be off-site and working.

"We knew then that our staff were going to be deemed essential workers," Silver recalled. "And so, they have to keep working." Agency management waited for guidance from city hall but decided that "at least those that worked in the parks, in maintenance, all the office workers" would report to work. They also prepared "for 20 to 25 percent of our workforce not to be in the office."

"Like most of the leaders, I made a determination that if staff is going to be in the field, I'm coming to work," Silver said. "I'm not working from home. Most of the agency's leaders felt the same way. Initially, we started stepping apart so if we did meet in here, we were six feet apart, but then we eventually just did all of our meetings on Zoom."

In Queens, Meira Berkower, a project manager, was getting text messages from her coworkers and husband in the critical early days. The situation was changing rapidly. At the time, she was a seventeen-year employee in the agency's planning office. She recalled, "As Commissioner Silver used to say, 'We're the happy agency.' The truth is, open space is just very important to living and sometimes its importance is overlooked. During COVID we learned that open space is really important. I think that's basically why I've stayed at Parks; it's a really important mission." Berkower recalled,

> My kids' school all of a sudden decided to close because they weren't sure what was going on. I was trying to figure out what I was going to need to do if their school seemed to be closed indefinitely. I had a lot of meetings, and kept asking what was going to happen? I was still on my phone taking conference calls. We secured a babysitter. . . . But we were saying, "It seems to be spreading. Should you be coming to work? Should you not be coming?" It was very stressful. I remember going to work and no one really knowing what was going on.

But soon agency leaders decided who would be working from home, including her. The decision had to be implemented rapidly without much time to get ready. She recalled that "I started, not really sure what was happening, I started to kind of collect my things. I don't remember when they said that work was going to close, but I do remember thinking, 'What do I take? Do I take everything?' I had no idea. So, I just started. I packed as much as I could and carried out as much as I could."

Working Remotely

Nicole Brooks works in the Stonehenge, the Staten Island Parks headquarters. A project manager, she had to balance working remotely with her school-age child at home as well as worrying about her father. "It was very scary," she said:

> At that time everything was uncertain. We didn't know what was happening. We were told to stay home. Schools were closed. I literally ran out, that same day, I think it was March 16, and bought a laptop, so I'd be able to have my daughter be able to do school from home. Laptops were flying off the shelves, and I needed to just get something. We didn't have one, so I ran to Best Buy and grabbed the first one I could get. I remember sitting in the parking lot and just thinking, "What else should I get? Where else should I go?" It was very disconcerting.

Brooks became one of the millions who now had to work from home for the first time. She had a full schedule that now seemed to stretch to twelve-hour days. Brooks also had to keep tabs on her daughter's school time:

> It was a lot. You think you can just set them up in front of the computer, and that's it. But it's not. I would have to be helping her with every class, making sure she's logged in on time, checking the schedule. When is she supposed to be on? When is she supposed to be off? Which teacher? Has she done the assignments? It wasn't as easy as I thought it would be or as easy as people made it seem. "Oh, you know, remote learning." She had a very difficult time doing remote learning. It is hard to focus for long periods of time. And get kids to sit and look at a screen for that long. Trying to teach anything. It must have been difficult, and I give the teachers all the praise because I don't know how they were able to keep kids learning as well as they were. They did they best they could; we did the best we could.

Thérèse Braddick, deputy commissioner for capital projects, has an office in the Olmsted Center in Flushing Meadows–Corona Park. Her office was filled with scores of plants left behind by office workers who departed, and the building was like a ghost town with so many vacancies.

"I actually made the decision that I was going to continue to work here in the office," Braddick said. "I did not enjoy working at home full time; I made the decision that I was going to come into work here. I also wanted to be supportive of those people that did come into work. There was a core group that came in with some regularity here."

Braddick was commuting to her job when most drivers were staying home, and the city parkways and roadways were a racecourse. "Oh gosh," she said. "It was just like a different world. People just started driving like lunatics and those people that were on the road were a little bit crazy. They drove way too fast because there was nobody else on the road. It was such a different period of time." Working in offices where so many colleagues were absent and working from home was a challenge too, she added. "It was a very lonely period of time because there were not very many people around you. You didn't have that personal interaction and you didn't have that human contact that you were so used to."

Feeding and Helping

As the COVID-19 era gripped New York, there were two areas that needed the government to step in and help the public. This was a dire situation, and these two major efforts were spun up for NYC Parks to manage: food distribution centers to feed families, and remote schools set up in NYC Parks buildings so children could connect with their schools while their parents went back to work. Neither had ever been tried before. The agency primarily used staff members from its recreation department to plan, staff, and manage both initiatives.

Ashanta Smith was the manager of the Hunts Point Recreation Center in the Bronx. A twenty-seven-year veteran of NYC Parks, he was on vacation when he was called and told he was to set up the first food distribution center in the state. "My specialty is basketball, outdoor adventure and sports," he recalled. He would have to quickly learn and apply new skills and strategies in this critical assignment.

Parks personnel worked with the National Guard, which the governor had called into service, and multiple city agencies to distribute the meals via taxicabs and hired car services.An effort on that scale required quick ramping up of processes and more people. Smith explained,

They sent me more staff, about eight people. My goal was to feed 100,000 people. That was the goal. Unrealistic goal. Now the city was shutting down, people can't leave. It's getting serious. People are scared. My mom was like, "Oh, why are you going to work? Everybody else is staying home." "Mom, it's just me. I'm going to run to the fire. I'm going to run to the fire, throw water on it, come back some more and do it again until it's gone, until it is out." That's just who I am. I can't help it.

The next thing you know, they are saying that we are going to try these initial routes. They started delivering the food. They got the cab drivers involved with the TLC [New York City Taxi and Limousine Commission]. I started off with a staff of six people. During that pandemic, I think I supervised over two hundred people at max, at one time.

During the day, maybe there would be eighty-five people in this building and outside, running in and out. That's not including the over three hundred cab drivers pulling up on a daily basis. The situation starts evolving. The first time, we sent out deliveries on maybe one hundred routes. Every route had six deliveries. That's six hundred deliveries. It started progressing. The staff was anxious now. We're doing more. The pace increased. "At one point we had around eight hundred, nine hundred and the next thing you know, at the height, maybe nine thousand routes in a day [approximately 54,000 meals]. We distributed, the last count I believe was 4.2 million meals. Let's say March to June.

This was the first-ever food distribution site in New York State history. Hunts Point. Chris Suarez and I were the first people, boots on the ground. No game plan, no nothing. Just figure it out.

That could describe the experience of many Parkies. They took initiative, learned by doing, adapted, and made things work.

Learning Bridges

During the pandemic, the NYC Parks and Recreation Centers were closed to the public, and all schools were closed. NYC Parks reopened some centers where schoolchildren could come and take part in remote learning. Recreation staff members who, pre-pandemic, were fitness instructors and aquatics teachers became one-on-one assistants with the children for many months. The Parkies helped the kids with their online lessons and provided fitness, exercise, and art classes.

When the New York City Department of Education opened the schools up in late January 2021—after they had been closed since March 2020—there was a need for places for children to take part in remote learning if they could not be home. NYC Parks employed the recreation staff and neighborhood recreation centers, which remained closed to the public, which allowed them to keep their staff drawing a salary while the centers were closed.

The Fort Hamilton Senior Recreation Center, in Bay Ridge, Brooklyn, was closed. NYC Parks told the city it would open for children to come in and connect with their teachers on days when they could not be in the classroom. The name of the program was Learning Bridges.

Teresa Mangan was an activities manager, running sports programs in parks. She was tasked with running a remote-learning center. A native of Cleveland, she threw herself into the task. Mangan recalled,

> When Learning Bridges started in September 2020, we were told it might be a two-month program and then the kids would be back in school. But it lasted the full year. We had all grades, kindergarten through eighth grade, until January of 2021. Then, the kindergarten, first grade, and third grade went back to school, and we had second grade, fourth grade, and all the way to eighth grade still at the center. Second grade and fourth grade went back to school around April of 2021. We had the fifth through eighth grade at the center. But the whole time we were at max capacity. When we lost some children who went back to school full time, we were able to pull some more kids off the roster and get more kids into the program.

Mangan was supervising staff members who were not teachers, who set up a school inside the rooms that had been used by seniors. She said,

> Almost all of my coworkers were programming recreational activities. They were teaching fitness classes or art classes. But some of them were only teaching seniors. Most of them were teaching classes to seniors. We had a center manager who unfortunately passed away. He was unfamiliar with the structure of a school day and kids' programs, because he had been at a senior center for a very long time. Pete was an amazing guy. We all missed him so much. He actually said, "We're doing amazing things here. One day, they're going to talk about what we're doing here." And he was right. He said, "I feel like I'm witnessing something." [Fort Hamilton Senior Center Manager Peter Lovett died April 6, 2021.]

Mangan recalled,

> We were originally told that we would just be watching the children on their screens and making sure that they were engaged with their teachers on the screens they used for remote learning. And then two o'clock, or 2:30-ish, whenever the school day ended, we would form recreational programs for them. This was not really what was happening. Mainly because every set of teachers had a different way of providing their remote learning with their class materials for the day. We also didn't have Wi-Fi until March 2021. . . . We had hotspots and sometimes employees had to use their—or they felt the need to use their—own phone as a hotspot for these children to make sure that they could submit their work on time and not freak out or get upset about getting on their meeting or not being in attendance. We also were able to figure out ways to use some of the DOE tablets as a hotspot for at least one other device.

Mangan continued,

> All of our participants had to be in masks. I felt we had to constantly check in with the kids because we had to say, "Are you okay?" And, "Are you breathing?" Because you can't tell when the only things you can see are the eyes. And if they are thirsty, they are not breathing well, it's very hard to perceive what is going on with them. Another thing is, the difference I noticed in kids is that they weren't speaking up. Once the mask was on their face, they were not talking as much. In my past experience with kids, they're loud. They're funny. They're speaking up. They are asking questions. A lot of these kids were very discipline oriented, wanted to do the right thing, didn't want to hurt anyone, get anyone sick. So, they were very much more following orders than exploring, questioning, and expressing. It was definitely different to see.
>
> When we would just be in the park and a little kid came up, and they just tried to hug you. And it was kind of like, "I know you're not supposed to be doing this, but how do I tell you it's not okay?" Everyone was, again, scared of . . . I wasn't personally scared, but I'm conscious of their emotions and what they were feeling. So, that was a weird moment when they would try to come up or just high five and stuff like that.

Vaccinations Begin

The race to find a vaccine dominated the news in 2020. On December 13, the first COVID-19 vaccination in the United States was administered, to a nurse in Queens. In 2021 a new era in the pandemic began. On January 26, worldwide COVID-19 cases surpassed 100 million. On February 11, New York City restaurants reopened for indoor dining with 25 percent capacity. On February 22, the US death toll passed 500,000. On March 29, the New York state death toll passed 50,000. And on March 30, the vaccine was available to New Yorkers aged thirty and older. New York used NYC Parks locations as vaccination-distribution sites, along with major locations such as the Jacob K. Javits Convention Center on the west side of Manhattan.

Max Soo was an associate urban park ranger who joined the agency in 2016. Park rangers were among the first to work at a vaccination site. Soo recalled,

> In addition to working as a Ranger, there was the Department of Health and Mental Hygiene. They asked other city agencies to help work at the vaccination PODs, which was "point of dispensation." They had emailed around and asked if anyone wanted to work there for overtime, and since the world was shut down anyway, and I wasn't hanging out with my friends on the weekend, I was pretty much just sitting in my apartment and thinking about COVID. I was like, "Well I may as well be productive and earn some money." I was working at the Bushwick Educational Campus POD, which was not too far from where I lived in Bed-Stuy; it's pretty close to Bushwick.
>
> The first day that I worked there, I had such a trippy moment where I walked in. It was a school that they had converted into a vaccination site, so you walk into the gym, and everything was kind of pushed off to the sides. They had set up these kind of lab tables and the lab tables were at least six feet apart. They were set up in these neat little rows, and you had teams of nurses sitting at each table wearing masks, face shields, and removable scrubs, and all of this gear. It was crazy, because I walked in, and I just remember thinking it was giving me the same kind of energy as a triage tent in the middle of a battlefield.
>
> When I walked in the door and saw it for the first time, I thought, wow, this is going to be in a history book one day,

and that's crazy, because if I have kids, my kids are going to ask me, "What was that like?" Because they're going to read about it. I'm going to say, "I remember walking into that room." If there is a picture of it somewhere in the textbook, I was there. I was there for that. That's pretty wild.

Lorenzo Calabrese, the director of the Buildings Construction Unit for Capital Projects, also worked at a site:

I volunteered. I also speak Italian fluently, so I volunteered as an interpreter if needed at the vax sites. There were twelve-hour shifts; that was mandatory. It was in January 2021, pretty much in the beginning of when they were doing the mass vaccinating. And back then, it was only open to, I believe it was people over sixty-five, and teachers, and essential workers. We would get assigned in the morning what your tasks were. I was always an interpreter, plus because I really didn't have any hospital skills, they would have me helping the crowd move along. So, you would line them up, make sure that they filled out the right paperwork.

You would have to sign yourself up for different dates, and it was always on your regularly scheduled days off from your regular job. It was over on Queens Boulevard. Aviation High School. I remember the excitement on these people's faces where the first day I was speaking to people, I remember speaking to an Italian couple. The husband said he was ninety. The wife was eighty-six or eighty-seven. They were frail, but they were happy-go-lucky. The husband says, "I haven't met my great-grandchild yet." I said, "How old is he?" He said, "Six months old. I haven't met him. I need to get this vaccine, and I need to come back and get the second dose, and I'm throwing a party at my house. I'm having all my kids and grandchildren over."

And it was emotional. It was really an emotional thing. I'm saying, wow, you don't think of what everybody's going through. So, it was excitement for them. A lot of the older people were excited to get back out to society. And these are people, they have lived through wars, they lived through recessions, and some of them even depressions, maybe not in this country, but from whatever country they came from, some of them have lived through hell, and now they are in line waiting to get that shot that is going to bring them back to society.

Moving Forward

Sue Donoghue became the commissioner of NYC Parks on February 28, 2022, appointed by Mayor Eric Adams at a time when the agency was under tremendous stress from the two years of the crisis. She also had to contend with the city hall policy of returning to work in person, when many companies were still allowing remote work. Parks were vandalized during civil unrest, and the agency struggled. Donoghue said,

> The last two and a half years showed just how important people's parks are. And in a way, it will sound odd, but in a way COVID was good in the sense that I think many people, many New Yorkers, could tend to take their parks for granted and go, "Oh, it is just something that's there." COVID showed that they weren't just a nice-to-have. They weren't just something that exist there. They were critical to people's quality of life. They're the only place people felt safe and comfortable, where they could gather with friends and family. They really became New Yorkers' everything, right? We talk about our parks being our backyards, but they were our classrooms, our gyms, our event spaces. They were incredibly critical.
>
> The pandemic coincided with the Black Lives Matter movement and social unrest around facing our demons in terms of inequity and police brutality. And so, there were protests in our parks, and it really led to some serious in-depth reckoning and conversations that we are continuing and a focus on diversity, equity, inclusion, and belonging. And how can we make sure we are providing an equitable, inclusive atmosphere for all of our employees? And that's something that is a big focus of mine.
>
> And that already started coming in the pandemic and that we're looking to further expand. And really the idea of diversity, equity, inclusion, and belonging, that aspect of it, that big "B" for belonging to me, I think again, it goes back to how do you come through challenging times and what's left, what's the after-

math. And for me, the hope is the aftermath is a stronger place, a place that feels like a community, a culture that supports that.

The months following the return of workers to jobs at the parks department were marked by change. Taking a page from other New York offices, a flexible work-from-home plan was tested and adopted. This was the same plan as Wall Street and other city industries used. "Listening sessions" were implemented for staff members to provide work/life balance feedback, and all-day, agency-wide off-site training sessions were undertaken to improve communication skills. As New York City pushed the reset button on everything from riding crowded subways to going into offices consistently, the lasting changes of COVID-19 are evident, five years later. Mayor Adams predicted tourism to the city would surpass pre-pandemic levels of 65 million annual visitors in 2025. Visits to NYC Parks increased along with greater awareness of the necessity for public parks. Commissioner Donoghue enthusiastically presided over many, many capital projects that were paused during the pandemic, cutting the ribbon on parks and playground improvements.

On May 8, 2022, the worldwide death toll from COVID-19 passed six million. On May 14, the US death toll from COVID-19 passed one million. As New York state looks to reflect on the commemoration of the 250th anniversary of the American Revolution, the series of events that began in 2020 in the state are not overlooked or forgotten. This history is so recent that some continue to wear face masks for their safety and new cases are reported daily to hospitals. New York continues to rise up in times of challenges, as it has for 250 years. The state motto has been "Excelsior" (Ever upward) since its adoption in 1778. In April 2020, "E pluribus unum" (Out of many, one) was added, further solidifying the state's reputation for community and strength in times of crisis.

Selected Bibliography

This bibliography lists the SUNY Press books that form the basis for several chapters of this volume (as noted at the beginning of those chapters). It also lists the books cited by the authors of *Revolutionary New York*. It does not list all their other sources, including articles and online sources. Sources cited in the chapters adapted from SUNY Press books are available in the respective books.

Atkins, Barton. 1898. *Sketches of Early Buffalo and the Great Lakes*. Buffalo: Courier.
Barbeau, Arthur E., and Florette Henri. 1974. *The Unknown Soldiers: Black American Troops in World War I*. Philadelphia: Temple University Press.
Barbuto, Richard V. 2014. *Staff Ride Handbook for the Niagara Campaigns, 1812–1814*. Fort Leavenworth, KS: Combat Studies Institute Press.
Basch, Norma. 1982. *In the Eyes of the Law: Women, Marriage, and Property in Nineteenth-Century New York*. Ithaca, NY: Cornell University Press.
Berton, Pierre. 1981. *Flames Across the Border: The Canadian-American Tragedy, 1813–1814*. Boston, MA: Little, Brown.
Blais, Allison Bailey, and Lynn Rasic. 2015. *A Place of Remembrance: Official Book of the National September 11 Memorial*. Updated ed. Washington, DC: National Geographic.
Bogad, Larry M. 2016. *Tactical Performance: Serious Play and Social Movements*. New York: Routledge.
Catt, Carrie Chapman, and Nettie Rogers Schuler. 1923. *Woman Suffrage and Politics: The Inner Story of the Suffrage Movement*. New York: Charles Scribner's Sons.
Chapin, Cyrenius. 1836. *Chapin's Review of Armstrong's Notices of the War of 1812*. Black Rock, NY: B. F. Adams.
Christman, Henry. 1945. *Tin Horns and Calico: The Thrilling Unsung Story of an American Revolt Against Serfdom*. New York: Henry Holt.

Cooney, Robert P. J. 2005. *Winning the Vote: The Triumph of the American Woman Suffrage Movement*. American Graphic Printing.

Cruikshank, Ernest A. 1912. *A Study of Disaffection in Upper Canada in 1812–5*. Ottawa: Royal Society of Canada.

Dangerfield, George. 1960. *Chancellor Robert R. Livingston of New York, 1746–1813*. New York: Harcourt Brace.

Dearstyne, Bruce. 2022. *The Spirit of New York: Defining Events in the Empire State's History*. Albany: State University of New York Press.

Deloria, Philip J. 2022. *Playing Indian*. New Haven, CT: Yale University Press.

Doctoroff, Daniel. 2017. *Greater Than Ever: New York's Big Comeback*. New York: Public Affairs.

Dowley, Kathleen M., Susan Ingalls Lewis, and Meg Devlin O'Sullivan, editors. 2020. *Suffrage and Its Limits: The New York Story*. Albany: State University of New York Press.

Eastman, Crystal. 1910. *Work Accidents and the Law*. New York: Russell Sage Foundation.

Ellis, David M. 1979. *New York: State and City*. Ithaca, NY: Cornell University Press.

Evans, Charles W. 1903. *History of St. Paul's Church, Buffalo, N.Y., 1817 to 1888*. Buffalo: Matthews-Northrup Works.

Flick, Alexander C., editor. 1926. *The American Revolution in New York: Its Political, Social and Economic Significance*. Albany: Division of Archives and History / State Education Department.

Gaffney, Dennis. 2007. *Teachers United: The Rise of the New York State United Teachers*. Albany: State University of New York Press.

Gero, Anthony F. 2009. *Black Soldiers of New York State: A Proud Legacy*. Albany: State University of New York Press.

Goodier, Susan, and Karen Pastorello. 2017. *Women Will Vote: Winning Suffrage in New York State*. Ithaca, NY: Cornell University Press.

Gould, David R. 1977. *Forces: Three Themes in the Lives of New Yorkers*. Albany: New York State Museum.

Gould, Jay. 1856. *History of Delaware County and Border Wars of New York, Containing a Sketch of the Late Anti-Rent Difficulties in Delaware*. Roxbury, NY: Keeny & Gould.

Hayes McAlonie, Kelly. 2023. *Louise Blancard Bethune: Every Woman Her Own Architect*. Albany: State University of New York Press.

Hickey, Donald R. 2012. *The War of 1812, A Forgotten Conflict*. Champaign: University of Illinois Press.

Hill, Henry W. 1923. *Municipality of Buffalo, New York: A History 1720–1923*. New York: Lewis Historical Publishing.

Hodge, William. 1885. *A Memoir of the Late William Hodge, Sen.* Buffalo: Bigelow Brothers.

Huston, Reeve. 2000. *Land and Freedom:Rural Society, Popular Protest and Party Politics in Antebellum New York*. Oxford: Oxford University Press.

James, William. 1818. *Full and Correct Account of the Military Occurrences of the Late War Between Great Britain and the United States of America*. London: Black, Kingsbury, Parbury, and Allen.

Jay, John. 1890. *The Correspondence and Public Papers of John Jay: 1763–1781*. Vol. 1, edited by Henry P. Johnston. New York: G. P. Putnam's Sons.

Johnson, Crisfield. 1876. *History of Erie County, New York; Being Its Annals from the Earliest Recorded Events to the Hundredth Year of American Independence*. Buffalo: Matthews & Warren.

Johnson, Joan Marie. 2017. *Funding Feminism: Monied Women, Philanthropy, and the Women's Movement, 1870–1967*. Chapel Hill: University of North Carolina Press.

Ketchum, William. 1854. *An Authentic and Comprehensive History of Buffalo*. Buffalo: Rockwell, Baker & Hill.

Ketchum, William. 1865. *History of Buffalo with Some Account of Its Early Inhabitants, Both Savage and Civilized*. Buffalo: Rockwell, Baker & Hill.

Koch, Daniel. 2020. *Land of the Oneidas: Central New York State and the Creation of America, from Prehistory to the Present*. Albany: State University of New York Press.

Kroeger, Brooke. 2017. *The Suffragents: How Women Used Men to Get the Vote*. Albany: State University of New York Press.

Lawson, Ellen NicKenzie. 2013. *Smugglers, Bootleggers, and Scofflaws: Prohibition and New York City*. Albany: State University of New York Press.

Lepore, Jill. 2005. *New York Burning: Liberty, Slavery, and Conspiracy in Eighteenth-Century Manhattan*. New York: Alfred A. Knopf.

Letchworth, William P. 1874. *Sketch of the Life of Samuel F. Pratt with Some Account of the Early History of the Pratt Family*. Buffalo: Warren, Johnson.

Little, Arthur W. 1936. *From Harlem to the Rhine: The Story of New York's Colored Volunteers*. New York: Covici-Friede.

McCullough, David. 2001. *John Adams*. New York: Simon & Schuster.

McCurdy, Charles. 2001. *The Anti-Rent Era in New York Law and Politics*. Chapel Hill: University of North Carolina Press.

McKenzie, Ruth. 1971. *Laura Secord: The Legend and the Lady*. Toronto: McClelland and Stewart.

McKinsey and Company. 2002. *Increasing FDNY's Preparedness*. Fire Department of the City of New York.

Morris, Richard B. 1967. *John Jay, the Nation, and the Court*. Boston, MA: Boston University Press.

NAWSA (National American Woman Suffrage Association). 1940. *Victory: How Women Won It: A Centennial Symposium 1840–1940*. New York: W. H. Wilson.

Neuman, Johanna. 2019. *Gilded Suffragists: The New York Socialites Who Fought for Women's Right to Vote*. New York: Washington Mews Books.

Newman, Nancy. 2025. *Songs and Sounds of the Anti-Rent Movement in Upstate New York*. Albany: State University of New York Press.

Patterson, Martha H. 2005. *Beyond the Gibson Girl: Reimanaging the American New Woman, 1895–1915*. Champaign: University of Illinois Press.
Patterson, Martha H., editor. 2008. *The New American Woman Revisited: A Reader, 1894–1930*. Rutgers, NJ: Rutgers University Press.
Pepper, Calvin, Jr. 1846. *Manor of Rensselaerwyck*. Albany, NY: Albany and Rensselaer Anti-Rent Associations.
Perry, Elisabeth Israels. 2019. *After the Vote: Feminist Politics in La Guardia's New York*. Oxford: Oxford University Press.
Pershing, John J. 1931. *My Experience in the World War*. New York: Frederick A. Stokes. 2 vols.
Pfeifer, Joseph. 2021. *Ordinary Heroes: A Memoir of 9/11*. New York: Portfolio.
Pratt, Julius W. 1925. *Expansionists of 1812*. New York: Macmillan.
Roseberry, C. R. 2015. *Capitol Story*. 3rd ed., with revisions by the New York State Office of General Services and Diana S. Waite. Albany: State University of New York Press.
Rosenblatt, Albert M. 2023. *The Eight: The Lemmon Slave Case and the Fight for Freedom*. Albany: State University of New York Press.
Rosenthal, Thomas C. 2025. *Cyrenius Chapin: Buffalo's First Physician and War of 1812 Hero*. Albany: State University of New York Press.
Santangelo, Lauren C. 2019. *Suffrage and the City: New York Women Battle for the Ballot*. Oxford: Oxford University Press.
Scott, Emmett J. 1919. *Scott's Official History of the American Negro in the World War*. n.p.
Sheriff, Carol. 1996. *The Artificial River: The Erie Canal and the Paradox of Progress, 1817–1862*. New York: Hill and Wang.
Silverstein, Larry. 2024. *The Rising: The Twenty-Year Battle to Rebuild the World Trade Center*. New York: Knopf.
Smith, Henry P. 1884. *History of the City of Buffalo and Erie County*. Syracuse, NY: D. Mason.
Sweeney, W. Allison. 1919. *History of the American Negro in the Great World War*. Chicago: G. G. Sapp.
Taylor, Alan. 2010. *The Civil War of 1812: American Citizens, British Subjects, Irish Rebels, and Indian Allies*. New York: Knopf.
Thompson, John H. 1897. *Jubilee History of Thorold: Township and Town from the Time of the Red Man to the Present*. Thorold, ON: Thorold and Beaverdams Historical Society.
Thomson, John L. 1818. *Historical Sketch of the Late War Between the United States and Great Britain*. Philadelphia: Thomas Desilver.
Trollope, Frances Milton. 1832. *Domestic Manners of the Americans*. 2nd ed., vol. 2. London: Whittaker, Treacher.
Turner, Orasmus. 1849. *Pioneer History of the Holland Purchase of Western New York*. Buffalo: Jewett, Thomas.

Utter, Brad L. 2020. *Enterprising Waters: The History and Art of New York's Erie Canal*. Albany: State University of New York Press.
Von Essen, Thomas. 2002. *Strong of Heart: Life and Death in the Fire Department of New York*. New York: Regan Books.
Wharton, Edith. 1905. *The House of Mirth*. New York: Charles Scribner's Sons.
Wharton, Edith. 1920. *The Age of Innocence*. New York: D. Appleton.
White, E. B. 1949. *Here Is New York*. New York: Harper & Brothers.
White, Truman C. 1898. *Our County and Its People: A Descriptive Work on Erie County, New York*. Boston, MA: Boston History.
Woods, Mary N. 1999. *From Craft to Profession: The Practice of Architecture in Nineteenth-Century America*. Berkeley: University of California Press.
Zahler, Helene Sara. 1941. *Eastern Workingmen and National Land Policy, 1829–1862*. New York: Columbia University Press.
Zinn, Howard. 2015. *A People's History of the United States*. New York: Harper.

Contributors

Bruce W. Dearstyne is the author of several books, including *The Spirit of New York: Defining Events in the Empire State's History*, *The Crucible of Public Policy: New York Courts in the Progressive Era*, and *Progressive New York: Change and Reform in the Empire State, 1900–1920: A Reader*, all published by SUNY Press.

Fourth-generation New Yorker **Kevin C. Fitzpatrick** is the author and editor of nine books, including *World War I New York: A Guide to the City's Enduring Ties to the Great War* (Globe Pequot Press) and *Dorothy Parker's New York* (3rd revised edition, SUNY Press Excelsior Editions). Fitzpatrick was the oral history project coordinator for the NYC Department of Parks and Recreation. He resides in Manhattan and Shelter Island. Visit fitzpatrickauthor.com.

Dennis Gaffney is a writer based in Albany, New York. He has written three history books, documentary scripts, and articles for publications such as *The New York Times*, *The Washington Post*, and *Mother Jones* as well as for the PBS websites *Antiques Roadshow* and *American Experience* (see dennisgaffney.wordpress.com). Gaffney was communications coordinator for Mayor Kathy Sheehan and the City of Albany for nine years. Previously, he was a writer and video producer at WGBH, Boston's PBS affiliate, as well as an adjunct journalism professor at the University at Albany, SUNY.

Anthony F. Gero of Auburn, New York, holds an MA in history from SUNY College at Cortland and is a fellow of the Company of Military Historians. He has had published over two hundred articles and six books on the New York State Militia, the National Guard in the State of New York, and African Americans in the military, and he is coauthor with Roger Sturcke of *The State of New York National Guard*. Gero is a retired high school teacher and former instructor at Cayuga Community College, SUNY.

Thomas X. Grasso was a geosciences professor at Monroe Community College from 1969 to 1990. He also served as president and later president emeritus of the Canal Society of New York State for a combined forty-three years.

Kelly Hayes McAlonie is an architect and director of campus planning at the University at Buffalo, SUNY.

Ashley Hopkins-Benton is a senior historian and curator of social history at the New York State Museum. Her research and collections work focuses on women's history, LGBTQ+ history, and immigration history as well as sculpture, decorative arts, and toys. Hopkins-Benton is coauthor, with Jennifer Lemak, of *Votes for Women: Celebrating New York's Suffrage Centennial* (SUNY Press), contributing author, with Brad Utter and Karen E. Quinn, of *Enterprising Waters: The History and Art of New York's Erie Canal* (SUNY Press), and author of *Breathing Life into Stone: The Sculpture of Henry DiSpirito* (Fenimore Art Museum).

Daniel Koch is the author of *Ralph Waldo Emerson in Europe: Class, Race, and Revolution in the Making of an American Thinker* and *Land of the Oneidas: Central New York State*. Originally from Oneida, New York, he currently lives and works in Cambridgeshire, England.

Daniel Kornstein is a lawyer in New York City. He couples a civil litigation practice with writing about the law and is currently working on a book about the Triangle Fire, to be published by SUNY Press.

Ellen NicKenzie Lawson was a professional historian and the editor of *The Three Sarahs: Documents of Antebellum Black College Women* (transcribed with Marlene D. Merrill).

Susan Ingalls Lewis is professor emerita of history at SUNY New Paltz, where she specialized in courses on New York state history and American Women's history. She is the author of *Unexceptional Women: Female*

Proprietors in Mid-Nineteenth-Century Albany, New York, 1830–1885 (Ohio State University Press, 2009, winner of the Hagley Prize in Business History) and has also published in the fields of twentieth-century girls' literature and college art appreciation. Dr. Lewis is a fellow of the New York Academy of History and a board member of the Women's Rights Alliance of New York State.

Nancy Newman is associate professor of music at the University at Albany, SUNY. She is the author of *Good Music for a Free People: The Germania Musical Society in Nineteenth-Century America*.

C. R. Roseberry was a journalist and writer who lived and worked in Albany. He was the author of many books, including *Glenn Curtiss, Pioneer of Flight* and *From Niagara to Montauk: The Scenic Pleasures of New York State*, published by SUNY Press.

Albert M. Rosenblatt teaches at the New York University School of Law and is a retired judge of the New York State Court of Appeals. His previous books include *Opening Statements: Law, Jurisprudence, and the Legacy of Dutch New York* (coedited with Julia C. Rosenblatt) and *Judith S. Kaye in Her Own Words: Reflections on Life and the Law, with Selected Judicial Opinions and Articles* (coedited with Judith S. Kaye and Henry M. Greenberg), both published by SUNY Press.

Thomas C. Rosenthal, MD, is emeritus professor of family medicine at the University at Buffalo, SUNY. He is the author of *Bloodletting and Germs: A Doctor in Nineteenth-Century Rural New York* and coeditor of *Office Care Geriatrics*.

Brad L. Utter is a senior historian and curator at the New York State Museum. He revised the second edition of *The Motorcycle Industry in New York State: A Concise Encyclopedia of Inventors, Builders, and Manufacturers*, by Geoffrey N. Stein.

Index

Act for the Gradual Abolition of Slavery, 28, 82, 88–91, 93, 96
AIDS, 237, 240–41
Albany, NY, South Mall. *See* Nelson A. Rockefeller Empire State Plaza
Algonquin, 35–37, 40
Altomare, George, 197–200, 204–206, 208–10
American Expeditionary Forces (AEF) 140–48, 154
American Federation of Labor, 125, 199, 212
American Federation of Teachers (AFT), 195–96, 199, 206
American Institute of Architects AIA), 106–109
American Revolution, 1–2
Anthony, Susan B., 157–61, 166, 170–72
Anti-Rent Wars, "Act Concerning Tenures by Lease," 75–79, 82; Boughton, Smith M., 74–76, 78–81, 83; "Calico Indians," 73–75, 77–80, 84; Coda, 83–84; end of manorial system, 81–82; Helderberg War, 71–73; movement, 71–78; Patroons, 71–75, 77–80, 83–84; settlement, 78–83; tenant farmers land system, 69–70

Architects, female, fighting for acceptance, 106, 109–11; American Institute of Architects (AIA), 105–109, 113–20; Bethune, Louise Blanchard, 103–106, 109–20; Board of Architects creation of, 117; Western Association of Architects (WAA), 106–20
Artcher, Michael Sheriff, 72

Battle of Saratoga, 10–11, 25–26, 29
Belmont, Alva Vanderbilt, 159, 163
Bethune, Louise Blanchard, 103–106, 109–20
Black Soldiers. *See* Hell Fighters
Blatch, Harriot Stanton, 159, 163–65
Bloomberg, Michael, 246–48, 250–56
Boerstler, Charles G., 34–37
Bootleggers, 177–79, 182, 185–86, 193
Bouck, William, 77–78
Boughton, Smith, 74–76, 78–81, 83
Brant, Joseph, 3, 7–15
Broadway Mob, 184–85
Buffalo, N.Y. battle. *See* War of 1812
Burgoyne, General, 9–11, 25–27
Burnham, Daniel, 105, 108–11, 115
Butler, John, 9, 11

281

"Calico Indians," 73–75, 77–80, 84
Carey, Hugh, 214, 227–28
Catt, Carrie Chapman, 157, 159, 162–73
Cayuga American Indians, 12, 15
Chapin, Cyrenius, 32–47. *See also* War of 1812
Christman, Henry, 76–77
Christopher Street Liberation Day March, 237, 240–41
Clingan-Burden Bill, 239
Clinton, DeWitt, 51–52, 55–57, 90
Clinton, George, 10, 14–15, 23–27, 215
Clintons Ditch. *See* Erie Canal
Committee for Action Through Unity (CATU), 206
Condon-Wadlin Act, 196, 210–11
Constitution, New York. *See* New York State Constitution
Continental Congress, 9, 14, 19–20, 22
Cooney, Robert J., 169
Corning, Erastus, 216–21
Costello, Frank, 182–83, 193
Council of Appointment, 22–23, 28
COVID-19 Era and New York City Department of Parks and Recreation; aftermath, 268–69; deaths, 257–58, 269; food and, 262–63; Learning Bridges, 263–65; 264–65; National Guard, 262; onset of pandemic, 257–61; programs, 264–65; recovery, 256; schooling and, 261–65; vaccinations, 266–67; working remotely, 259–62
Culver, Erastus, 93, 95–97
Cuomo, Andrew, 258

Daughters of Bilitis (DOB), 230, 232
Declaration of Independence, 17, 19, 22, 58, 102, 137

Dewey, Thomas E., 215
Discrimination Laws, 22, 239–41
Doctorow, Daniel, 252
Dutch West India Company, 70, 74

Eastern Regional Conference of Homophile Organizations, 237
Eighteenth Amendment, 75–76, 185–87
Empire State Plaza, Albany. *See* Nelson A. Rockefeller Empire State Plaza
The Empty Closet, 239
Erie Canal, 49–51, engineering, 53–56; funding, 51–53; industrial growth, 58–61; operation, 61–66; success of, 64–66; wedding the waters, 56–58

Farmers' Rebellion. *See* Anti-Rent Wars
Fire Department, City of New York (FDNY), 9/11 attacks on World Trade Center and, 244–46; changes after attacks; 246–47; Pfeifer, Joseph, 247, 256
Fish, Hamilton, 143, 154
FitzGibbon, James, 35–37
Fort George, 32–35, 38, 44
Fort Niagara, 9, 12, 35, 38–39
Fort Schuyler, 9–13
Fort Stanwix, 3–4, 7, 9–10, 14–15
Fort Ticonderoga, 10, 25
Freedom Tower, 248–51, 255
French and Indian War, 2
Fugitive Slave Law (1850), 86–87, 92, 94–95, 97–98, 100

Gage, Matilda Joslyn, 159–60
Gangsters, 178–79, 180–85, 190–93
Gay Activist Alliance (GAA), 237–39
Gay Liberation Front (GLF), 236, 238
Gay Rights. *See* Stonewall Uprising
Geddes, James, 54–55

282 | Index

Giuliani, Rudolph, 245, 248, 252–54
Gompers Samuel, 125, 131
Goodier, Susan, 161, 164, 167–68, 173
Greater than Ever: New York's Big Comeback (Giuliani), 252
Greeley, Horace, 81
Ground Zero, 244, 252 See also World Trade Center (WTC)

Hamilton, Alexander, 28, 70, 90
Harlem Hell Fighters. See Hell Fighters
Harriman, Averill, 220
Haudenosaunee American Indians, 1–2, 5, 8, 10–16
Hay, Mary Garrett, 162–65
Hayward, William, 142–44, 146, 148–51
Helderberg War. See Anti-Rent Wars
Hell Fighters, after the war, 149–55; American Expeditionary Force (AEF), 140–48, 154; combat, World War I, 145–49; German propaganda, 141–42; Harlem, 140–42, 150–51; officers, 140–41, 143–50; Pershing, John J., 141, 145–48; Red Summer, 152, 155; segregation, 139–41, 153–55
Holley, Myron, 52–53

International Ladies Garment Workers Union (ILGWU), 125–26
Iroquois, 1–2, 8, 14, 16. See also Haudenosaunee Indians

Jay, John, 19–20, 23–24, 28, 90–91
Jefferson, Thomas, 27, 51, 86
Johnson, Guy, 7–8
Johnson, Henry, 147
Johnson, William, 2–4, 7–9, 13

Kanonwalohale, 5–7, 9, 11–13
Kennedy, John F., 212

King George III, 3–4, 8, 22, 45
Kirkland, Samuel, 7–9, 14–15
Koch, Daniel, 1–2

Lanigan-Schmidt, Thomas, 233–34
Learning Bridges, 263–65
Lemlich, Clara, 126
Lemmon Slave Case. See Slavery
Leslie, Miriam, 163, 168
Levitt, Arthur, 222–23
Lewiston, N.Y., 38, 44
LGBT+. See Stonewall Uprising
Libeskind, David, 248, 250
Livingston, John, 70, 74–78, 83
Lower Manhattan Development Corporation (LMDC), 248, 250, 255

Mangan, Teresa, 264–65
Marquis de Lafayette, 11
Marriage Equality Act, 240
Mattachine Society, 230–36
McClure, George, 32–34, 38–39, 45

Napoleon, Louis, 92–94
National American Woman Suffrage Association (NAWSA), 160–71
National Educational Association (NEA), 199, 206, 210
National Guard, 139–45, 152, 155, 262
National Labor Relations Act, 136
National Reform Associating (NRA), 76
National September 11th Memorial & Museum, 250–51
Nauman, Fred, 196–97, 208–209
Nelson A. Rockefeller Empire State Plaza, Beatrix, Princess of Netherlands, 215–16; Commission, 216–17; concept, 213–16; construction, 219–26; Corning,

Nelson A. Rockefeller Empire State Plaza *(continued)*
  Erastus, 216–21; cost, 222–23; design, 213–16, 220; financing of, 218–23; ornamental aspects, 226–27; Rockefeller, Nelson, 213–16
Neuman, Johanna, 162–63, 172
New Deal, 122, 134–35
New York City Board of Education, 196
New York City Fire Department. *See* Fire Department of, the City of New York (FDNY)
New York City Human Rights Law, 239
New York Court of Appeals, 85, 102, 230
New York City Department of Parks and Recreations, 262–63, *See also* COVID ERA and New York City Department of Parks and Recreations
New York Society for the Manumission of Slaves, 90–91, 97
New York State Assembly, 131, 143, 176
New York State Capitol, 213–14, 248
New York State Constitution (1777), architects of, 19–21; bicameral legislature, 22; creation, 19–21; Continental Congress and, 18–20, 22; Council of Appointment, 22–23, 28; Council of Revision, 22–23; Declaration of Independence, 17, 19, 22; defending, 24–27; drafting, 19–23; enduring, 28–29; John Jay and, 19–20, 24–25, 27–28; provisions of, 20–21; religious freedom; revisions of 1821, 28–29
New York State Executive Mansion, 213, 215
New York State Liquor Authority, 230
New York State Office of General Services, 213
New York State Suffrage Association, 159, 163
Newark, N.Y., *See* War of 1812
Newman, Nancy, 70–72
9/11 attacks. *See also* World Trade Center (WTC)
Nineteenth Amendment, 20, 158, 170–71
Norris-LaGuardia Act, 135

Obergefell v. Hodges, 240
Occupational Safety and Health Administration (OSHA), 136
One World Trade Center, 248, 250–51
Oneida Carry, 3–4, 8
Oneida American Indians. *See* Oneida Rebellion
Oneida Rebellion, 1–5, American Revolution and, 8–13, British, colonists: 8–10; end of, 13–16; Kanonwalohale, 5–7, 9, 11–13; Line of Property, 3–4; Native Americans wars, 10–13; Oriskany Patent, 3–4, 10, 25; religion and, 5–6; Treaty of Paris, 13–14
Ordinary Heroes (Pfeifer), 256
Oriskany Patent of 1763, 4, 10, 25

Pastorello, Karen, 161, 164, 167–68
Patroon system, 70–74, 77, 79–80, 84
Paul, Alice, 162, 165, 171–72
Pavlic, Gary, 237–38
Perkins, Frances, 126, 128–36
Pershing, John J., 141, 145–48
Pfeifer, Joseph, 247, 256
"A Place of Remembrance," 247
Pontiac, Chief, 3
Porter, Peter, 32, 34, 46
Prigg v. Pennsylvania, 98

Prohibition, bootleggers, 177–85, 188; Broadway mob, 184–85; Eighteenth Amendment and, 175–77; Gangsters, 177–82, 192–93; Harlem, 189–92; Little Italy, 182–83; repeal 176; smuggling, 177–80; speakeasies, 185–89

"Reflecting Absence," 249
Riall, Phineas, 39, 42–44
The Rising: The Twenty-Five Year Battle to Rebuild the World Trade Center (Silverstein), 251
Rockefeller, Nelson, 213–16, 244; *See also* Nelson A. Rockefeller Empire State Plaza
Roosevelt, Franklin D., 122, 134–36, 176

St. Leger, Barry, 9–10, 25
Santangelo, Lauren, 162, 167–68, 173
Schneiderman, Rose, 129–30, 159–60, 169
Schuyler, Philip, 9, 23–26
Schuyler, Pieter, 4
Secord, Laura, 35–36
Selden, David, 200–10
Seneca Falls, 103, 157, 172
Seward, William H., 71–74
Sexual Orientation Non-Discrimination Act (SONDA) (NYS), 239–40
Shanker, Albert, 198–211
Shaw, L. Edward, 151, 154–55
Siegel, Benjamin "Bugsy," 179
Silverstein, Larry, 251
Slavery, Fugitive Slave Law (1850), 86–87, 92, 94–95, 97–98, 100; fugitive slaves, 91–94; Lemmon Slave Case, 95–102; Manumission and, 90, 91, 97; Natural law and, 93, 97, 100; New York and, 87–93;

Quakers and, 88, 90; Somerset Case, 96–97
Smith Al, 131, 134, 150, 170, 188
Sojourner Truth, 159
Somerset v. Stewart, 96–97
South Mall. *See* Nelson A. Rockefeller Empire State Plaza
Stonewall Inn. *See* Stonewall Uprising
Stonewall Uprising, 235–36; AIDS epidemic, 237, 240–41; discrimination laws, 230; Daughters of Bilitis (DOB), 230, 232; Gay Activist Alliance (GAA), 237; Gay Liberation Front (GLF), 236–37; gay rights, 229–30, 235–38; incarceration, 235; Mattachine Society, 230–36; non-discrimination laws, 238–39; police, 230–35; Pride Parade, 237–38; raids, 229–34; rebellion, 229–30; riots, 230–36; sip-ins, 231
Sullivan, John, 11–12
Superstorm Sandy, 247, 256

Tammany Hall, 167, 176, 178, 181–82
Tenant farmers. *See* Anti-rent wars
Theobald, John J., 196, 205, 207, 210
369th U.S. Infantry. *See* Hell fighters
Ticonderoga, NY, 10, 25
Triangle Shirtwaist Factory Fire; cause of, 123–28; Factory Investigating Commission (FIC), 121, 131; history of, 124–24; investigation following, 133–35; legislation and, 136, 203; National Labor Relations Act, 136, 203; Velvet revolution, 122–23, 136–37
Treaty of Paris, 13–14, 27
Tuscarora American Indians, 2, 10, 12, 14–16

United Federation of Teachers (UFT), 195–210; Condon-Wadlin Act, 196, 210–11; High School Teachers Association (HSTA), 204–206; Nauman, Fred, 196–97, 208–209; New York City Board of Education, 196, 202, 205–11; New York City Teachers strike, 195–205; Shanker, Albert, 198–211; Strike, 196–99; strike settlement, 211–12; Teachers Guild, 199, 211

U. S. Supreme Court, 22, 24, 75, 89, 93, 98, 124, 136, 176, 240

United States v. Stanley, 89

Van Rensselaer, Killiaen, 70–71, 74
Van Rensselaer, Stephen III, 71–72
Van Rensselaer, Stephen IV, 70, 72–73, 75–76, 83–84
Van Rensselaer, William, 73–78, 83–84
Velvet revolution, 122–23, 136–37

Wagner, Robert, 131–32, 134–36, 203
Wagoner Act. *See* National Labor Relations Act
Waite, Richard, 104–105
Walker, Peter, 249
War of 1812, Battle at Beaver Dam, 35–37; burning of Newark, 32–34; British attacks on Buffalo, 34, 43–44; *See also* Chapin, Cyrenius; Federal Government and, 45–47; Fort George, 32–35, 38, 44; *See also* McClure, George; Riall, Phineas, 39, 42–44; Secord, Laura, 35–36
Washington, George, 9, 11–14, 19, 26–27

Western Association of Architects (WAA), 106–20
Whig party, 73
Whitehouse, Vira Boarman, 159, 162–64, 168
Wilkerson, George, 32, 35
Willard, Frances, 160
Woman Suffrage, Anthony, Susan B., 157–61, 166, 170–72; "Banner Parade,"165; Catt, Carrie Chapman, 157, 159, 162–73; first wave, 159–60; National American Woman Suffrage Association (NAWSA), 160–71; New York State and, 157–59; 1915 Campaign, 163–64; Nineteenth Amendment, 158, 170–71; road to, 161, 163–64; voting rights, 172; tactics, and, 161–69
Women's Christian Temperance Union (WCTU), 160
World Trade Center (WTC), 243–44, 247–48, 251; *See also* Bloomberg, Michael; City wide Incident Management System, 247; *See also* Fire Department, of New York (FDNY); Lower Manhattan Development Corporation (LMDC), 248, 250, 255; memorial, 244–50; National September 11 Memorial & Museum, 250–55; "Reflecting Absence," 249; terrorist attacks, 244–47; rebuilding, 251–55; resilience, 255
Workplace Safety, *See* Triangle Shirtwaist Factory Fire
Wright, Benjamin, 54

www.ingramcontent.com/pod-product-compliance
Lightning Source LLC
Chambersburg PA
CBHW032035150426
43194CB00006B/282